Judging Economic Policy

The Political Economy of Global Interdependence
Thomas D. Willett, Series Editor

Judging Economic Policy

Selected Writings of Gottfried Haberler

EDITED BY

Richard J. Sweeney, Edward Tower, and Thomas D. Willett

Routledge
Taylor & Francis Group

NEW YORK AND LONDON

First published 1997 by Westview Press

Published in 2021 by Routledge
605 Third Avenue, New York, NY 10017
2 Park Square, Milton Park, Abingdon, Oxon OX14 4RN

Routledge is an imprint of the Taylor & Francis Group, an informa business

Copyright © 1997 Taylor & Francis

A CIP catalog record for this book is available from the Library of Congress.
ISBN 0-8133-8906-2

ISBN 13: 978-0-3670-1699-9 (hbk)
ISBN 13: 978-0-3671-6686-1 (pbk)

Contents

Acknowledgments

The editors are grateful to Oliver Goldstein, who read through the original essays and helped devise a structure for the volume; Barbara Johnston, Haberler's longtime secretary, who helped coordinate the project; Sven Arndt, who helped design the project; Vivian Bourselian, Dorothy Ellis, Michael Lofgreen, Wells Dawson Tower, and Junette Wrathall, who commented on earlier versions; and Dora Fisher and Mary Kaempfer, who prepared the camera ready copy.

Dick Sweeney
Ed Tower
Tom Willett

1

Introduction

Dick Sweeney, Ed Tower, and Tom Willett

This volume collects edited versions of selected essays of Gottfried Haberler, most of them written after he retired from Harvard shortly after the mandatory age of 70 and joined the American Enterprise Institute, in Washington, D.C., where he continued to work until shortly before his death on May 6, 1995. Tower used to assign these annual volumes to his Duke undergraduates to evaluate; the students would grade and critique the essays in these volumes. Consistently, Haberler was credited with producing the best essays, besting his colleagues who were sometimes 50 years younger. This admiration for Haberler's recent work by students who never knew him but found his arguments compelling indirectly suggested the project to us.

To those who know Haberler's work well it is difficult to disagree with Paul Samuelson's judgment that they:

> qualify him for about two-and-a-half Nobel Prizes in Economics--one for his quantum improvement in trade theory beyond Ricardo's paradigm of labor's comparative advantage, one for his definitive synthesis of business cycle theory, and beyond these his policy wisdoms over a period of six decades.[1]

This "policy wisdom" is the basis for this volume. Two collections of Haberler's technical contributions have been published and the

February 1982 issue of the *Quarterly Journal of Economics* contains detailed summaries and perspectives on the body of his technical work.[2] We shall not attempt to repeat these appreciations here. Our focus is on Haberler's contributions to economic policy analysis, both as recognition and to make his contributions more easily available for readers interested in international and macroeconomic policy.

We also believe that having these writings pulled together in one place enables the reader to develop more easily an understanding of how Haberler went about analyzing policy. Haberler's mastery of the policy essay is something that all of us who are interested in economic policy should seek to emulate.

Gottfried Haberler was unquestionably one of the great economists of the twentieth century. Both the quality and breadth of his contributions are exceptional. His work contributes importantly to our understanding of international trade theory and policy, domestic and international monetary and macro economics, and the international trade aspects of economic development. Clarity of thought and exposition characterize Haberler's work, as well as the ability to distinguish the important insight from the flashy detail. As his brother-in-law, Herbert Furth, has written:

> In his view, economic activity and economic science are based on common sense; philosophy, mathematics, even statistics are valuable and important, but--like drugs in medicine--always to be applied with caution. Otherwise we risk that they might obscure instead of clarifying the underlying real relationships.[3]

Herbert Stein characterizes Haberler as follows:[4]

> Gottfried was a policy wonk, but he was an exceptionally scholarly one. He was not content to spin out his own thoughts of the moment, however justified he might have been in doing so by his long immersion in economics. He wanted to cite facts and authorities. Much of his writing while at the AEI consisted of essays in the annual volume, *Contemporary Economic Problems*, edited by William Fellner and containing essays by seven or eight other people. Gottfried's articles always contained about twice as many footnotes per page as any of the others. The footnotes had a wide range, running from the classics to the latest pamphlet from a Washington think-tank. He read everything and remembered everything he read. Many of the foot-

notes were I think, exceptionally generous, giving credit to younger economists for ideas that Gottfried was quite capable of having on his own.

Most of the articles that Gottfried wrote while at the AEI dealt either with stagflation or with the international financial situation, both leading issues of the time . . . These papers served to clarify many issues. And they still remain as models of how to write a paper on economic policy--explaining the reasoning at every step of the way and giving due attention to competing points of view.

Rereading his great books, *The Theory of International Trade, With Its Applications to Commercial Policy* (1936) and *Prosperity and Depression* (1937), one is struck by how relevant much of the analysis remains. Of immense importance when they were written, they have also stood the test of time.

While the writings reprinted here often deal with specific historical policy episodes, the writings have been selected and edited to illustrate important policy insights that are of equal relevance today, and which we strongly believe will still be so tomorrow. For example, we are struck by the similarity of Haberler's positions on the critical role of rigidities and distortions in labor and capital markets (discussed in his "Overview" essay, and the section, "Inflation: Causes and Cures") to the positions taken by *The Economist* in the Spring of 1994, especially in its "Schools Briefs," which compare American and European labor markets.

The essence of Haberler's approach is openness and principled eclecticism. His eclecticism is not that of the true believer who picks and chooses among approaches and evidence to present the best case for preconceived conclusions, but rather one who starts with basic principles and studies how their application may need to be modified under varying circumstances. For this reason, he often sounds like a monetarist to Keynesians and like a Keynesian to monetarists.

In truth, his position is a logically consistent and powerful one. He remains convinced of the power of monetary forces at a time when they were ignored or downplayed by most Keynesians, but he refuses to believe that controlling the money supply is all that one need worry about. Thus, he also gives considerable attention to the possibilities of cost-push pressures in the economy. He maintains skepticism that government intervention in the economy would work as well in practice as in the world of ideal theory. For example, while he acknowledges cases in which free trade might not be the ideal solution, he wishes to put a significant burden of proof on those advocating government intervention.

In another example, his innovative proposal for a government incomes policy stresses the potential gains from government activism to reduce regulations and promote more competitiveness of the economy, at a time when most proponents of incomes policy were advocating more direct government intervention in wage and price decisions.

With his background in international economics, it is not surprising that Haberler was a leader in emphasizing international dimensions of domestic macroeconomic policy and highlighting the importance of macroeconomic stability in the United States for global economic stability. He is far from dogmatic on exchange rate issues. He was one of the key contributors (along with Milton Friedman) to the postwar reevaluation of exchange rate regimes by international monetary economists that led to support for flexible exchange rates. His primary emphasis is on the need for consistency between domestic macroeconomic conditions and policies and the exchange rate regime. He is skeptical of popular arguments that flexible exchange rates cause inflation and was one of the first to raise the possibility that a depreciating exchange rate might do as much to discipline domestic macroeconomic authorities as a loss of international reserves under pegged exchange rates.

In his later years, Haberler no longer did technical research, but he kept up with the latest developments in his fields and often offered cogent criticisms. Drawing on his immense knowledge of both the development of theory and its use in policy applications he frequently presented politely worded, but intellectually devastating perspectives on the latest theoretical developments which claimed undue novelty and/or overlooked basic truths. For examples, see his essays in this volume on "Rational Expectations" and "Strategic Trade Policy and the New International Economics: A Critical Analysis."

On development policy issues, Haberler was a firm critic of the views of those who were extremely pessimistic about the development prospects of low income economies and argued that a special economics needed to be developed for the analysis of these economies. For Haberler there was "only one economics," but one that needed to be applied thoughtfully, taking into account the possibilities of differences in circumstances between countries and across time. It is gratifying that he lived to see his once lonely call for liberal trade policies in developing countries eventually become widely accepted by development economists and over the past decade by many governments in the developing countries.

Haberler is one of those rare writers of English who learned it as an adult but mastered it so completely that he serves as an exemplar to writers whose birth language is English.[5] Joseph Conrad and Vladimir Nabokov are other examples. Nabokov can stun the reader with his sharp, pictorial images and immense vocabulary. Haberler writes with simplicity and spareness that make clear his powerful thoughts in debates where little seems clear.[6]

A brief biography helps put these essays into perspective. John Chipman writes in his biography of Haberler:[7]

> Gottfried Haberler was born on 20 July 1900 in Purkersdorf, near Vienna. He studied economics at the University of Vienna under Friedrich von Wieser and Ludwig von Mises, where he received doctorates in law (1923) and economics (1925). After two years in the United States and Britain he returned to Vienna, received his habilitation in 1928, and was appointed lecturer, later Professor of Economics, at the University of Vienna, from 1928 to 1936. He was appointed professor at Harvard University in 1936 where he remained until his retirement in 1971. Since that time he has been a resident scholar at the American Enterprise Institute, Washington, D.C. He was President of the International Economic Association (1950-51), the National Bureau of Economic Research (1955) and the American Economic Association (1963). In 1980 he was awarded the Antonio Feltrinelli prize.

Some Appreciations

We cannot conclude this introduction without offering a few brief comments about Haberler the person. For all of his greatness as an economist, Haberler was first and foremost a wonderful human being. His many friends have views that span the range of non-Marxist economic and policy views. His friends know his views and when their views differ from his. His wide circle arose and continued because he was a gentleman who believed that critical comments could be presented in a civil manner, because he was humble in his views and open to change, and because he differentiated between bad ideas and bad people. He was always on the lookout to give younger scholars a helping hand. We are fortunate to have had the opportunity to be befriended by him and hope that this collection of essays will provide a much broader group some exposure to his approach to doing economics and analyzing policy.

Max Corden in a comment which concludes this volume assesses Haberler's career as a development economist. He notes that "Haberler is not a development economist as this term is usually understood." But his work is highly relevant to the developing economies.

> Indirectly, his contributions to trade theory have probably had a greater effect on their policies and the analysis of their policies, than the contributions of some of [those conventionally understood to be development pioneers. . . . He] sorted out (and usually demolished) many arguments for protection. Another important contribution is that . . . immobilities of factors of production . . . do not affect the case for free trade, but factor price rigidities do. . . . Many of the criticisms he made seem obvious today, but it is worth noting that Haberler was right *at the time*, not afterwards. . . . In effect, Haberler was a precursor, who kept the free market or liberalization flame alight. Now, when one rereads him, one finds much that is obvious, quite moderate, and close to the mainstream. In assessing him, one should assess the whole of this school of thought and its battles with the protectionists.

Some vignettes give a sense of him. A letter from his sister written in November 1994 and translated from the German:

> Dear Gottfried,
>   My thoughts are often about you and especially on November 8th, the day commemorating your name. This day in our childhood and youth was almost celebrated like a birthday. Maria always made something special for dinner and there were small presents. I always think on these episodes.
>   I remember when you were attending the Schotten Gymnasium (high school) and that you were thrown out because you said *die Reichspost*, the clerical daily newspaper, was like a piece of trash. Poppa was called to school and told about your bad activities, and Momma was shaking from fear over what had happened. When Poppa came home he just sat himself down on a chair and made a kick as a sign you had been kicked out of school. Then you went to the Döblinger Gymnasium (high school) and you were one of the best students.

I also think about the time Poppa was close to dying and was in his death bed, he said quietly to Momma and me that something very special is going to come of Gottfried.

I think we have done much to make our parents proud and that our offshoots can continue on.

After a hot summer we have beautiful fall days with splendid color and I am enjoying this very much on my walks.

Take care dear Gottfried and be warmly embraced.

Maria

Greetings from Priska.

From Robert Solomon:[8]

Although he was no Keynesian, Haberler of course respected Keynes and liked to tell the story of his initial correspondence with him when Gottfried was still in Vienna. He had written to Keynes but Keynes could not read the signature. So in his reply, he cut Gottfried's signature from the bottom of the incoming letter and pasted it to the envelope containing his reply. . . Gottfried was a great economist, a good friend, a gentle person, gifted with a sense of humor and a wealth of stories out of his long experience and wide acquaintanceship. He will be missed and remembered.

From Herbert Stein:[9]

For those of us who worked here during Gottfried's stay his chief value was not only in his writing but even more in his presence. He had a large number of associates and acquaintances--former colleagues and students, foreign journalists and some foreign government officials--whom he used to invite here to the AEI for lunch. We who joined in these lunches at what came to be known as the economist's table got much pleasure and some education from the conversations that went on there.

We got something much more important from Gottfried's presence. We got the experience of being in touch with the great tradition of economics--and here I must also add the name of William Fellner, who made the same contribution. We were reminded that we were, or could be, part of a discipline that had standards of its own, including respect for the facts, responsibility to the reader, openmindedness, devotion to the general welfare and independence of parties, interests or ideologies. Persons who can represent those qualities are rare and we who worked with Gottfried at the AEI are fortunate to have known him.

From James Tobin:[10]

In the hotly contested issues of the day, he was thoroughly and patiently logical, fair- and open-minded, impeccably analytical. His painstaking and stiff Germanic manner often delightfully gave way to a dry and subtle wit. He contributed a great deal to economics. I particularly admired his survey of cycle theory and what we would now call macroeconomics, a powerful contribution in its own right. I was proud to evolve from student to friend, and we kept in contact, though not always in agreement, in correspondence and occasional personal encounter. His career spanned most of this century, of which he was one of the truly great economists.

From John Chipman:

My favorite story has to do with a walk at Harvard. One Sunday, one of many Sundays, we went for a walk in Vermont, so he came to pick us up in his car, and after driving about five miles out of the way to get gasoline at one cent per gallon lower price, we went up to Vermont and began climbing the mountain. And we reached just about the pinnacle, or the last stage and Friedl was exhausted. I was exhausted. My wife was exhausted, and the dog was exhausted, Tasso. So what did Gottfried do? Well, Friedl decided she would just stay there, and not walk up to the top. Gottfried picked up the dog, and began walking up to the top of the mountain. Of course, I had to follow him. So we went all the way up to the top.

But that image of Gottfried climbing the mountain with his dog, I think says everything about the man.[11]

From Wolfgang Stolper:[12]

The best horse in the Viennese stable. This is how Schumpeter characterized the young Haberler in a letter to Gustav Stolper in which Schumpeter asked Stolper to use his political influence to secure Haberler a call to the University of Königsberg . . .

Incorruptibility of judgement was accompanied by incorruptibility of personal behavior. When I was his first teaching assistant in his course on international trade theory, I had to persuade him to prescribe his own *Theory of International Trade*. He thought that he should not profit from the fact that he was the teacher. He felt the use of his own book to be a conflict of interest. I, on my part, argued that it would be unfair towards the students to keep the best book from them, just because he was its author . . .

And there was . . . his willingness to help younger and less experienced colleagues. He suggested that I join him in teaching the course on International Trade Theory in Radcliffe, where I would be responsible for half the lectures and would be paid for half a course. This was important for the extra income, but it also meant that my name was printed in the catalogue. It was still the Great Depression and jobs were scarce. Hence Haberler's invitation greatly improved prospects for employment. But then he added: 'If this becomes too much for you, I'll give more than half the lectures, and you will still be paid for half the course. . . .'

I remember the many walks in the beautiful surroundings of Boston and the mountains of southern New Hampshire, the joint meals and more formal receptions in his house. And I remember with a certain nostalgia a telephone call at 5 o'clock in the morning which began with the question, in Viennese, of course: 'Did I wake you up?' and when I answered that indeed he had, continued: 'Well, I just came from New York, and now that you are awake, how about some tennis?' So as a dutiful assistant I got out of bed to play tennis.

With Gottfried Haberler many of us have lost a faithful friend. And all of us have lost a voice of reason in a world which is more and more deafened by ideological noise, a world, which would need such a voice of reason more than ever.

From Paul Samuelson:

Jobs in post-World War I Vienna economic circles were scarce. Gottfried was found at his maternal uncle's bank. On the second day, when he picked up his coat and hat, he left behind the laconic message: 'I'm not coming back. I really don't like it here.'[13]

Here is another story. Some of us at sherry before a Fiscal Policy dinner in the Harvard Faculty Club were beefing about certain tax loopholes in the IRS code. Gottfried whispered quietly, 'Capitalism breathes through those loopholes.' The next day I told him how much I had liked his aphorism. Always the straight-arrow scholar, he said, 'Yes, but the words are those of Ludwig von Mises not Gottfried Haberler.'[14]

Scientific innovation is of course what counts and Gottfried richly earned the top honors that came his way. I hope it is not inappropriate for me to add a personal opinion. Gottfried Haberler, Jacob Viner, and Bertil Ohlin were the magnificent triad who converted international trade theory from is Ricardo-Taussig classical phase to its modern general equilibrium apotheosis. All three fully deserved a Nobel Prize for that. But by mere luck neither Haberler nor

Viner chanced to be so honored. *Ex post facto* I personally rectify this miscarriage and set things aright for my two great teachers and before God and this company I bestow on them posthumously the Nobel Awards that should have been theirs. Hail Apollo! Hail Haberler![15]

A Reader's Guide

The following is designed to serve as a readers' guide to the volume. We have highlighted the major themes in the essays included here. This guide is designed to help the reader who wants a quick summary, and also the reader who is interested in particular issues. In some cases we quote directly from the articles (although we do not use quotation marks and footnotes), and in others paraphrase.

An Overview of Economic Policy:
"A Positive Program for a Benevolent
and Enlightened Dictator"

Haberler succinctly summarizes his macroeconomic world view in this essay. Macroeconomic ills are the child of distortions in factor and product markets. We need policies to foster more effective markets and competitiveness throughout the economy: more price stability to mitigate the distortion of the tax structure which inflation brings; tighter budgets to shrink the crowding out of investment that easy fiscal policy generates; lower marginal tax rates to keep incentives strong; less protection of union power and favored sectors to keep wages and prices flexible; deregulation and free international trade to keep industry competitive; the elimination of farm price supports and acreage restrictions to keep agriculture productive; and a floating dollar to facilitate convertability between currencies regardless of inflation differentials.

Inflation: Causes and Cures

Explaining Stagflation. Budget deficits, by creating an incentive for inflationary finance, cause inflation. Labor unions, minimum wages, monopoly, and government regulations that make the economy less flexible all raise the natural rate of unemployment. This stimulates monetary expansion and worsens inflation.

Micro Foundations of Employment and Inflation Theory. The literature on the micro-foundations of inflation and employment theory is of little help for explaining the stagflation dilemma, because it abstracts from the most important factors--wage rigidity, wage push, real wage resistance from labor unions, similar activities of other pressure groups, and the effects of the widespread government regulation of industry. A tight monetary and fiscal policy must be supplemented by measures designed to make the economy more competitive. If we rely on monetary and fiscal restraints alone, we will create so much unemployment that the fight against inflation will be broken off prematurely.

Curing Stagflation (How to Make the Economy More Flexible and Competitive). The preceding essay argues the need to make the economy more competitive and flexible. This essay suggests ways to do so, simultaneously increasing output and employment. It too stresses the micro policy roots of our macro problems.

Tax-based Incomes Policy. This essay defines "Incomes Policy II" as a bundle of policies of different kinds designed to bring the economy closer to the competitive ideal. It is a vastly superior alternative to "Incomes Policy I" (what usually is called incomes policy). The latter ranges from comprehensive wage and price controls, wage freezes, and price stops to guidelines for noninflationary wage and price setting. Tax-based incomes policy (TIP) tries to attack the problem of inflation with a combination of taxes and subsidies, taxing agents for inflationary behavior. TIP cannot do anything that cannot be done as cheaply, efficiently, and without any red tape and administrative cost by a combination of Incomes Policy II and monetary-fiscal restraint.

Rational Expectations. The basic insight of rational expectations is correct, namely that people do not simply extrapolate current and past rates of inflation and that they try to form a judgment on what the government's policy is and how this policy is likely to change the course of events. But, the common, concrete rational expectations assumption--namely that all private agents have the same perceptions of the government's policy and draw the same (correct) monetarist conclusion--is highly implausible. A worrisome feature of the rational expectations literature is the complete neglect of institutional rigidities, in particular rigidity of money wages and increasingly of real wages. Money illusion tends to become progressively eroded in a long period of inflation. But money illusion is a fairly hardy plant. There is still some left, which can be exploited by monetary policy and misused by politicians to win the next election.

Fiscal Policy and the Supply Side

Do Budget Deficits Raise Interest Rates? The Ricardian Equivalence Theorem. Ricardian Equivalence is wrong. Budget deficits do raise interest rates and crowd out investment. Many people will assume, rightly or wrongly but not irrationally, that large budget deficits will lead to inflation. The development of inflationary expectations will make a shambles of any equivalence of taxes and borrowing. Ricardo in proposing and rejecting "Ricardian Equivalence" was more realistic than his modern enthusiasts.

The Decline in Productivity Growth. The causes are (1) an increased share in the labor force of teenagers and women whose productivity is much less than prime-age males, (2) lagging investment, and (3) the enormous growth of the public sector: the sharp increase in government employment, and the exploding propensity of the government to control and regulate the economy. The lagging investment is caused by regulation and high effective marginal tax rates (due to high marginal tax rates, double taxation of dividends and faulty accounting rules that fail to adjust for nominal, not real, profits caused by inflation). But low productivity growth causes neither inflation nor unemployment. Only government policies that foster or tolerate both union power and wage push and yield to other pressure groups make inflation or unemployment, or both, the inevitable consequence of lagging productivity growth and low investment.

International Macro Policy Coordination

A Critique of the Locomotive and Convoy Strategies. The so-called locomotive or convoy strategies of pressuring the strong currency country or countries to expand faster is tantamount to an attempt to eliminate the inflation differential by inflating the low-inflation countries rather than disinflating the high-inflation countries--a policy of curing the healthy rather than the sick. This would intensify worldwide inflation and ultimately cause worldwide recession.

The only way to prevent trend movements in exchange rates is to have all countries inflate at the same rate. Countries can transmit current account impulses to one another through adjusting the monetary-fiscal mix, and thereby shifting the exchange rate, without altering their own level of economic activity. However, where one decides to peg the unemployment rate does not influence the net stimulus one gives one's trading partners.

International Policy Coordination: Do We Need It? Proposals for international policy coordination are superfluous. All that is needed is an agreement to maintain free international markets, and follow the rules of the IMF and the GATT; under floating exchanges the level of employment should not be an issue for international diplomacy. Policy coordination that results in an elimination of the U.S. trade deficit without curing the U.S. budget deficit will simply crowd out U.S. private sector investment.

International Criticism of the U.S. Budget Deficit. The budget deficit in the U.S. resulting in a mix of easy fiscal policy and tight monetary policy has raised U.S. interest rates, but by causing the dollar to appreciate, the net influence on Europe has been expansionary. Thus the U.S. budget deficit has not caused European unemployment. The European economies have their own structural rigidities and inefficiencies to thank for their poor recent performance (e.g. unemployment compensation, labor market rigidities, high taxes, inefficient nationalized industries, exchange control and zealous customs enforcement), not the U.S. budget deficit. Similarly, the higher U.S. interest rates have increased the debt burden on LDCs, but LDCs have their own macroeconomic mismanagement (squandered oil revenues, wasteful government spending, state enterprises, coddled trade unions, military expenditures and galloping inflation) to thank for their problems. The strong dollar has helped LDCs; the only important grievance LDCs have is protectionism by the developed world, but many LDCs compound their problems by protectionism of their own.

Exchange Rates and Inflation

The Vicious Circle Argument Against Floating. The proponents of the vicious circle argument against floating argue that under a float, an inflationary impulse depreciates the currency which worsens inflation. This further depreciates the currency and so forth. A vicious circle cannot be said to exist when a currency depreciates at the rate by which domestic inflation exceeds the foreign rate. The roots of the vicious circle, if it exists, are to be sought in domestic arrangements-- accommodating monetary policy and wage indexation. Floating exchange rates help fight inflation, because an exchange rate change is a clear and immediate signal of inflationary pressure, which puts some pressure on monetary authorities to step on the break.

Flexible Exchange Rates and Inflation. Floating exchange rates cause neither recession nor inflation. Nor do they insulate an economy from real disturbances. A floating rate means that a country will feel the consequences of an internally generated inflationary impulse more quickly than under fixed exchange rates, but it insulates a country from foreign inflationary impulses. It also grants a country the freedom to select its own inflation rate, without fear of consequences for the balance of payments.

The International Monetary System

The Present International Monetary System in Historical Perspective. This essay traces the pressures and responses leading up to the current system of flexible exchange rates. Differential inflation rates and real shocks like oil-price changes mean that floating rates are here to stay, although small, open economies will continue to peg their currencies to those of larger countries.

The Present International Monetary System in Perspective. The major benefit of the Bretton Woods system was the relative ease of changing exchange rates. It was the rising tide of world inflation after 1965, especially in the United States, that killed Bretton Woods and forced the adoption of widespread floating on reluctant governments. It was not the other way around; the death of Bretton Woods did not bring on inflation. Though floating rates do not insulate an economy from real disturbances, they do allow countries to pursue differing rates of inflation. Floating rates also obviate the need to use import restriction and exchange control for balance of payments adjustment, as can be seen by contrasting the relatively liberal international policies today with the restrictions of the thirties and those proposed to cope with the balance of payments deficit by President Johnson during his administration.

Gold, the European Monetary System and the Need to Float. Floating exchange rates enable countries to adjust to differential disturbances affecting the domestic price level without having to drag other countries' price levels along. Among the conditions for fixed rates to work smoothly, particularly important is a common monetary policy.

International Liquidity in a World of Floating Exchange Rates. Floating exchange rates simultaneously solve the adjustment, confidence and liquidity problems. Because adjustment is so much more efficient under floating rates, less liquidity is needed, even under a managed float. Also, because currencies are no longer convertible at a fixed rate into some ultimate reserve medium such as gold, a confidence problem never develops.

Under floating, global reserves become a less important determinant of world inflation. Small countries inflate when they peg their currencies to a large country that inflates. The International Monetary Fund (IMF) can fight inflation, however, by using conditional lending to encourage countries to put their financial houses in order and to curb inflation. Unconditional lending is counterproductive, because it is likely to tempt countries to delay needed structural reform and anti-inflationary measures and to postpone needed changes in exchange rates or inflation.

Exchange-Rate and Balance of Payments Policy

Managed Floating. An important distinction exists between managed and dirty floating. This essay defines dirty floating as policies like split exchange markets, multiple exchange rates, import deposit schemes, taxes on the purchase of foreign currencies differentiated according to the prospective use of the foreign currency, and the like. These are policies which violate one of the basic objectives of the IMF, to avoid restrictions for balance-of-payments purposes on current account transactions. The essay defines managed floating as official trading of foreign exchange in a free exchange market to prevent or moderate sharp and disruptive exchange-rate fluctuations as well as to moderate, though not suppress or reverse longer run movements.

Reference exchange rates and target zones for exchange rates would present the same speculative problems as the old par value system. Moreover, a tradition of political stability and responsible financial and monetary policy is enough to keep floating exchange rates stable. The IMF's job of guiding interventions under a managed float should be restricted to discouraging "aggressive" interventions. Such a role is less important than trying to dissuade countries from engaging in dirty floating as defined above.

The Case Against Capital Controls. Capital controls breed wasteful efforts to circumvent them by legal and illegal means, and wasteful measures to tighten and expand controls. Because there is no way to distinguish between legitimate and illegitimate speculative capital flows, effective control of capital flows requires the distorting control of current account transactions. Finally, because the adoption of floating exchange rates has discouraged destabilizing speculation, it would be most unwise to use the heavy weapon of controls as a supplement to floating.

Exchange Rate Policy and the Strong Dollar of 1984. Lingering doubt that inflation had been curbed, along with current and projected budget deficits in the absence of Ricardian equivalence, kept American nominal and real interest rates high during the early 1980s. The high interest rates, combined with a favorable climate for investment in the U.S., kept the American dollar high in 1984. The strong dollar, contrary to American criticism, did not significantly hurt the American traded goods sector. Nor did it cause American recession. Rather, it was a valve for releasing American inflationary pressure. This meant that to contain inflation interest rates had to rise by less than would have been the case without the dollar's appreciation. Moreover, the appreciation prevented the inflation which would have directly hurt the American traded goods sector, and it obviated the need for a future recession to drag down the inflationary momentum that would have otherwise developed.

Given the huge size of the international capital market, sterilized intervention (i.e. intervention without changes in domestic or foreign money stocks) would have to be massive or else be regarded as the precursor (or signal) of nonsterilized interventions to have any significant effect on the dollar. Consequently, all the internationally coordinated sterilized intervention designed to lower the dollar was almost completely economically ineffective. Such intervention can be politically efficacious, however, for it permits participating central banks to claim, when the dollar stops appreciating, that it was they who turned the tide.

Trade Policy

Current Account Deficits Under Floating—Burden or Benefit? Under fixed exchange rates a large current account deficit that is financed by a loss of international reserves is a burden, because under the rules of the game it forces the central bank to tighten money; and when wages are imperfectly flexible, tight money deflates the economy. Under flexible exchange rates, however, there is no such requirement, and a trade deficit permits domestic absorption to be higher than it would otherwise be. Moreover, under flexible exchange rates, current accounts do not cause unemployment, because they can always be matched with expansionary monetary and fiscal policy. Finally, some of the distressed tradeable sectors in the U.S., like steel, are unlikely to rebound even when the trade deficit disappears; their problems arise from a lack of comparative advantage or the consequences of permitting domestic wages to rise above the competitive level.

Strategic Trade Policy and the New International Economics: A Critical Analysis. Free trade is not passé. The new economics has added one more item to the list of theoretically possible exceptions to the free trade rule, to wit the possibility of shifting, under certain circumstances, excess profits from foreign to domestic firms. But as Krugman himself has shown, this in practice is of very dubious value and should be ignored: free trade is still the right policy. To help industry to do better in the world market there is a lot to do in the domestic area to foster innovation and entrepreneurship, for example, in education and industrial R&D, removing restrictions and rigidities in the labor market and elsewhere, not to mention taxation and macroeconomic policies.

Development Policy

Liberal and Illiberal Development Policy. Like any economist who is interested in economic policy, I could not avoid thinking and writing about economic growth and development in general. It was then quite natural to apply the general principles of economics to the problems of the developing countries. If one samples casually the literature on economic development, one might easily get the impression that trade is a most destructive force that locks developing countries in a vicious circle of poverty. I believe in what some development economists call "monoeconomics"; that is to say, the same economic principles apply to developing and developed countries alike.

The Federal Reserve's horrendous policy mistakes which caused or permitted the money supply to contract by 30% combined with restrictions on international trade, designed to preserve employment, and the gold standard mentality which made it difficult for deficit countries to relieve deflationary pressures by devaluation of the currency, let alone by floating, turned what would have been a recession into a catastrophic slump. The Great Depression was not "a crisis of capitalism," as Prebisch says, but was a crisis of largely anticapitalistic government policy, the consequence of horrendous policy mistakes. The Great Depression combined with the immunity of the Hitler reich and the USSR to it, caused intellectuals in developing countries, to believe in the superiority of controls and central planning over free markets and private enterprise. Subsequent decades where there was no contraction of the money stock helped turn the consensus back to more liberal policies. The liberal resurgence went into high gear in the late 1940s and 1950s when monetary restraint and liberal policies produced economic miracles in several countries.

Several arguments for protection in developing countries are reviewed and found wanting. There is no secular deterioration of the terms of trade for developing countries. The demonstration effect shows an unbecoming and unjustified patronizing attitude toward the "natives" on the part of development economists from abroad and their disciples in the developing countries. Haberler expresses strong doubts that disguised unemployment ever existed anywhere on a considerable scale. The terms of trade argument simply does not hold any more, now that the world economy is so competitive, if it ever did. The infant industry argument holds only when there are institutional rigidities and distortions, for in a fully competitive economy, where factors of production are remunerated according to their marginal productivity, untrained labor would receive a correspondingly low wage. If a "big push" to simultaneously expand many industries is needed, the best policy is to let free markets do what they do best--develop new industries. Haberler concludes that the mills of the market often ground slowly, but they always ground powerfully.

Gottfried Haberler as Development Economist, by W. Max Corden. Haberler is not a development economist as this term is usually understood. But his work is highly relevant to the developing economies. Indirectly, his contributions to trade theory have had a greater effect on their policies and the analysis of their policies, than the contributions of some of those conventionally understood to be development pioneers. He sorted out (and usually demolished) many arguments for protection. Another important contribution is that immobilities of factors of production do not affect the case for free trade, but factor price rigidities do. Many of the criticisms he made seem obvious today, but it is worth noting that Haberler was right *at the time*, not afterwards. In effect, Haberler was a precursor, who kept the free market or liberalization flame alight. Now, when one rereads him, one finds much that is obvious, quite moderate, and close to the mainstream. In assessing him, one should assess the whole of this school of thought and its battles with the protectionists.

Notes

1. Paul Samuelson, "Paul Samuelson's Remarks for Gottfried Haberler's Ninetieth Birthday Party Lunch at American Enterprise Institute, Washington, D.C., 18 July 1990," *The Journal of International Trade and Economic Development* vol. 1, number 1 (June 1992), 101-103.

2. Malcolm Gillis, "Gottfried Haberler: Contributions Upon Entering His Ninth Decade," pp. 139 140; Robert Baldwin, "Gottfried Haberler's Contributions to International Trade Theory and Policy," pp. 141-148; Lawrence H. Officer, "Prosperity and Depression--and Beyond," pp. 149-160; Thomas D. Willett, "Gottfried Haberler on Inflation, Unemployment, and International Monetary Economics: An Appreciation," pp. 161-171, all *Quarterly Journal of Economics*, vol. 97 (February 1982); Wolfgang Stolper, "Gottfried Haberler, 20 July 1990 - 6 May 1995," *Neue Züricher Zeitung*, May 13-14, 1995; Paul A. Samuelson, "Gottfried Haberler (1900-1995), *Economic Journal*, forthcoming. See also the tributes to him delivered at his American Enterprise Institute Memorial Service, September 18, 1995 by Christopher C. DeMuth, John S. Chipman, Wolfgang Stolper, Robert Solomon and Herbert Stein.

3. In p. 4 of Herbert Furth, English translation of "Gottfried Haberler: Ein Persönliches Lebensbild," *Wirtschafts Politische Blätter: Herausgegeben von der Bundeskammer der gewerblichen Wirtschaft*, 1990.

4. Herbert Stein, "Life with Gottfried at the AEI," Remarks at Haberler's AEI Memorial Service, September 18, 1995.

5. McCloskey cites Haberler as one of the economists whose writings are models for others. "When you read any of these [authors] in economics, pay attention: this is as good as it gets." Donald N. McCloskey *The Writing of Economics*, (New York: Macmillan, 1987), p. 9.

6. Haberler's birth tongue is German. The gymnasium he attended followed a classical curriculum; he studied Greek and Latin there, but not modern languages. In 1918, when he was eighteen, he was drafted into the Austrian army, but was stationed in a quiet zone. In his spare time, he taught himself English. In reading his essays from both the early 1930s and the early 1990s, it is clear that his powerful, effective style was something he worked hard to perfect. As an example, Robert Solomon at Haberler's AEI memorial service cites footnote 7 of the essay reproduced here as "Rational Expectations."

7. John S. Chipman, "Gottfried Haberler" in *The New Palgrave Dictionary of Economics*, John Eatwell, Murray Milgate, and Peter Newman (eds.) (London: Macmillan Press Ltd.), p. 581.

8. Robert Solomon, "Gottfried Haberler, 1900-1995," delivered at Haberler's AEI Memorial Service, September 18, 1995.

9. Herbert Stein, "Life with Gottfried at the AEI," Remarks at Haberler's AEI Memorial Service, September 18, 1995.

10. From a letter to Christopher C. DeMuth, August 16, 1995.

11. From John S. Chipman's Tribute to Gottfried Haberler, at the AEI Memorial Service (prepared from a tape recording).

12. Excerpted from Wolfgang Stolper, "Gottfried Haberler: 20 July 1900 - 6 May 1995," the *Neue Züricher Zeitung*, May 13-14, 1995.

13. Paul A. Samuelson, "Gottfried Haberler (1900-1995)," *Economic Journal*, forthcoming.

14. Paul Samuelson, "Paul Samuelson's Remarks for Gottfried Haberler's Ninetieth Birthday Party Lunch at American Enterprise Institute, Washington, DC, 18 July 1990," *The Journal of Intentional Trade and Economic Development*, Volume 1, Number 1, June 1992, pp. 101-103.

15. Paul Samuelson, "Tribute to Gottfried Haberler for American Enterprise Institute Memorial 18 September 1995."

2

An Overview of Economic Policy:
"A Positive Program for a
Benevolent and Enlightened Dictator"[1]

Summary

The economic malaise that gripped the Western world in the 1970s, after the euphoria and optimism of the 1950s and 1960s, continued and deepened in the 1980. All recent economic reports by national and international agencies are tinged with pessimism and gloom--seemingly intractable inflation and low productivity and GNP growth are the outlook. How would a benevolent and enlightened dictator deal with this problem?

The monetary authorities would be instructed to reduce monetary growth to the potential growth of real GNP. Although it is true that sufficiently tight money can bring down inflation irrespective of the size of the budget deficit, our dictator would realize that the combination of tight money-soft fiscal policy would drive up interest rates, crowd out private investment, and slow productivity growth, which in turn would make the fight against inflation more difficult. This is why most monetarists insist that anti-inflationary monetary policy must be supported by tight fiscal policy. Easy money-tight budget is the appropriate anti-inflationary policy.

The importance of fiscal policy, however, goes far beyond balancing the budget. The growing size of the budget, the mounting tax burden, and the inflation-distorted tax structure have become a formidable road-block for economic growth. Tax reduction and tax reform--especially lowering of high marginal tax rates, which blunt the incentives to work, would realize that the beneficial effects of lower taxes would be slow in coming. Therefore, in order to avoid larger budget deficits, tax cuts must go hand in hand with expenditure cuts. This amounts to saying that our dictator would practice supply-side economics in the broad sense of the term, to wit, that he would take steps to stimulate output and employment. He would, however, reject supply-side economics in the narrow sense, now so popular, which claims that the beneficial effects of tax cuts on output and employment will materialize so fast that no reduction in tax revenues will result.

Growing rigidity of wages and prices has become a more serious obstacle to a successful anti-inflationary monetary policy than soft fiscal policy. Money wages are almost totally rigid downward, and real wages, too, have become rigid through formal or de facto indexation. Labor unions are not the only culprits. Numerous other pressure groups do for their constituents through political pressure what unions do for workers. Organized agriculture is the most important example. As a consequence, monetary restraint causes so much transitional or even long-lasting unemployment that it is almost impossible to bring it to a successful conclusion. In a truly competitive economy stagflation on the present scale would be impossible.

In this paper, the view of some monetarists that stagflation and persistent unemployment are possible even in a perfectly competitive economy is analyzed and found invalid, because of the failure to make the crucially important distinction between involuntary and voluntary unemployment.

Measures to make the economy more competitive are discussed. The most difficult problem will be curbing union power. Withdrawing special privileges will go a long way toward reducing wage pressure, but more drastic measures, such as abrogating inflationary wage contracts, should visibly be kept in reserve.

As far as nonlabor monopolies, oligopolies, and price rigidities are concerned, free international trade is the most potent and administratively easiest measure for restoring and maintaining competition. Deregulating industry and eliminating farm price supports and output restrictions would help to restore flexibility, to stimulate output, and to smooth the transition to a noninflationary growth path.

Two other reasons for chronic inflation and near-zero productivity growth that are often mentioned are the enormous rise of crude oil prices by OPEC and a dearth of entrepreneurial talents combined with a

slowdown of technological progress. On closer analysis these explanations of intractable inflation are found invalid.

International complications are next considered. For the United
States the proper policy is to concentrate on domestic stability and
growth. If inflation is curbed, the dollar will strengthen all by itself, and
the foreign exchange market can be left to manage itself. A unilateral
return to a Bretton Woods-type regime of "fixed but adjustable"
exchange rates, let alone the gold standard, is out of the question. Such
a reform would require consensus among the leading industrial countries
that does not exist.

Our dictator would cooperate with the International Monetary Fund
to see that other countries keep their currencies freely convertible in the
foreign exchange markets either at fixed rates (if they prefer to peg their
currency to that of a major country) or at floating rates. The many
countries that peg their currencies will have to keep their inflation rates
approximately to the level prevailing in the country to whose currency
they peg. The numerous highly inflationary countries, mostly in the
third world, have no choice but to let their currencies float in one form
or another.

In conclusion, it is pointed out that the present paper's concern with
inflation as the most serious economic problem confronting the United
States and other industrial countries is not meant to deny that the real
economy, output and employment, are intrinsically more important than
price stability. But we have learned that satisfactory, steady real growth
and full employment cannot be achieved in an inflationary environment.
There is a widespread view that the "North-South" confrontation is a
more serious problem than inflation and slow productivity growth. This
view, which has been dramatized by the Brandt commission report on
international development issues, is briefly analyzed and rejected.

Introduction

In my contribution to the 1979 edition of "Contemporary Economic
Problems," I analyzed the economic malaise that in the 1970s had
gripped the United States and other Western industrial countries after a
long period of rapid growth, optimism, and euphoria in the 1950s and
early 1960s. The malaise continued and became more intense in 1980.
All recent reports on the state of the world economy and the prospects
for the coming year from national and international agencies--the Inter-

national Monetary Fund, the Organization for Economic Cooperation and Development, the European Community, the Bank for International Settlements, the Kiel Institute, and so forth--are tinged with pessimism and gloom, predicting more inflation, near-zero productivity growth, stagnating or declining GNP, and high unemployment.[2] The Reagan Administration has been warned of the danger of an "economic Dunkirk," requiring the declaration of an economic emergency. Even some of those who, rightly in my opinion, reject the idea of declaring an economic emergency call the present outlook frightening.

In my 1979 article I traced the malaise to two related developments, first, a seemingly intractable chronic inflation in its modern vicious form of stagflation and, second, near-zero productivity growth and GNP stagnation. I argued that these twin afflictions are not due to a basic flaw of the free-market, free-enterprise capitalist system; on the contrary, they are the result of the fact that the Western industrial economies have moved too far away from the competitive ideal.

In the present article I discuss how a benevolent and enlightened dictator would deal with the problem. This approach permits me to concentrate on the economics of the problem and to bypass the admittedly important question of the political feasibility of such a program in a democracy.

A benevolent dictator is one who respects consumer sovereignty, who does not, as actual dictators usually do, impose on the people his own views of what is good for them. An enlightened dictator is one who realizes that to get the best results, to achieve rapid growth, full employment, and price stability, he has to rely on free, competitive markets-- that is, real competition with private property of the means of production and respect for adequate profit margins. In other words, an enlightened dictator does not try to substitute central planning for free markets and recognizes the theories of democratic, competitive socialism à la Oscar Lange and H. D. Dickinson[3] as what they are--unrealistic utopias.

How Much Power to the Dictator?

The power of the enlightened dictator must be circumscribed in a reasonable way. Simply to endow him with omniscience and omnipotence would beg too many questions and would stamp the approach as a utopian exercise.

It is not unreasonable, however, to assume that the dictator would be in full control of monetary and fiscal policies. That would make it possible for him to solve the credibility problem. It would exclude political interference by a recalcitrant parliament swayed by pressures from special interest groups. Thus, the public could be persuaded that the announced policies will be carried out consistently.

Monetary Restraint

The central bank would be instructed to reduce monetary growth to approximately the potential or normal rate of growth of real GNP.[4] That leaves open technical questions such as the choice of the monetary aggregates, the speed of the reduction of monetary growth, and occasional minor deviations from the norm. These decisions can be left to the monetary experts, who would be freed from political interference and the pressures of special interest groups.

The Need for Fiscal Restraint

The enlightened dictator would realize, however, that for optimum results monetary policy needs to be supported by fiscal policy. Inflation can be brought down by different monetary-fiscal policy mixes; tight money (high interest rates)--easy budget (large budget deficits), or easy money (low interest rates)--tight budget (low deficits or budget surpluses). Consider the first alternative. It is true that sufficiently tight money could do the job of bringing down inflation irrespective of the size of the budget deficit. Still, side effects on productivity and investment of tight money and an easy budget (large deficits) would be serious. This policy mix would drive up interest rates and would crowd out productive private investment, thus slowing down the growth of productivity and GNP.[5] This in turn would make the fight against inflation more difficult, for in a stagnating economy it is much harder than in a growing one to accommodate rising claims on the national product and to shift resources from obsolescent, declining industries to those showing new growth.

It follows that the other alternative, easy money-tight budget, is much to be preferred; large budget deficits must be scaled down. It could even be argued that in order to stimulate investment and productivity growth, the most effective policy would be to aim at a budget surplus, channeling the surplus funds through the capital market into productive private investments. This policy option, however, has gone out of fashion.[6] Today a balanced budget is regarded as the maximum achievable.

The importance of a tight fiscal policy as a supplement to anti-inflationary monetary policy goes far beyond balancing the budget. The size of the budget and the tax structure are equally important for productivity growth and thus indirectly for the fight against inflation. Therefore our enlightened dictator would do his best to reduce government expenditures, expenditures on goods and services as well as transfer payments, in order to free resources for productive investment in the private sector and to lighten the tax burden. The magnitude of the tax burden and the tax structure have become a major impediment for the attainment of maximum growth. The tax structure has been greatly distorted by inflation. Inflation has pushed taxpayers into higher and higher tax brackets and has led to the taxation of inflationary phantom profits and of negative interest rates--thus discouraging saving and investment. A radical reform of the tax system to eliminate the existing distortions would be a high-priority task. Reducing the progressivity of the income tax, indexation of the income tax, and realistic depreciation allowances would go a long way to reforming the tax structure.

The beneficial effects of such reform measures on the flow of savings and investment, on productivity and GNP growth, would be substantial and thus could be expected eventually to result in an increase in tax revenues. Still, our enlightened dictator would realize that these beneficial effects are likely to emerge only slowly. He therefore would carefully watch the impact on the budget. In the short and medium run, tax revenues will decline, and the budget deficit will increase. Therefore, to avoid inflationary effects, tax reductions and tax reform should go hand in hand with expenditure cuts.

In other words, our dictator would practice supply-side economics in the broad sense of adopting measures, in the tax field and other areas, that stimulate productivity growth and increase supply. In particular, he would remove existing obstacles to innovative investment, such as over-regulation of industry and taxation of inflationary phantom profits and of negative interest rates. This approach does not imply acceptance--on the contrary, it means rejection--of supply-side economics in the narrow (extreme) sense that has become popular in recent years, namely, in the sense that reduction of tax rates will almost instantaneously induce a greater work effort and stimulate savings and investment to such an extent that tax revenues will not decline and the budget deficit will not increase.

Monetarists, who rightly stress the monetary nature of inflation and the primary responsibility of monetary policy for winding down inflation, usually add that it is imperative that tight money be supplemented by a tight fiscal policy. They concede that in order to avoid side effects of monetary restraint on output, employment, and investment, and to improve the growth performance of the economy, budget deficits must be scaled down, the size of the government reduced, and the tax structure reformed.

The Role of Wage and Price Rigidity

This qualification of pure monetarism has very important implications. It raises the question: Are there no factors other than a soft fiscal policy that also aggravate the side effects of an anti-inflationary tight money policy on output, employment, and productivity? The answer is: There are indeed such factors, and in a sense that will become clear presently, they are even more basic and important than the budgetary and fiscal-policy problem. Our enlightened dictator would understand that the fight against inflation would not be so difficult, in fact, that stagflation on the present scale would be impossible, if our economy had not moved so far away from the competitive ideal. He would realize that changing that trend, making the economy more competitive and flexible, is of great importance for curbing inflation and promoting growth.

Let us compare the solution of the problem of unemployment in an ideally, or even a moderately, competitive economy with the actual situation. If monetary-fiscal restraints initially cause unemployment, in a fully competitive economy money wages and labor cost would decline, so that the level of employment could be quickly restored. In a moderately competitive economy, money wages would at least stop rising and would gradually decline so that wage costs could decrease. Actually, money wages have become almost totally rigid downward, both in the aggregate and in particular industries. Striking examples are provided by the U.S. automobile and steel industries. These industries pay the highest union wages in the economy, although they are in deep trouble and suffer from high unemployment and slack. Wages in these industries are more than 50 percent higher than the average wage in manufacturing industries. This would be impossible in a competitive economy. Furthermore, real wages, too, have become increasingly rigid downward through formal and de facto indexation, and unions often push up real wages in the face of substantial unemployment. Labor unions are, of course, not the only culprits. Other pressure groups often force the government, through political action, to do for their members what unions do for workers. Organized agriculture is the most conspicuous and important example.

Monetarists in general have neglected, ignored, downplayed, or even denied the importance of this development for the fight against inflation. Still, there are exceptions. For example, the great monetarist Harry G. Johnson in one of his last papers wrote:

> Over the period since World War II governments have been assuming wider and wider responsibilities. In particular, their commitment to full employment has been carried to absurd lengths, well beyond the limits of feasibility. In some countries, there now appears to be a commitment not only for every man to be employed, but for him to be employed in the occupation of his choice, in the location of his choice and, it would sometimes seem, at the income of this choice.

In a footnote to the second sentence of this passage, Johnson added: "This has been a significant factor in the inflationary tendencies that have developed in a number of industrialized countries--especially in the United Kingdom."[7]

The older generation of Chicago economists, Frank H. Knight, Henry Simons, Jacob Viner, and others, unlike most modern monetarists did not ignore or minimize the great importance of the growing rigidity of wages and prices for the smooth working of the monetary system. Frank H. Knight wrote: "In a free market these differential changes [between prices of "consumption goods" and "capital goods" on the one hand and the prices of "productive services, especially wages," on the other hand] would be temporary, but even then might be serious, and with important markets [especially the labor market] as unfree as they actually are, the results take on the proportion of a disaster."[8] Knight wrote with the *deflation* of the 1930s in mind, but what he says about wage and price rigidity applies equally to the case of disinflation, and the rigidification of wages and certain prices has made much progress since Knight wrote.

A good example of the neglect of the problem of institutional rigidities by most monetarists and rational expectations theorists is provided in an article by Karl Brunner, Alex Cuikerman, and Allan H. Meltzer.[9] The gist of the article can be given and evaluated without wading through the flood of mathematical formulas with which the argument is presented. According to the authors, "persistent unemployment" and stagflation "can occur in a neo-classical framework . . . in which all expectations are rational and all markets clear instantaneously."[10] In other words, perfect competition is compatible with persistent unemployment and stagflation.

For the problem at hand, the relevant part of the authors' theory is the supply function of labor. It goes like this: To determine the amount of labor that workers are willing to supply, they "compare the currently prevailing wage to the wage they currently perceive as permanent." If the prevailing wage is equal to the perceived permanent wage, there is full employment. Now suppose the economy is subjected to a "shock"-- the authors usually speak of "a change in productivity." If productivity goes up, the actual real wage is raised "on impact." Still, the workers cannot know immediately whether the change is permanent or transient. Therefore, "the currently perceived permanent wage" will for some time be below the actually ruling wage. This will induce workers to supply more labor, which means "to work now and substitute future for current leisure," resulting in "negative unemployment."[11] In other words, there will be what is usually called "overfull employment."

If the shock is unfavorable, if productivity declines, the actual real wage will be reduced "on impact." Again, however, the workers cannot be sure what the permanent wage will be. Therefore, the actual wage will for some time be below the currently perceived permanent wage. This will induce "part of the labor force which looks for work [to] abstain from accepting current employment. This group is counted as unemployed in the official statistics."[12] If "negative unemployment" means "substitution of future leisure for current leisure," then positive unemployment means substitution of current leisure for future leisure.

To describe unemployment as leisure is rather odd. At any rate, it is voluntary unemployment: If workers "substitute current leisure for future leisure" or vice versa, the leisure that they freely choose because they expect the future wage rate to be different from the current one represents *voluntary* unemployment and has nothing to do with real, *involuntary* unemployment.[13] But the authors do not mention the indispensable distinction between voluntary and involuntary unemployment.

The essential distinction between voluntary and involuntary unemployment has been made popular by Keynes's *The General Theory*. Keynes criticized the "classical school" for recognizing only voluntary unemployment. As far as his contemporary classical economists were concerned, Keynes's criticism was clearly unjustified. For example, A. C. Pigou makes the distinction between voluntary and involuntary unemployment,[14] although using different words. Still, Keynes's criticism was prophetically right as far as many modern monetarists are concerned.

That Brunner, Cuikerman, and Meltzer are a little uneasy about their definition of unemployment is suggested by the fact that although they speak repeatedly of *persistent* unemployment, in a footnote they suddenly say: "Since the focus of the paper is on cyclical unemployment, we do not discuss types of unemployment that arise for other reasons."[15] It seems that despite the talk about *persistent* unemployment, the authors had all along the comparatively mild and short-lived postwar recessions in mind. It is true that in these recessions, due to generous unemployment benefits and welfare payments, the official unemployment figures contain a significant amount of spurious, that is, voluntary unemployment. It is also well known that generous unemployment benefits have increased frictional unemployment (which occurs when workers who have lost their jobs take more time to look for suitable new jobs) and have reduced the hardship of unemployment. Still, it is surely an exaggeration to say, as the authors seem to imply, that all or the great bulk of registered unemployment is of the voluntary kind and that unemployment no longer involves any hardship.

In defense of the proposition that unemployment can occur even in the absence of strong unions, it can be argued (and has been argued, though not in the article under discussion) that unorganized workers often behave as if they were organized. Thus, in the depression in the nineteenth century, or in the 1930s, when unions were nonexistent or weak, workers resisted wage cuts. Declining demand for labor in a depression is a strong inducement for workers to organize themselves in order to strengthen their bargaining power. For this and other reasons, employers, on their part, are reluctant to push hard for wage cuts. The reason for the stickiness of wages even in the absence of powerful labor unions--why there is rarely "thoroughgoing competition" among workers --was thoroughly analyzed by A. C. Pigou in *The Theory of Unemployment*, a pre-Keynesian work, and repeated in the post-Keynesian *Lapses from Full Employment*. Pigou, of course, attributed much importance to the activities of labor unions and to government policies, especially generous unemployment benefits. In the preface to *Lapses* he says, "Professor Dennis Robertson has warned me that the form of the book may suggest that I am in favor of attacking the problem of [mass] unemployment by manipulating wages rather than by manipulating demand. I wish therefore to say clearly that this is not the case."[16]

In recent years the problem of wage rigidities, the seeming collusion of employers and workers, has been thoroughly examined by Arthur Okun. He speaks felicitously of the "invisible handshake" and the "implicit contract" between management and labor, both being fully aware that they have a valuable investment in their amicable relationship.[17]

In short, wages were not entirely flexible downward even before unions became as powerful as they are now. This is what Knight had in mind when he wrote that even when the economy was more free than at the time of his writing, monetary deflation was a serious matter.[18]

There surely is truth in all this, but the point must not be pushed too far; we must keep a sense of proportion. After all, in the great depression of the 1930s and the depression of the nineteenth century, money wages did decline sharply despite the workers' resistance. This situation has changed completely. Today's almost total downward rigidity of money wages, both in the aggregate and in particular industries, combined with real wage push, often in the face of heavy unemployment, would be inconceivable without the existence of strong unions, fostered and abetted by government policies.[19] The power and aggressiveness of other pressure groups, too, has increased sharply. This accounts for stagflation on the present scale. To ignore these institutional changes and rigidities is like playing Hamlet without the Prince of Denmark.

How to Make the Economy More Competitive

Since government policies are to a large extent responsible for the power of the various pressure groups to push up wages and prices, our enlightened dictator should be able to reduce the pressure on wages and prices considerably without taking such drastic steps as prohibiting collective, industrywide bargaining, outlawing indexation of wages, abrogating existing union wage contracts, and the like. Merely withdrawing privileges, protective measures, and subsidies that are now lavishly accorded to numerous pressure groups would go a long way to promote price stability and to reduce the transitional unemployment resulting from monetary-fiscal restraint, thus taking some of the burden of fighting inflation off the shoulders of the monetary authorities. But keeping visibly in reserve to be used if necessary some of the drastic measures, such as the possibility of abrogating or modifying inflationary wage contracts that run for several years, would have a restraining effect on wage contracts and thus would help to smooth the transition to a noninflationary growth path.

As far as industrial monopolies and oligopolies are concerned, freer trade is the most powerful and administratively the easiest method of restoring and strengthening competition. Given the enormous growth of world trade in manufactured goods during the postwar period and the fact that numerous new industrial centers have sprung up in developed and less developed countries, few significant monopolies or oligopolies could survive under free trade (outside the public utility area, where prices are controlled anyway). In addition to ensuring competition, freer trade would also increase GNP through more extended international division of labor. The increased flow of goods would have an anti-inflationary effect. Since high tariffs, import quotas, and other nontariff barriers to trade are still widespread, despite the liberalization of international trade that has taken place under the aegis of the General Agreement on Tariffs and Trade (GATT), there is here a rich field for our enlightened dictator to exploit in moving the economy closer to the competitive ideal. The concept of nontariff barriers should be interpreted broadly to include "voluntary" restrictions imposed on foreign exporters (often called "orderly market agreements," or OMAs) and subsidies to noncompetitive firms and industries, including subsidies in the form of taking over noncompetitive firms and operating them with great losses at the expense of the taxpayer.

Curbing the power of labor unions is the most difficult part of a policy of liberalization of the economy. Still, opening up the economy to foreign competition would go a long way to reducing the power of unions. Unions know, or find out quickly, that striking against world markets is risky. This is the reason why in small countries, where international trade is a large fraction of the economy, labor unions are usually much more moderate than in large countries.

Specific measures to reduce the power of unions to push up wages are abolition of the Davis-Bacon Act, which forces the government to buy exclusively from industries paying the highest union wages; elimination of minimum-wage laws;[20] prohibition of closed-shop agreements; restriction of the right to picket; and withdrawal of unemployment benefits from striking workers. Deregulation of industries will obviously rank high on the list of urgent tasks. The regulatory explosion of the last ten years or so should be stopped and rolled back as far as possible.

Doing all these things would reduce monopolistic wage and price pressures, promote labor mobility, enlarge international division of labor, stimulate growth, and reduce government expenditures by eliminating the vast bureaucracies that are now needed to administer the existing restrictions, privileges, subsidies, and controls.

The question arises--is that all there is to it? Or are there other causes of inflation that have not been mentioned so far? Does our dictator not need additional power to deal with those factors?

The Oil Price Rise

What comes to mind first is the Organization of Petroleum Exporting Countries (OPEC) and the recent and prospective rises in the oil price. In the United States, and lately also in Germany, the second oil shock of 1979-1980 is frequently mentioned as the major, if not decisive, cause of inflation and stagnation.

That the rise in the oil price as such was not decisive is demonstrated by the fact that some countries that depend much more on imported oil than the United States--for example, Germany, Switzerland, and Japan-- have managed to reduce the rate of inflation far below the American level despite the increase in the oil price. Furthermore, there are other energy-rich and oil-exporting countries that had even more inflation than the United States, for example, Canada and Venezuela.

According to OECD, "The quadrupling in 1973, and the more than doubling of the oil price between the end of 1978 and early 1980 represented a shock on the OECD economies equivalent to roughly two percent of GNP on each occasion."[21] After the first oil shock in 1973, the burden was lightened by inflation, because the dollar price of oil was kept stable for several years; this is not likely to happen after the second oil shock.[22]

A two percent reduction in real GNP is a shock, but it is not a crushing burden. In an ideal, fully competitive economy, if the monetary authorities keep the price level stable, prices of commodities other than oil and oil-related commodities would decline slightly, and there would be a once-for-all roughly two percent decline of money wages (or more generally, money incomes). In a growing economy a short pause in the growth would take care of the problem. In a perfectly competitive economy, there would be no unemployment, or if we relax the assumption and assume some stickiness of wages, there would be some transitional unemployment.

Now suppose money wages are rigid downward, whereas real wages are not (the Keynesian assumption). In this case, to maintain full employment, a small once-for-all increase in the price level, a slight extra spurt of inflation, would be necessary to accomplish the unavoidable once-for-all reduction in real wages. At the other extreme, if *real* wages too are rigid downward through indexation, the only remedy, that is to say, the only way to maintain equilibrium in the balance of payments, would be unemployment and slack, which would reduce the demand for oil. In the real world the outcome will probably be somewhere in the middle, some unemployment, merely transitional it is to be hoped, and some inflation.

This analysis, rough and simple though it is, permits us to draw an important conclusion: If, and to the extent to which, our enlightened dictator is able to bring the economy close to the competitive ideal, he will also solve ipso facto the problem of the oil shock. No additional powers are needed.

Secular Stagnation?

Another factor that is often mentioned as a cause of low productivity growth and indirectly of inflation is reminiscent of the theory of secular stagnation that flourished in the 1930s. Today, no one would argue, as the proponents of secular stagnation did, that we are suffering from over-saving, that is, an excess of saving over investment with deflationary consequences. Still, it is said, as in the 1930s, that investment has declined partly because of a lack of entrepreneurship, the absence of a technological breakthrough, or the slowing down of technological progress. Symptoms or aspects of this development are a declining trend in expenditures on research and development and an increasing share of lawyers and accountants among corporate executives, reflecting a decreasing share of businessmen.

The enlightened dictator would strongly doubt that there is a lack of entrepreneurial talents[23] and a decrease in the flow of usable inventions, as distinguished from actual innovations.[24] But, he would recognize that innovative investments by Schumpeterian entrepreneurs have been seriously impeded and reduced by the growing web of government controls and regulations, the low level of profits due to chronic inflation and stifling taxation, and the growth of government expenditures. This is the reason for the decline of expenditures on research and development and the tendency of lawyers and accountants to replace businessmen as directors of corporations.[25] These same factors are responsible for stagflation and low productivity. Therefore, our dictator would redouble his efforts to reduce the size of the public sector, cut government expenditures, reform the tax structure, deregulate industry, and so forth and thus would make the economy more competitive and flexible.

The enlightened dictator would understand that the creative job of introducing innovations, of "revitalizing industry," as the modern phrase goes, is best done by private entrepreneurs, large and small. Our dictator would resist the temptation of trying to speed up growth by government interventions, government commissions, or bureaucrats trying to identify growth industries as candidates for special subsidies, tax rebates, and other privileges. Such attempts almost always lead to the creation of white elephants and waste of resources. The dictator would also understand that the widespread practice of propping up uncompetitive, obsolescent firms and industries by subsidies and import restrictions is the very opposite of a rational growth policy.

The proper method to stimulate saving, investment, and growth is to provide a favorable climate for saving and investment through cutting government expenditures, lowering taxes, curbing inflation, and dismantling controls and regulations.

Problems of an Open Economy

So far I have assumed essentially a closed economy. In an open economy with substantial foreign trade and capital flows across the border, there arise additional complications the importance of which varies from country to country, depending on the size and structure of the economy.

The Case of the United States

In a large country where the foreign trade sector is relatively small, the additional complications are minor. Thus, in the United States, if our enlightened dictator is successful in subduing inflation, there would be no reason to worry about the foreign exchange value of the dollar and the balance of payments. The dollar, as the world's foremost international reserve currency, weakened by the long period of high inflation, would be restored to its former strong role. A larger inflow of foreign official funds could be expected. The U.S. share in "petrodollars" from

OPEC countries would increase. The United States may have to accept a larger current account deficit corresponding to the OPEC surplus, but that should be regarded as a blessing rather than a burden.

Of course, there could be changes in that picture. The OPEC countries may again turn out to be better spenders than was expected. That is to say, their surplus may shrink, and the flow of petrodollars may contract, and other countries may draw down their dollar reserves. Still, given the huge size of the U.S. capital market, such changes would hardly cause more than a ripple. No massive switches from the dollar to other currencies are likely, so long as reasonable price stability is maintained.

Our dictator would continue the present system of floating exchange rates. The United States could not, even if it wanted, unilaterally return to the Bretton Woods system of "stable but adjustable" exchange rates, let alone to fixed rates under the gold standard. This would constitute a major reform of the international monetary system. It would require agreement among the leading industrial countries and would take years to negotiate even if there existed a basic consensus that a move in that direction was desirable--a consensus that surely does not exist at the present time. If miraculously an international agreement on the restoration of a system of fixed exchange rates could be reached, the successful operation of such a regime would require continuous extremely close coordination of macroeconomic policies. Postwar experience has shown that in the present-day world this is impossible among sovereign states. The closely linked members of the European Community (EC) have not been able to reach the required degree of policy coordination. Nor has the problem been solved by the members of the European Monetary System (EMS), an even more tightly knit subgroup of the EC.[26]

Our enlightened dictator would conclude that the best strategy is to concentrate on domestic policy objectives--price stability, growth, employment--and leave the foreign exchange market to manage itself. He would cooperate with the International Monetary Fund, helping the Fund to discharge its statutory duty of "exercising firm surveillance over the exchange rate policies of members,"[27] to make sure that countries keep their currencies freely convertible in the foreign exchange market either at fixed rates (if they wish to peg their currencies to some major currency or to a basket of currencies) or at a floating rate and refrain from imposing exchange control and from "manipulating exchange rates . . . in order to prevent effective balance of payments adjustment or to gain an unfair competitive advantage over other members."[28]

The Case of Smaller Countries

I will now discuss very briefly some of the complications arising for some other countries or groups of countries from the openness of their economy.

There are, first, many, mostly medium-sized or small, countries that peg their currencies to the dollar or to some other major currency or basket of currencies. To stay out of balance-of-payments troubles, these countries have to keep their inflation rate approximately at the level prevailing in the country or countries to whose currency their own is pegged. I say "approximately" because comparative inflation rates, like purchasing-power parity, are but a very rough criterion of equilibrium. There is, furthermore, a large group of countries, mostly developing countries, with very high inflation rates, such as Argentina, Brazil, Israel, and Turkey. These countries have no choice but to let their currencies float in one form or other, including a crawling, trotting, or galloping peg. Much more complicated is the situation in Japan and the industrial countries in Europe.

Concluding Remarks

The emphasis in this chapter . . . has been on inflation. This is not to deny that the *real* economy--output, employment, income distribution, and so forth--is intrinsically more important than a stable price level. But, we have learned that the prospects for attainment of maximum growth, full employment, and price stability are inextricably interrelated. Whatever is true in the short run, in the long run inflation is incompatible with satisfactory growth. The longer inflation lasts, the less can be achieved even in the short run by sudden unexpected spurts of inflation. In technical terms, even in the short run the Phillips curve tends to become vertical. Moreover, as we have seen, largely the same type of policy is indicated for bringing down inflation and for promoting growth.

The statement that inflation and the associated low productivity growth is the major problem confronting the industrial countries will perhaps be questioned by the many people who have become greatly alarmed by what is now called the North-South dialogue or confrontation allegedly resulting from a growing income gap between the developed industrial countries, the "North," and the less developed countries, the

"South." This problem has recently been dramatized by the report of a prestigious "independent commission on development issues" under the chairmanship of Willy Brandt, former chancellor of the Federal Republic of Germany. The title of the report is: "North-South: A Program for Survival."[29] The subtitle, "A Program for Survival," indicates the alarmist tone of the report. No one can fail to be appalled by the stark poverty in some less developed countries. Still, the Brandt commission's statement that poverty in less developed countries and the great inequality between the North and the South are responsible for wars, violence, and tensions in the world cannot be taken seriously. None of the recent wars had anything whatsoever to do with the North-South income gap--not the two world wars, nor any of the many local postwar conflicts--the wars in Korea and Vietnam, the Israel-Arab wars, the Persian Gulf war between Iran and Iraq, or the conflicts between Greece and Turkey or Ethiopia and Somalia. The *East-West* tensions and confrontations are a real global threat compared with which the *North-South* skirmishes are of minor importance.[30] The so-called South, or third world, is a very heterogeneous group. It comprises many countries (Argentina, Brazil, Taiwan, and so forth) that are well on the way to joining the industrial North. The really poor countries, sometimes called the fourth world, are but a fraction of the South.

Here is not the place to discuss the commonly proposed policies to deal with that problem ("resource transfer" from the rich to the poor countries, foreign aid and international charity, commodity price stabilization, and so on).[31] I confine myself to saying that if the industrial countries put their economic houses in order, curb inflation, resume normal growth, and liberalize trade, they will make a great contribution on the development of the less developed countries, including the very poor, by providing markets for third world exports, thus enabling them to continue the remarkable progress that, according to World Bank statistics, the less developed countries as a group have made during the prosperous period after World War II.[32]

Notes

1. Reprinted in abridged form from "The Economic Malaise of the 1980s: A Positive Program for a Benevolent and Enlightened Dictator," *Essays in Contemporary Economic Problems-Demand, Productivity, and Population, 1981-1982.* William Fellner, Project Director. (Washington, D.C.: American

Enterprise Institute, 1982), pp. 214-244.

2. A lame-duck economic report is an exception. An outgoing administration likes to depart on an at least moderately cheerful outlook, leaving the blame for future troubles and disappointments squarely on the shoulders of its successor. Of course, the incoming party has the opposite bias.

3. H. D. Dickinson, *The Economics of Socialism* (London: Oxford University Press, 1937), and Oscar Lange, "On the Economic Theory of Socialism," in B.E. Lippincott, ed., *On the Economic Theory of Socialism* (Minneapolis: University of Minnesota Press, 1938).

4. A few words should perhaps be said about the meaning of "potential" GNP growth. This concept refers to long-run growth, abstracting from cyclical fluctuations. "Potential" growth should not be interpreted as growth under ideal conditions such as perfect competition, absence of institutional rigidities, and optimal government policies. Normal long-run growth would perhaps be a better description." On the difficulties of estimating potential output, see William Fellner, "Structural Problems Behind Our Measured Unemployment Rates," *Contemporary Economic Problems 1978*, pp. 84-93. Successive reports of the Council of Economic Advisers, under both Democratic and Republican administrations, have estimated potential GNP growth to be between 3 and 4 percent per year. Whatever the defects of these estimates, monetary growth of 3 to 4 percent surely would not have been inflationary.

5. Two possible objections should be considered. First the question may be asked whether the crowding out of private investment by large government deficits can be prevented by easy money; in other words, whether "easy money and easy budget" would be a viable option. The answer is that from a narrow static viewpoint the impact of a given government deficit on private investment can always be offset by sufficiently easy credit to private industry. But this policy is, in general, incompatible with a stable price level; in other words, it is possible only at the cost of rising inflation. I say "in general" to allow for the exception of a Keynesian situation of high unemployment. In that case public deficit spending need not crowd out private investment. This was the case in the 1930s, when Keynesian theory was born. In the 1980s, however, we do not live in a Keynesian world. True, we have over 7 percent unemployment, but there is general agreement that the "natural" (incompressible) unemployment rate is higher than it used to be, perhaps as high as 5 or 6 percent. And equally important, inflationary expectations have become very sensitive, so that an expansionary policy quickly translates into higher prices; in other words, the Phillips curve has become almost vertical, even in the short run.

The second objection is that the larger deficit caused by the tax cut need not drive up interest rates and crowd out private investment because the taxpayers will be induced to save all or almost all of the additional disposal income resulting from the tax cut. This is, however, unlikely to happen on a sufficient scale, especially since the tax reduction is intended by the policy makers to be permanent and is so regarded by the taxpayers. A temporary tax reduction would be much more likely to elicit substantial savings than a permanent one because taxpayers would not want to raise the level of consumption if they knew that the higher level of consumption could not be maintained.

6. This policy raises, moreover, several difficult problems of which only two can be briefly mentioned. First, the policy obviously requires that the surplus be achieved without reducing the flow of private savings and investment and without impairing essential productive public services. Second, the question may be asked whether in a free market economy the determination of the volume of savings and investment should not be left to market forces, that is to say, to the collective decisions of households and firms to save and invest. This raises the deeper question: Is a growth policy justifiable that goes beyond removing impediments to growth created by public policies and tries to raise the rate of growth to a higher level than that implied by the collective savings and investment decisions of the market participants? In other words, is a policy of compulsory saving defensible in a free enterprise, capitalist economy? I have tried to give an answer in my book *Economic Growth and Stability: An Analysis of Economic Change and Policies* (Los Angeles: Nash, 1974), pp. 26-29.

7.   Geoffrey Denton, Seamus O'Cleireacain, and Sally Ash, *Trade Effects of Public Subsidies to Private Enterprise* (London: Holmes and Meier, 1975), pp. xiii, xxxiii.

8.   Frank H. Knight, "The Business Cycle, Interest and Money," in Frank H. Knight, *On the History and Methods of Economics* (Chicago: University of Chicago Press, 1956), p. 224. See also p. 211: "Wages are notoriously sticky, especially with respect to any downward change of the hourly wage rates."

9.   "Stagflation, Persistent Unemployment and the Permanence of Economic Shocks," *Journal of Monetary Economics*, vol. 6, no. 4 (October 1980), pp. 467-92.

10. Ibid., pp. 483, 490.

11. Ibid., p. 470.

12. Ibid.

13. The authors seem to assume that there is a basic symmetry between negative and positive unemployment in the sense that deviations of actual employment from the full employment level, what they call the "zero unemployment" level, are of the same order of magnitude on both sides of full employment. This surely is unrealistic, although it is consistent with the authors' neglect of institutional rigidities. In the real world there is a strong asymmetry between deviations on the up side and the down side of full employment, due to the fact that wages (and to a lesser extent, prices) are rigid downward but more or less flexible upward. With labor unions and other

pressure groups as strong as they are now, this asymmetry is pronounced. Still, it existed even in earlier periods when labor unions were weak. (See below.)

14. See Pigou's excellent discussion of the problem in his monograph *The Theory of Unemployment* (London: Macmillan & Co., 1933), chapter 1, "Definition of Unemployment." Actually, Keynes's definition of involuntary unemployment is unnecessarily complicated. The entirely satisfactory common-sense definition is: A worker is involuntarily unemployed if he cannot find a job, although he is willing and able to work at the ruling wage for the type of work for which he is qualified. A man is voluntarily unemployed if he does not work because he finds the ruling wage too low and prefers leisure. For the actual application of these concepts, further specifications are required, and the borderline between voluntary and involuntary unemployment is not always clearly marked. On this point, see the careful analysis by Herbert Giersch, *Konjunktur- und Wachstumspolitik in der offenen Wirtschaft* (Wiesbaden: Dr. Th. Gabler-Verlag, 1977), pp. 254-57.

15. "Stagflation, Persistent Unemployment," footnote 12, p. 470. What the other types of unemployment are is not explained. Could it be that the other types of unemployment are nothing else but real, involuntary unemployment? In this connection it would be interesting to know whether the authors regard the mass unemployment of the depression of the 1930s as cyclical. Can that unemployment be described as a "substitution of present for future leisure?"

16. A. C. Pigou, *Lapses from Full Employment* (London: Macmillan & Co., 1944), p. v.

17. See especially Arthur Okun's posthumously published book *Prices and Quantities: A Macroeconomic Analysis* (Washington, D.C.: Brookings Institution, 1981).

18. Knight, *On the History and Methods of Economics*.

19. For statistical evidence of the changes that have taken place, see Jeffrey Sachs, *The Changing Cyclical Behavior of Wages and Prices, 1890-1976*, National Bureau of Economic Research, Working Paper 304 (Cambridge, Mass., 1978).

20. Minimum wages are largely responsible for the shockingly high unemployment among teenagers, especially black ones, and other under-privileged unskilled workers. The victims of this antisocial legislation are thus deprived of the on-the-job training that is essential for their future careers. See Masanori Hashimoto, *Minimum Wages and On-the-Job Training* (Washington, D.C.: American Enterprise Institute, 1981).

21. OECD, *Economic Outlook*, July 1980, p. 114. For the United States it is less than 2 percent.

22. I ignore another factor that postponed and potentially lightened the burden for some countries (for example, the United States), namely the fact that they received a large share of the petrodollars, in other words, that they could run a balance-of-payments deficit corresponding to the OPEC surplus.

23.   A striking example of lively entrepreneurial activity is the economic rejuvenation of New England. In the last two decades or so the economy of the region has undergone a basic transformation. It has emancipated itself from the traditional, obsolescent textile and shoe industries. Their place has been taken by high-technology industries--micro-ball bearings, computer hardware and the like. These industries are composed of numerous small and medium-sized firms. See John R. Meyer and Robert A. Leone, "The New England States and their Economic Future: Some Implications of a Changing Industrial Environment," *Papers and Proceedings of the American Economic Association*, 68 (May 1978), pp. 110-15, and Lynn E. Browne and John S. Hekman, "New England's Economy in the 1980s," *New England Economic Review* (Federal Reserve Bank of Boston), January/February 1981.

24.   It will be recalled that since Schumpeter, economists distinguish between inventions, that is, discoveries of new or improved products or methods of production in the scientist's study or laboratories on the one hand, and the actual production of new products or use of new methods of production or marketing by innovating, risk-taking entrepreneurs on the other hand. (J. A. Schumpeter, *The Theory of Economic Development*, trans. Redvers Opie [Cambridge, Mass.: Harvard University Press, 1934]; first German edition, 1912).

25.   Since business management has to spend more and more time and effort to cope with the rising flood of government regulations and to find ways to reduce the tax burden, it is quite natural for lawyers and accountants to play an increasing role in corporate board rooms.   These basically unproductive activities drain scarce human resources away from the creative and productive entrepreneurial activities.

26.   It has often been demonstrated that a system of "stable but adjustable" exchange rates à la Bretton Woods is in the long run unworkable because it opens the floodgate to destabilizing speculation. See, for example, Gottfried Haberler, "The International Monetary System after Jamaica and Manila," in *Contemporary Economic Problems 1977*, William Fellner, ed. (Washington, D.C.: American Enterprise Institute, 1977), pp. 244-45, excerpted in this volume as section IV.A.1.

27.   *Articles of Agreement*, article IV, section 3.

28.   *Articles of Agreement*, article IV, section 1.

29.   Cambridge, Mass.: MIT Press, 1980.

30.   For recent U.S. and other Western policy statements (especially but not only before the Russian invasion of Afghanistan) that take the opposite position, see the article by the great historian and Soviet expert Adam B. Ulam, "How to Restrain the Soviets," *Commentary*, vol. 70, no. 6 (December 1980), p. 99.

31.   The largely dubious policy proposals of the Brandt commission have been critically analyzed by P. T. Bauer and B. S. Yamey in "East-

West/North-South: Peace and Prosperity?" *Commentary*, no. 4 (September 1970), and P. D. Henderson in "Survival, Development and the Report of the Brandt Commission," *The World Economy: A Quarterly Journal on International Economic Affairs*, vol. 3, no. 1 (June 1980). For a thorough discussion of the so-called New International Economic Order, see Ryan C. Amacher, Gottfried Haberler, and Thomas D. Willett, eds., *Challenges to a Liberal International Economic Order* (Washington, D.C.: American Enterprise Institute, 1979).

     32. On this point see Gottfried Haberler, "The Liberal International Economic Order in Historical Perspective," in *Challenges to a Liberal International Economic Order*, pp. 43-65 and 85-90.

3

Domestic Macroeconomic Policy

Inflation: Causes and Cures

Explaining Stagflation[1]

Introduction. I take it for granted that inflation is a monetary phenomenon in the sense that there has never been a serous inflation without an increase in the quantity of money and that a serious inflation cannot be slowed or stopped without restrictions on monetary growth. Recognition of this fact does not, however, imply the assumption of a strict parallelism between changes in M and P, however these terms may be defined. Nor does it preclude going behind changes in M and analyzing the economic, social and political forces that shape the observed changes in M, in other words, identifying causes of inflation more remote than changes in M. Nor does it mean that anti-inflation policy must be confined to monetary policy, i.e. measures to restrict monetary growth. Changing or eliminating some of the factors which cause excessive monetary growth may be an indispensable ingredient, along with monetary restraint, of an economically effective and politically feasible anti-inflation policy.

Monetarists are fully aware that the parallelism between M and P is not quite strict. There is in the short-run a sizable and variable lag between changes in M and P, and there are longer-run, structural changes in the correlation. In other words V, the velocity of circulation of money, although neither a volatile nor a plastic magnitude as Keynesians assume, is subject to change. It changes cyclically and it seems to have a secular downward trend; occasionally it displays longer swings. For example, during World War II, price control, rationing and a sharply reduced supply of durable goods induced a sharp increase in consumer savings; and a decrease in consumer credit depressed V to an abnormally low level. This was followed by a longish period of rising V after the war. Prolonged inflation naturally has the effect of speeding up velocity, as recent developments have again demonstrated. The rise in V in an inflation[2] is a very important matter to which I shall briefly return later. Here I note that it marks one way by which "inflation feeds on itself" and that it has given rise to a dispute and confusion among monetarists: I am referring to the controversy on whether nominal or real balances are the proper target for monetary policy.

I do not propose to pursue the subject of the precise correlation between M and P any further. Suffice it to say that it is only in rare, extreme circumstances that V moves out of a fairly narrow range.[3] Such extreme cases apart, changes in V are sufficiently large to create policy dilemmas and opportunities for confusion, but they do not destroy the basic connection between changes in the quantity of money and changes in the price level.

It is easy to point to certain latter day economic, political, social and intellectual developments that help to explain the modern proneness to inflation. The rise of Keynesian thinking, preoccupation with full employment and growth, and intolerance to comparatively low levels of unemployment have without doubt greatly increased the propensity to inflate. Today a slight increase in slack and unemployment which might have gone unnoticed in former years is enough to trigger loud demands for expansionary monetary and fiscal measures to speed up growth and increase employment. The recent anti-growth movement and rising concern about the environment and pollution have not reduced but increased the pressure; for environmental concerns express themselves largely in measures that reduce output, increase cost and require additional expenditures to protect the environment.

A related development that is often mentioned as a source of inflation is the enormous growth of the public sector in all countries. In the broad sense, this includes increasing interventions in, and regulations of, private business, rapidly growing transfer payments (for social security and welfare purposes, subsidies of all kinds, etc.) and a growing number of firms and industries owned and operated by the government.

Still another change, largely a consequence of government policies, is the rise of monopoly or market power, labor unions and big business. It is a widely held view that wage-push by powerful unions and monopoly pricing has made inflation much more intractable than it used to be in former years.

Each of these various developments has, no doubt, some bearing on inflation. But the important thing is to identify the channels through which they exert the inflationary pressure.

If we accept the proposition that there can be no serious inflation without an increase in the quantity of money, it follows that these various developments operate via inducing monetary expansion. Some of the factors mentioned merely explain why there is greater readiness on the part of the monetary authorities actively to expand, or passively to permit an increase in the money supply. Larger government deficits due to the growth of the public sector provide a powerful inducement for monetary expansion. Cost push by unions and monopolistic price rises, by threatening unemployment, are perhaps an even stronger pressure to expand the monetary circulation. (I realize that this is a controversial statement and shall come back to it presently.)

There is still another channel through which inflationary pressure may be exerted. A sharp reduction in output (aggregate supply or real GNP) could lead to a price rise. (This could be an exception to the rule that no serious inflation is possible without an increase in M.) "Special factors" such as the oil price rise, a poor crop, the disappearance of the anchovies from the coast of Peru which have been said to have greatly contributed to the price explosion in 1973 and 1974, belong to this category. As I shall try to show, the depreciation of the dollar is analytically closely related to the special factors just mentioned.

I take it for granted that any inflation, however it is brought about-- by credit expansion for private business, government deficit, wage push, "special factors" or what not--can be slowed or stopped by monetary restraints. But the side effects on overall activity, on particular sectors and on long-run growth will be different. For brevity let me concentrate on overall activity (unemployment and idle capacity) and mention sectoral and long-run side effects only in passing.

I shall now discuss the different cases starting with (1) what is often called the "classical" case of demand inflation, and cost-or wage-push inflation, (2) "special supply-reducing factors," and (3) international aspects ("imported inflation"). Actually the different factors usually operate concurrently. Demand and cost inflation are especially difficult to separate, but it is sometimes possible to find periods when the one or the other factor was dominant.

Demand Inflation and Cost Inflation. There is agreement, shared by monetarists and anti-monetarists, such as James Tobin, that monetary restraint is the specific cure for demand inflation as distinguished from a cost- or wage-push inflation. That holds for an inflation which has its root in expanding bank credits to private business as well as for one which finances a government deficit. If the monetary authorities stand firm, a government deficit will drive up interest rates and "crowd out" private investment. Alternatively, a deficit can be eliminated by raising taxes or cutting government expenditures. As far as the effect on overall activity is concerned, there is probably not much difference between fighting a government-induced inflation by monetary policy (higher interest rates), raising taxes or cutting expenditures. But the sectoral impact (e.g., on the construction industry) and long-run effects on productivity growth will of course be very different depending partly on which taxes are raised and which expenditures are cut.[4] It is often assumed that the transition from an inflationary to a non-inflationary (or less inflationary) situation can be accomplished without side effects on overall activity if it is brought about by fiscal rather than by monetary measures.[5] I cannot see the difference--apart from the different sectoral or long-run impact.

But how do we distinguish a demand-pull inflation from a cost-push inflation, conceptually and in reality? The standard phrase which has been used again and again by economists and policy makers in the course of the current inflation is that when "excess demand" has been "squeezed out," but prices continue to rise, demand inflation has been transformed into a cost inflation. But this is a very misleading expression. What is "excess demand?" Whenever the price level rises, aggregate demand rises faster than aggregate supply. In that sense demand is excessive whenever there is a rise in the price level. A better description is the Keynesian term "profit inflation," used in *The Treatise on Money*. What is being squeezed (though not squeezed out) is profits.

Let us speak then of a demand-pull inflation when prices stay ahead of wages, salaries and often costs so that profits continue to rise. A demand inflation is, thus, an essentially unstable disequilibrium situation. Sooner or later wages and other incomes will adjust, and inflationary profits will be whittled down. But while it lasts, a demand inflation is comparatively easy to stop by monetary restraint with only mild repercussions on economic activity because inflationary profits act like a cushion. When profits have been sufficiently reduced, but wages and other incomes and prices go on rising we have a case of cost-push inflation. Obviously it is often difficult to identify a period of rising prices as being definitely a case of cost or demand inflation. But the price explosion in 1973 had nothing to do with a wage-push, while in 1974 the inflation clearly acquired a strong cost-push element (and was aggravated by supply scarcities). The 1974 inflation was no longer a profit inflation. There is general agreement, I believe, that profits had fallen to a very low level if the inflationary factor (insufficient depreciation of fixed capital and inventory adjustments) is eliminated.

What is the role of labor unions and other monopolies? For brevity I shall express my views somewhat dogmatically and shall concentrate on unions, saying a few words about other monopolies later. This is a highly controversial question. While many economists from different camps have reached the conclusion that in many democratic countries unions have become a major threat to price stability, some monetarists-- Milton Friedman, Harry Johnson and their numerous followers--flatly deny that unions have anything to do with inflation. There are strange agreements and unexpected disagreements on this issue. For example, Friedrich v. Hayek and Lord Balogh agree that unions have become a major inflationary force. Herbert Giersch is a monetarist who in his theory of inflation[6] allots to monopolies including labor unions a large role. On this point I have a longstanding disagreement with Johnson and Friedman.

But the disagreement should not be exaggerated. There is full agreement that a wage-push inflation, too requires permissive monetary policy. There is also agreement that the recent militancy of unions, in Great Britain and elsewhere, is largely a consequence of inflation and that the upsurge of inflation in 1973 was a case of demand inflation (aggravated by "special factors" which I shall discuss presently) and had nothing to do with wage-push; in fact, unions, like everybody else (including most monetarists I believe) were taken by surprise and reacted surprisingly late. Another very important point of agreement is that any once-for-all increase in monopoly or market power of unions as well as a monopolization of business will push up the price level. This happened on a large scale when the New Deal in the early 1930s, through the Wagner Act, AAA and NRA, greatly strengthened union power and fostered business monopolies. The consequence was that an abnormally large part of the sharp increase in money GNP from 1933-1937 went into prices and a correspondingly small part into output and employment. This was indeed an extreme case of a monopoly and wage-push inflation in the midst of very high unemployment. I would add that, if unions are able to push up wages in a deep depression, they are in an even stronger position without any further increase in monopoly power, when there is little unemployment.

There is furthermore agreement I believe, that labor unions have made money wages almost totally rigid in the downward direction. This is, in my opinion, a very important matter which makes stabilization policy much more difficult. It is true that even in the absence of unions, in a free competitive labor market wages display a certain stickiness compared with commodity prices. Wages will not immediately fall to the market-clearing level when demand declines, because workers will take their time to look for a suitable job before they accept a wage cut.[7] But unions have made money wages completely rigid.

Where is then the disagreement? Briefly it is this: monetarists say there is no such thing as a *continuous* push for higher wages by unions. When a union is first created or when its monopoly power is increased, there will be a once-for-all increase in wages and labor cost and presumably a larger spread between union and non-union wages, but there is no continuing upward pressure. Applied to the present situation, the monetarist will say that there has been recently no increase in monopoly power of unions similar to what happened in the early 1930s. The percentage of the labor force that is unionized has not increased; it is still around 20-25 percent. Furthermore the monetarist will point to the fact that, in the short-run, union wages are sticky even in the upward direction, so that on several occasions non-union wages have risen faster than union wages.

I find these arguments unconvincing for the following reasons. Although there have been no additional legal immunities and privileges granted to the unions since the New Deal, there have been very important changes in public policy and attitudes which have given the unions much more power to press for higher wages than they used to have. Most important, much more liberal unemployment benefits and welfare payments make it possible for unions to hold out in long crippling strikes to obtain large wage increases. In fact, to a large extent, the government finances strikes; in some states the strikers themselves are eligible for unemployment benefits if the strike lasts longer than a certain number of weeks.

The fact that, compared with other countries, in the United States only a small part of the labor force is unionized, does not prove the unimportance of unions. For one thing, higher union wages obtained by threat of strike spread more or less rapidly to the rest of the labor force. Non-union firms and industries are under strong pressure to match union wages for workers of similar skills; for in order to maintain morale and efficiency and to prevent unionization, employers find it necessary not to let the spread between wages of unionized and non-unionized workers and of workers of different skills, etc., become too large.

Another very important recent development is the spread of unionization to groups that were not unionized in the past, to public officials and employees in all levels of government. Today teachers, policemen, firemen, civil servants and so on are organized in unions and do not hesitate to use the strike weapon to boost their salaries. True, these developments have been speeded up, if not originally caused by inflation; but there can be no doubt that they are here to stay even if inflation abates.

That union wages in the short-run are usually stickier than non-union wages and therefore on some occasions have lagged is an unimportant frictional phenomenon which occurs because union wages are determined by a cumbersome and time-consuming process of collective bargaining and are thus fixed in contracts which run for several years. In a prolonged inflation, however, such lags and frictions are quickly eliminated.

On another occasion I have tried to formulate the problem in static, monetarist terms as follows. Unions (and other monopolies) increase what Milton Friedman calls the "natural rate of unemployment," defined as the rate which "would be ground out by the Walrasian system of general equilibrium equations provided there are embedded in them the actual characteristics of the labor and commodity markets," including the existing labor unions and other monopolies.[8] It is surely not farfetched to assume that the "natural" or "equilibrium" rate of unemployment is thereby raised to a level which modern society does not accept without fighting back by means of expansionary policies.

It is true that this merely explains a once-for-all effect. But we should keep in mind that ours is not a Walrasian world where general equilibrium is instantaneously reached, but one where equilibrium is merely approached (without ever being fully realized) by the interaction of many markets with different, overlapping lags. In such a world, what in static theory looks like a once-for-all change becomes a multiratcheted, self-propelling, dynamic process which for all practical purposes is equivalent to a continuous push. The situation would perhaps be different if labor were organized in one large union and the overall wage level were determined in one, country-wide collective contract. In that case the connection between wage levels, price levels and employment would be much clearer than it is now, and unions might moderate their demands. But we do not live in this kind of a world.

How about monopolies other than labor unions? In principle what was said of labor monopolies also holds for business monopolies; they too tend to raise the level of natural unemployment. But for reasons which I have explained elsewhere,[9] and shall not repeat here, I believe that outside the public utility area--transportation, communication, etc.--business monopolies are *not* a serious threat to price stability--except when they are created and protected by government policies.

Government regulations, restrictions and subsidies are a very potent source of inflation. They operate like private monopolies, by raising prices, making them rigid downward and reducing output. In many cases where private producers, for example, farmers, are unable to organize themselves in effective monopolies, the government steps in and in effect makes them behave more or less like monopolists. This is being achieved in many ways, by import restrictions including anti-dumping and countervailing duties, export subsidies, farm price supports, the so-called "voluntary" restrictions forced on foreign exporters, government guaranteed loans to producers to prevent a fall of livestock prices, regulation of wellhead prices of natural gas,[10] minimum wages which cause high unemployment among underprivileged workers, etc. Hendrik Houthakker, Thomas Moore and Murray Weidenbaum[11] have presented a long list of such cases. Ironically the regulatory agencies themselves, which are supposed to prevent public utilities from exploiting their monopoly positions, have in many cases become their powerful protectors who shield them from competition.

Wage-push by labor unions and pressure exerted by various groups, through government restrictions, regulations and subsidies, to increase their rewards help to explain why inflation, once it has continued for a while, always tends to accelerate. The acceleration mechanism is so well known that I need not elaborate. Suffice it to say that there would be acceleration even in a competitive economy. Interest rates rise, people reduce the size of their cash balances in relation to their income by spending money faster, so that the velocity of circulation of money goes up as was already mentioned, etc. But it stands to reason that price setters--monopolists of all description--are in a better position to anticipate expected price increases than price takers under competition.

Saying that inflation tends to accelerate does not imply that every creeping inflation inexorably must become a trotting and eventually a galloping one. What it does mean is that an expected and anticipated inflation loses its stimulating power unless it is allowed to accelerate beyond the expected rate and that, at a later stage, slowing down the rate of inflation has the same depressing effect on economic activity as stopping it altogether would have had earlier. This is, I believe, the real meaning of stagflation. We have reached a stage in the process where measures to slow down the rate of inflation, or perhaps merely to reduce the rate of acceleration produce slack and unemployment. If we do not act now to curb inflation we merely postpone the day of reckoning. Those who clamor for expansionary measures now in the midst of a two digit inflation close their eyes to the virtual certainty that if we follow their advice in a year's time, although unemployment may be lower, the rate of inflation will be still higher and the pains of stopping it correspondingly greater.[12]

Looking at the whole picture--labor unions and other pressure groups trying to increase their share in the national product[13] and the government itself increasing its demands steadily--one is lead to regard inflation as society's method of reconciling and scaling down inconsistent claims of the various groups on the national product.

Although this way of looking at inflation is not incompatible with monetarism, monetarists often reject it. They believe that a tolerable amount of unemployment for a not too lengthy period would induce unions and other pressure groups to moderate their demands. Some anti-monetarists take an equally relaxed position. Tobin clearly sees the problem but says complacently "there are worse methods of resolving group rivalries and social conflicts than inflation;" inflation has the great advantage that it works "blindly, impartially and nonpolitically."[14] He visualizes a steady, or at least a non-accelerating inflation that keeps unemployment permanently lower than it would be with stable prices. But it is difficult to believe that the various monopolies and pressure groups would not raise their monetary claims when they see their expectations again and again frustrated by inflation.

Even in a largely competitive economy it is not always possible to stop a prolonged serious inflation without a temporary rise in unemployment and idle capacity.[15] But the existence of labor monopolies and numerous other pressure groups and the absence of an adequate buffer of profits makes the job undoubtedly much more difficult.

I wish--and hope--that the optimists, Tobin and the monetarists, are right. But I am afraid there is much truth in what the pessimists, such as F.A. v. Hayek and Friedrich Lutz (both closely allied in many respects with the monetarists) say. v. Hayek recently expressed the view that inflation can be "successfully" stopped "only in collaboration with the unions."[16] Lutz believes that tight money, in the present environment, does not prevent price increases any more, but produces unemployment on top of inflation. The only way to solve the inflation problem would be to dissolve the pressure groups and make the economy more competitive. But only a strong government could do that and democracy is likely to perish in the process.[17]

Micro Foundations of Employment and Inflation Theory[18]

There exists a substantial modern literature on the "Microeconomic Foundations of Employment and Inflation Theory."[19] This theory is essentially one of frictional or structural unemployment, inasmuch as it describes and analyzes in detail the search for suitable jobs on the part of employees who have lost their previous job and the search for suitable candidates for job openings on the part of employers. Stress is laid on the cost (both money and opportunity cost) of gathering information about jobs, including the income foregone by not accepting second- or third-best options that may present themselves. One aim of most contributors to this literature is to explain unemployment without reference to labor unions and money illusion. It is unquestionably true that the picture of a perfectly competitive labor market in which wages immediately adjust to the market-clearing level does not correspond to reality. Even if there were no unions and no money illusion, workers who have lost their jobs would not immediately accept wage cuts in their old employment (if that were an option) or inferior job offers elsewhere. They would take their time and invest time and money to search for acceptable openings. What is true of labor markets is also true of many commodity markets, especially of the market in durable manufactured goods where seller-buyer and manufacturer-customer relationships are important. In these markets prices are sticky and respond sluggishly to changes in demand, even in the absence of monopolies and oligopolies. This stickiness implies that in the short run quantity adjustments resulting in ups and downs of employment and of capacity utilization play a great role. All that is well described in Okun's paper.[20]

This analysis of frictional or structural unemployment is an extremely useful exercise. It has greatly enriched our knowledge of the way the economy works. The perfectly competitive economy in which all prices and wages immediately adjust to any change in the data and in which markets are cleared continuously at the full-employment level is an ideal never fully realized--even in the absence of monopolies or oligopolies in commodity and labor markets.

What I find unfortunate and unacceptable is the tendency in that literature to obliterate the distinction between general depression or recession unemployment (often called Keynesian unemployment) on the one hand and frictional or structural unemployment on the other hand, to play down the importance of labor unions, to ignore the fact that unions have made money wages almost completely rigid downward, to neglect the inflationary implications of the fact that the unions often push up wages even in the face of heavy unemployment.

I find equally unconvincing the reinterpretation of Keynes's theory of involuntary unemployment. It runs as follows: Unemployment is the "consequence of a decline in demand when traders do not have perfect information on what the new market-clearing price will be. No other assumption . . . needs to be relinquished . . . in order to get from the Classical to Keynes' Theory of Markets."[21] If, as Keynes says, workers do not accept a reduction of their *real* wage when it comes in the form of a reduction of their money wage, while they do accept it in the form of a rise in prices, it is not because unions rule out money wage reductions or because of money illusion. The real reason is said to be different: A rise in the price level "conveys" the information that "money wages everywhere have fallen relative to prices." Workers reject an equal cut in their real wage in the form of a money wage reduction because "a cut in one's own money wage does not imply that options elsewhere have fallen."[22] Tobin offers the same interpretation of Keynes's theory of involuntary unemployment. "Rigidities . . . of money wages can be explained by workers' preoccupation with relative wages and the absence of any central economy-wide mechanism for altering all money wages together."[23]

This interpretation is in my opinion unconvincing. Keynes was confronted with the mass unemployment and misery of the 1930s; he surely did not want to say that workers were unemployed (more or less voluntarily) because they were shopping around for better opportunities or that they were "preoccupied" not so much with their own plight as with the possibility that if they accepted a lower money wage other groups might get away with a better bargain. Keynes was, of course, opposed to *general* wage reduction as a recovery measure. But even at that time few economists favored that policy.[24]

The upshot of this discussion is that the literature on the micro-foundations of inflation and employment theory is of little help for explaining the stagflation dilemma, because it abstracts from the most important factors--wage rigidity, wage push, real wage resistance from labor unions, similar activities of other pressure groups, and the effects of the widespread government regulation of industries. I find Frank H. Knight's explanation much more convincing. With the Great Depression in mind Knight wrote in 1941: "In a free market these changes [in demand and prices of different types of goods] would be temporary, but even then they might be serious; and with important markets as unfree as they actually are . . . the results take on the proportion of a social disaster."[25] Since 1941 the economy has moved much farther away from the competitive ideal.   There are many more powerful unions--for example public employees (including not only bus drivers, subway personnel, garbage men but also teachers, civil servants, firemen, policemen) are now unionized and do not hesitate to use the strike weapon to push up their wages.   Many other pressure groups have organized themselves and government regulation of more and more industries has made more prices rigid downward while they remain elastic upward.   In addition the public sector has grown enormously-- which is bound to slow GNP growth.[26]   Slower growth of aggregate supply collides with ever increasing claims on the available national product.   This puts heavy pressure on the monetary authorities to make a choice between giving way and financing an inflation or standing firm and bringing on a recession.   Monetarists are right when they say that stagflation like any other type of inflation cannot be stopped without an appropriate monetary policy. Monetary restraint is a necessary condition for stopping an inflation but it is not a sufficient condition for an economically efficient and politically feasible anti-stagflation policy.   I agree with William Fellner, Herbert Giersch, Friedrich Hayek, Hendrik S. Houthakker[27] and others that a tight monetary and fiscal policy must be supplemented by measures designed to make the economy more competitive.   If we rely on monetary and fiscal restraints alone, we will create so much unemployment that the fight against inflation will be broken off prematurely.   This premature breaking off has in fact taken place in country after country.   The result will be more inflation and more unemployment, a stop-and-go cycle around a steepening price trend.   The great danger is that the cry for comprehensive wage and price controls will become irresistible despite the dismal failure of controls whenever and wherever they have been tried. Since the people will remember from the last time how to anticipate and evade the controls, the next time around the system of controls will run its course rapidly: that is, it will break down, merely disrupting the economy, or (perhaps more likely) will be quickly followed by consumer rationing and allocation, leading straight into a fully planned and regimented economy.

Curing Stagflation
(How to Make the Economy More Flexible and Competitive)[28]

In recent years government polices and regulations that restrain competition, protect (or even create) private monopolies, restrict production, and raise or fix prices have come under closer scrutiny. Economists have unearthed and described dozens of such cases.[29] Phasing out these restrictions and changing these policies would go a long way toward making the economy more competitive and flexible than it is now, thus making macroeconomic recovery and anti-inflation policies more effective. Here only a few examples can be mentioned.

In the field of agriculture, although output restrictions on some basic foodstuffs were belatedly lifted after food prices had exploded in 1973 and 1974, such restrictions still exist on several important products. Furthermore, interregional trade in many agricultural commodities (especially dairy products, fruits, and vegetables) is severely restricted by federal and state marketing orders or by producers' privately organized--organizations in restraint of trade that are government-sponsored, government-licensed, government-enforced, and of course exempt from antitrust laws. Imports of many agricultural products from abroad, especially of meats and fruits, are sharply restricted. Such policies freeze and distort prices and reduce output because they prevent a rational interregional and international division of labor. There exist, furthermore, many import restrictions on industrial products, apart from tariffs, including the so-called "voluntary restrictions" imposed on foreign exporters, ranging from exporters of steel to exporters of textiles. These "voluntary" restrictions are especially damaging and costly because they force foreign producers to organize themselves in export monopolies at the expense of the American consumers. There is, furthermore, the Buy American Act which prevents foreign competition and costs the U.S. taxpayer many hundreds of millions of dollars. The field of trans-portation and energy is full of government-imposed restrictions on competition.[30]

Most difficult to deal with but crucially important are restrictions in the labor market imposed by labor unions. The importance of unions has been often questioned on the ground that in the United States only 20-25 percent of the labor force is unionized. But it has been demonstrated many times that, for various reasons that need not be repeated here, nonunion wages tend to follow union wages although at a distance and usually with a lag.[31] Leaving aside far-reaching structural reforms of the present methods of wage determination by industry-wide collective bargaining under the constant threat of crippling strikes, there exist a number of policy changes that could reduce wage pressure, increase competition, and expand output and employment. Houthakker mentions the following:

> Unions should be prevented from restricting membership by apprenticeship requirements, nomination procedures, or excessive entrance fees; nor should they be allowed to operate hiring halls. The Davis-Bacon Act and similar laws requiring excessive wages to be paid under government contracts have interfered seriously with the performance of the construction market [and cost the taxpayer hundreds of millions of dollars]; they should be phased out not only at the federal but also at the state level.[32]

Today, moreover, the government finances strikes by generous unemployment benefits and welfare payments. In some states such benefits go even to the strikers themselves, and in that connection a proposal of Arthur Burns should be mentioned. In an important speech he has recommended that "public employment" be offered "to anyone who is willing to work at a rate of pay somewhat below the Federal minimum wage." Burns stressed that a low rate of pay in such public service employment is essential to prevent "such a program from becoming a vehicle for expanding public jobs at the expense of private industry."[33] Public service employment would largely take the place of the present system of unemployment benefits which have become so generous that they "blunt incentives to work."[34] It has been found that in many cases unemployment benefits and various welfare grants (all of which are tax-free) exceed the income after taxes that a person could earn if he accepted a job for which he was qualified.

Minimum wage laws cause considerable unemployment among teenagers and other underprivileged groups, especially blacks and high-school dropouts. The minimum wage laws deprive thousands of young people of their first crucial on-the-job training and may seriously damage their whole future working career. These laws are a social and economic crime and should be phased out.[35] Unions strenuously object to the phasing out of minimum wage legislation. They even reject a reduction of the minimum wage for teenagers on the grounds that such a change would give employment to some teenagers at the expense of adult workers; "sons would displace their fathers on the jobs." This argument completely misses the purpose of policies designed to make the economy more competitive and flexible. Such structural reform is not a zero-sum game: The purpose is not a redistribution of a given pie but the enlargement of the pie. Overall employment and output would increase, and so would real wages, partly because more expansionary and more effective monetary and fiscal policies would be possible if the threat of rekindling inflation were eliminated (or at least sharply reduced) by measures that would make the economy more competitive and flexible.

What about incomes policy? A policy along the lines indicated above, designed to make the economy more competitive, is sometimes called an "incomes policy." Arthur Burns has used that terminology. In earlier publications I have called it "incomes policy II" as distinguished from incomes policy I in the usual sense of wage and price guidelines, price stops, wage freezes, and similar measures. Because of these connotations of the term incomes policy, it is perhaps better not to use it for the policy here recommended.

Keynesians and monetarists alike should be able to agree on the desirability of structural reform for the purpose of making the economy more competitive and more flexible. The Keynesian (or, more precisely, the Phillips-curve advocate) would say that such a reform would improve the terms of the trade-off between unemployment and inflation, while the monetarist would assert that the reform would reduce the level of "natural" unemployment.[36]

Concluding Remarks. I am painfully aware that structural reform along the lines sketched here will be at best a very slow process. Vested interests fiercely resist any attempt at deregulation and liberalization and the beneficiaries of present policies hold on, tooth and nail, to their privileges and monopoly positions. What, then, are the policy options if quick relief through structural reform is beyond our grasp?

There is, I believe, no other choice but to continue the present policy of letting the economic expansion proceed slowly in the hope that inflation will not accelerate too rapidly. In my opinion it would be a great mistake to speed up the expansion in order to reduce unemployment quickly, whatever the political appeal of such a policy may be in an election year. Quick expansion surely would speed up the ongoing inflation. The consequence would be either that the monetary brake would be applied and the expansion give way to a new inflationary recession or (perhaps more likely) that the call for wage and price controls would become so strong that the system of controls would be tried once more despite the dismal failure of earlier attempts. The controls would either soon become ineffective, merely further disrupting the economy and burdening it with a new bureaucracy without preventing a recession, or worse (but perhaps more likely) lead to consumer rationing, compulsory allocation of factors of production, and full regimentation of the economy in the guise of economic planning.

The many Keynesians who argue that large unemployment and slack in the economy make a quick expansion safe at present forget that the experiment has been made: much unemployment and slack has *not* prevented the rapid inflation of the last three years. (The operation of "special" inflationary factors can, as we have seen, "explain" only a fraction of the price rise that has occurred.) To say as some do that a more rapid monetary expansion would reduce the rate of inflation because it would stimulate production and so increase aggregate supply is like saying that one can make a drunk sober by forcing whiskey down his throat to pep him up. True, if the poison is withdrawn from him too rapidly a situation may arise where one must increase the dose of the stimulant temporarily to forestall an imminent collapse. But I do not believe that the economy faces that danger now. The economic recovery that started a year ago has gathered momentum and is likely to continue for a considerable period without any additional monetary or fiscal stimulation.

Tax-Based Incomes Policy[37]

There is almost general agreement that an indispensable condition for winding down inflation is a gradual reduction of monetary growth. Most experts, including many monetarists, add fiscal restraint (reduction of government deficit spending) to monetary restraint. There is, however, disagreement on whether monetary-fiscal restraint is not only a necessary but also a sufficient condition for regaining price stability. Monetarists insist that monetary-fiscal restraint is all that is needed and all that can be done to bring down inflation, while many others believe--with some justification in my opinion--that exclusive reliance on monetary-fiscal policy would create so much unemployment, at least in the short and medium term, that the policy of disinflation is unlikely to be carried to a successful close. Monetarists and nonmonetarists should be able to agree that monetary restraint to bring down inflation would work much better with less transitional and permanent unemployment if it were possible to bring the economy closer to the competitive ideal, if there were no powerful labor unions which, with the help of government policies, are able to push up wages even in the face of heavy unemployment, if there were fewer other pressure groups such as the farmers or the steel industry which force the government by political pressures to raise their incomes by restricting imports or output, if there were no minimum wages which are raised from time to time, and the like.

It is understandable that policy makers are looking desperately for means to break out of a vicious wage-price spiral: prices cannot be stabilized because labor costs are rising too fast and wage push cannot be eliminated because the cost of living is going up rapidly. Incomes policy is again being recommended with increasing urgency as a way out of the dilemma. But incomes policy means different things to different people. On several occasions I have proposed to distinguish two basic types of incomes policy, incomes policy I and incomes policy II.[38] The first type is what usually is called incomes policy, ranging from comprehensive wage and price controls, wage freezes, and price stops to guidelines for noninflationary wage and price setting. The second type of incomes policy is defined as a collection or bundle of policies of different kinds designed to bring the economy closer to the competitive ideal. It includes such diverse measures as freer trade, antimonopoly policies, restraint of union power, deregulation of industry, and elimination of minimum wages.

Incomes policy in the usual sense (incomes policy I) has never worked for any length of time. Incomes policy II is an entirely different matter. It is the type of incomes policy that the present writer favors.[39] A particular kind of incomes policy that has found impressive sponsorship recently will be briefly analyzed in the next few pages. It is the so-called tax-based incomes policy (TIP), which tries to attack the problem of inflation with a combination of taxes and subsidies.[40] Henry Wallich and Sidney Weintraub have proposed that firms that grant wage increases exceeding a certain norm be subjected to an excess wage tax, and Arthur Okun has turned the Wallich-Weintraub penalty into generous tax incentives, which would benefit employers who avoid widening gross profit margins and employees who keep their wage demands below a clearly defined noninflationary standard.[41] The proposal of the "carrots" and "sticks" cure for inflation has been endorsed, in principle, by an impressive group of experts.[42]

In my opinion it would be a great mistake if policy makers in their desperate search for a way out of the stagflation dilemma were to embrace the gadget of the tax-subsidy scheme instead of applying monetary-fiscal restraint, grasping the nettle of standing up to the various pressure groups, and changing government policies which are at the root of the trouble.

Although ingenious and greatly superior to direct wage and price controls (because it does not destroy the price mechanism), TIP is subject to two very serious objections: First, as Gardner Ackley has convincingly demonstrated, the administrative complications and costs of the scheme would be formidable, hardly less than those of full-blown wage and price controls.[43] Ackley's paper is so convincing because he is, in principle, for an incomes policy and because his paper is based on personal experience as a price controller during World War II and again during the Korean War. Passages from Ackley's paper indicate the complexities of the problem.

> I retain keen, and sometimes bitter memories [from my wartime experience] of great ideas about ways to restrain wage and price increases for which the fine print could never be written--or, if it could be written, filled endless volumes of the *Federal Register* with constant revisions, exceptions, and adjustments necessary to cover special situations that could never have been dreamed of in advance by the most imaginative economists, accountants, and lawyers. Okun's proposal raises some of these old problems . . . For example, Okun's firms must be told how to define each wage rate, and thus how to measure its increase--presumably to include all benefits, including pension rights, dental-care plans, executive stock options, and changed eligibility for overtime pay. Whose estimates of these costs would be accepted? How would cost-of-living escalators in contracts be evaluated? Instructions must then be given as to how to compute an average wage rate increase . . . How does one visualize a union bargaining with an industry composed of many firms differently affected by a given wage increase? How could an employer assure a union that a proposed agreement would or would not qualify its workers for the tax rebate, until much bookkeeping (and IRS review) had been completed? Indeed, could it give any assurances before its tax year was finished? . . . Are exceptions to be made for that portion of wage increases that merely lets workers "catch up" with wage increases

already granted to other workers, or that remove long-standing "inequities"? Is it possible to deny all exceptions to the wage standard? . . . It [would take] a growing army of economists, commodity experts, statisticians, and lawyers to deal with the question and the problems that [arise] not about the general principle, but about how to define, apply, and measure it in all the infinite variety of its applications . . . And would it [Congress] not need to write into the tax code the equivalent of a complete wage control system in order to define the wage increases which would qualify workers for their tax rebates?

It will perhaps be said that the administrative costs, though high, are small compared with the enormous costs of inflation which the tax-subsidy scheme is supposed to eliminate. But will it achieve its objective? This brings me to the second basic objection to the scheme.

The wage tax is supposed to stiffen the employers' resistance to excessive wage demands. The proponents of the tax-subsidy scheme are surely right that one of the principal causes of stagflation is the power of labor unions to impose by threat of crippling strikes wage increases that far exceed what would be compatible with stable prices. The proponents of the scheme are also right that monetary-fiscal restraint alone does not offer a completely satisfactory solution of the stagflation problem; it can stop inflation but only at a high cost of unemployment. True enough, but it must be asked: Why should excess-wage taxes succeed where tight money fails? I see no reason why unions would moderate their excessive wage demands if the resistance of the employers stems from a wage tax and not from tight money, which prevents an increase in overall demand that would enable the employer fully to pass on higher costs to the consumers. If union pressure for higher wages persists despite the wage tax, the employer has no choice but to pass on to the consumers the tax along with the higher wage costs in the form of higher prices, an expansionary monetary policy permitting; or to cut output and employment if tight money prevents the pass-through of the tax to the consumer. It follows that TIP cannot do anything that cannot be done cheaply, efficiently, and without any red tape and administrative cost by monetary-fiscal restraint.

In addition, TIP is bound to have a distorting, growth reducing effect on the economy because it would penalize expanding, dynamic, inno-vating firms and industries that have to bid labor away from other less dynamic sectors of the economy. Since the dynamic, innovating firms and industries are saddled with an additional cost--the wage tax--output and employment are bound to suffer. The proponents of the wage tax will perhaps answer that exceptions will have to be made for innovating, expanding firms and industries. But that presents formidable administrative problems as described by Gardner Ackley. It means substituting decisions of a government bureaucracy for the price mechanism.[44]

The basic objection to the subsidy scheme is somewhat different. The tax benefits are supposed to persuade unions to moderate their wage demands and business firms to refrain from utilizing monopoly power they may possess. Wages are now rising more than three times as fast as would be compatible with price stability. To make it worthwhile for unions to moderate their wage demands sufficiently to reduce appreciably inflationary wage pressure, very large tax subsidies would be required. This would create a formidable budgetary problem, in addition to the enormous administrative costs and the distortions any such scheme is bound to produce because it would be practically impossible to apply it generally in a uniform, nondiscriminatory manner.

The first reaction to this criticism may well be that it is defeatist. Since the costs of unemployment and inflation keep piling up and nothing else seems to work, isn't it worth trying the tax-subsidy approach? This type of argument always reminds me of the story of the man who during the Lisbon earthquake walked the streets trying to sell anti-earthquake pills. When somebody argued with him that pills could not possibly protect anyone from earthquakes, the man answered: "But my dear fellow, what would you put in their place?"

Fortunately, even in the form of stagflation, inflation is more amenable to remedy than earthquakes, but unfortunately, from a certain point on, inflation has a strong tendency to accelerate. If inflation is not curbed now it will become worse and more difficult to deal with later. The only remedy that can be applied quickly is monetary-fiscal restraints. These restraints should be applied immediately to prevent a further acceleration of inflation, although this policy will cause some transitional increase in unemployment. These side effects can be minimized by applying the restraint gently and gradually. By making it clear at the same time that the policy will be firmly pursued, it will be possible to dampen inflationary expectation. The side effects on employment can be further reduced by avoiding price and wage boosting measures and by eliminating as many as possible of those that have been taken earlier, thus making the economy more competitive and flexible.[45] Although it would be unrealistic to expect quick results from such reforms the application of monetary-fiscal restraint should not be delayed, or else we would find ourselves in an even more difficult situation a year later.[46]

Rational Expectations[47]

How does the rational expectations theory fit into the picture of the post-Keynesian consensus? This is not an easy question to answer, because the literature on rational expectations has proliferated enormously. There exist almost as many versions as there are members of the school, and later versions of the same author often are different from, and are more qualified than, earlier ones.[48]

The rational expectations school is an offshoot of Chicago-monetarism and can be described as the radical wing of monetarism. It is best known for the startling policy conclusions that are often attributed to it--to wit that macro-economic policies, both monetary and fiscal, are ineffective, *even in the short run*, to influence the real economy (output and employment); that these policies merely change the price level and the nominal interest rate. The adjustment in the nominal magnitudes (prices, interest rates) occurs without delay because the rational private agents correctly foresee and anticipate the outcome. This is indeed an amazing conclusion: the rational expectations theory is the extreme antithesis of orthodox Keynesianism with its assumption of rigid wages and prices, it contradicts what is sometimes called the Austrian theory of money and the business cycle (of Hayek and Mises) which asserts a basic *unneutrality* of money and it goes beyond Friedman's monetarism, which assumes a long lag, up to two years, of the effect of monetary measures on prices and does not exclude quick though transitory effects on output and employment.

In reality the results of the rational expectations theory are not quite as startling nor do they deviate so much from the consensus as stated above. The claim that monetary and fiscal measures influence only the nominal economic variables (prices) but not the real economy applies only to "systematic," "perceivable" and "predictable" policy measures of the government. In fact, Robert E. Lucas, a prominent member of the rational expectations school, has shown how, "unsystematic monetary-fiscal shocks" with the help of an "acceleration effect" (similar to the old-fashioned acceleration principle) can produce business cycles with the usual features of "pro-cyclical" price and investment movements and "in somewhat limited sense pro-cyclical movements in nominal interest rates."[49]

This leaves open serious questions, some of which have not been faced squarely in the rational expectations literature, let alone satisfactorily answered. To begin with, it is not quite clear what the "systematic" policies are, and it must be questioned whether modern democratic governments are able to pursue truly systematic and consistent monetary-fiscal policies.[50] Be that as it may, as William Fellner has pointed out, systematic policies and unsystematic shocks usually come in a package and are difficult if not impossible to separate. In fact, the distinction between systematic and unsystematic government policies is essentially not a sharp but a fuzzy one. It is a drastic simplification to divide government actions into just two sharply distinct categories--systematic fully predictable policies and unsystematic entirely unpredictable shocks. In reality, government policies are spread out over the whole range between the two extremes. In other words, it is a question of more or less predictability and not one of either-or.

It follows, first, that it is impossible to determine whether the actual cycle is, as Lucas says, the result only of the unsystematic shocks and, second, that it is most unlikely that all, or the great majority of, private agents will interpret governmental policies or intentions identically and draw the same conclusions for the future course of events. As Arrow says, in "the rational expectations hypothesis, economic agents are required to be superior statisticians capable of analyzing the future general equilibrium of the economy" resulting from systematic government policies.[51] I would add that the economic agents are also assumed to be convinced monetarists who draw the same monetarist conclusions from identically perceived information. Actually, it would seem much more plausible to assume, as Arrow argues at some length, that, "the anticipations of the different agents are not only not based on the same general model but [that] they should in general differ considerably from each other."[52]

This criticism does not imply that the basic idea of the rational expectations theory is wrong, namely that people do not simply extrapolate the current rate of inflation (or its recent acceleration) and that they do try to form a judgment on what the government's policy is and how this policy is likely to change the course of events. What the criticism does mean is that the concrete rational expectations assumption--namely that all private agents (or the great majority) have the same perceptions of the government's policy and draw the same (that is to say, the correct monetarist) conclusion--is highly implausible.[53]

A worrisome feature of the rational expectations literature is the complete neglect of institutional rigidities, in particular rigidity of money wages and increasingly of real wages. Rational expectations theory is competitive theory in the strict sense of the word. What Lucas says of his business cycle model, "that prices and quantities at each point of time are determined in *competitive equilibrium*,"[54] holds pretty much for the whole rational expectations literature. Competitive theory has very important positive and normative uses.[55] But the unemployment problem, the business cycle, especially recession and depression, would be very different if all markets were competitive auction markets. Anti-inflation policy would become a much easier task if wages were less rigid. Arrow raises basically the same complaint when he says, "They [the rational expectations theorists] have put, for the most part at any rate, most exclusive stress on prices. Individuals are regarded as responding solely and exclusively to present and anticipated prices. . . ."[56] The neglect of institutional rigidities greatly impairs the relevance of the rational expectations theory for the real world. Institutional rigidities make it impossible for government monetary-fiscal policies, even if entirely systematic and correctly perceived by the public, to be neutral with respect to the *real* economy as the rational expectations school claims.

It is instructive to consider a concrete example where the total neglect of rigidity has led to questionable policy recommendations. In his very interesting paper, "Rational Expectations and the Role of Monetary Policy,"[57] Robert J. Barro discusses the oil price rise and the shortfall of agricultural harvests in 1973-1974.

> These shocks can be represented by a downward movement in aggregate real supply. . . . It follows that output . . . would fall while prices would rise. What is the proper role for monetary policy in this situation? The present analysis suggests that there is a substantive role only to the extent that the monetary authority has better information than the public about the disturbance, or, possibly, about their implications for the economy. Perhaps the most obvious observation about the oil and agricultural shocks is the extent to which they are perceived. Hence, this paper argues that there is no role for monetary policy in offsetting these real shifts. Adverse shifts like the oil and agricultural crises will reduce output and cause painful relative adjustments no matter what the reaction of the monetary authority. Added monetary noise would only complicate and lengthen the process of adjustment (p. 26).

I suggest that by taking explicit account of the fact that in the present-day world money wages are almost completely rigid downward, one gets a better and more realistic picture of the consequences of the OPEC oil price rise and the shortfall of farm output. There is agreement that those changes constitute, as Barro says, a decline in aggregate real supply. This implies that if full employment is to be preserved, real wages (or more generally real incomes) must decline. In the ideal competitive world assumed by the rational expectations school this could be accomplished without a rise in the price level by reducing the money supply. Oil and food prices would go up, other prices would go down, and money wages would decline slightly. With money wages rigid downward, keeping the price level stable would create unemployment. It is, therefore, not unreasonable to argue that the authorities should increase the money supply so as to let the price level rise a little in order to bring about the unavoidable decline in *real* wages by higher prices rather than by lower money wage rates.[58]

This argument assumes, of course, that money illusion has not completely disappeared, while the rational expectations models are, without exception as far as I can see, "derived within a framework from which all forms of money illusion are rigorously excluded" and "all prices are market clearing."[59] True, money illusion tends to become progressively eroded in a long period of inflation. This is implicit in the consensus that I have described. It follows that money illusion cannot be used to justify a policy of permanent inflation. But money illusion is a fairly hardy plant.[60] In the short run, in the context of a single shock such as the oil price crisis in 1973-74, it was not illegitimate or unrealistic to proceed on the assumption that there was still some money illusion left.

Even the highly inflationary period of the last five years offers many examples of stepped-up monetary-fiscal expansions that have been quite effective *in the short or medium run* in bringing about a rapid expansion of the *real* economy, of output and employment. The U.S. cyclical expansion from March 1975 to 1979, which started with an inflation rate of almost 6 per cent, is one example. Britain and Italy with much higher inflation rates than the United States offer more striking examples. The upshot is that, contrary to what the rational expectation theory tells us, monetary-fiscal measures still are effective in the short run. The examples just cited suggest that the short run has been two years or so. But one would expect it to become shorter if the inflationary trend continues. In other words, there is still some money illusion left, which can be exploited by monetary policy and misused by politicians to win the next election.

Fiscal Policy and the Supply Side

Do Budget Deficits Raise Interest Rates?[61]

The Ricardian Equivalence Theorem. In the United States, supply-siders and many monetarists, especially in Treasury circles, are arguing that budget deficits do not raise interest rates. This statement seems to defy the basic economic law of demand and supply, specifically that an increase of supply depresses the price: if the government increases the supply of government bonds by running large budget deficits and printing bonds, the price of bonds will decline, that is to say, interest rates will go up.

Those who deny that deficits raise interest rates have to show that any increase in the supply of government bonds will be matched by an increase in demand. (Before going into that question, I should point out that putting the problem in terms of demand and supply of bonds does not imply the adoption of what is now often called, disparagingly, a "flow" rather than a "stock" analysis of the budget deficit and its effect on interest rates.) It is indeed possible to think of circumstances in which this will be the case. It has been argued, for example, that if a tax cut has caused the deficit, it is possible that the tax cut will stimulate savings and thus increase demand for bonds. Supply-siders are fond of this argument. It is most unlikely, however, that this will happen on a sufficient scale to obviate a substantial rise in interest rates.

An obvious possibility of additional demand for bonds to match the increased supply is capital inflows from abroad. This has indeed happened on a considerable scale. The projected U.S. budget deficits are so large, however, it is most unlikely that capital inflows from abroad will be large enough for interest rates to remain unchanged. It would at any rate require high interest rates to induce such large capital imports.

A sophisticated argument purporting to show that deficits in general do not raise interest rates and do not crowd out private investment is the so-called Ricardo equivalence theorem, which David Ricardo supposedly put forward. This theorem, which has become popular among members of the rational expectations school in recent years, states that under certain reasonable assumptions, it makes no difference whether the government finances its deficit by taxing or by borrowing.

This surprising theory has been spelled out by Robert J. Barro in a widely quoted article "Are Government Bonds Net Wealth?"[62] Barro supposes that, with government expenditures unchanged, taxes are reduced, and the resulting deficit is financed by issuing bonds. The unsophisticated analyst would argue that the public will react to the tax cut by spending the larger part of the windfall on consumption and saving only a small portion. Only part of the increased supply of bonds will, therefore, be matched by additional demand; and the price of bonds will decline, that is to say, interest rates will rise.

No, say the sophisticated rational expectations theorists. People will realize that the increased public debt will have to be serviced. This means that future tax liabilities will increase, and the discounted present value of the additional future tax liabilities must be equal to the additional debt. It follows that consumption will not increase. In other words, the increase in disposable income will be saved; thus the additional supply of bonds will be fully matched by additional demand.

The unsophisticated analyst would perhaps reply that the additional taxes to service the debt may not fall on the present generation of tax payers, but on posterity. To counter this argument Barro has developed an intergenerational model showing that the present generation will save exactly enough to make sure that future generations will not suffer from the profligacy of the present.

I must confess that this theory strikes me as rational expectations gone wild, carried to extremes, if not to say *ad absurdum*. People just do not think that way. Nobody knows what his or her share, if any, in future tax liabilities will be, let alone that of their children and grandchildren, and it would not be rational to spend scarce time and brainpower trying to figure it out.

What is very likely to happen, however, is that many people will assume, rightly or wrongly but not irrationally, that large budget deficits will lead to inflation. The development of inflationary expectations will make shambles of any equivalence of taxes and borrowing.

In an important paper James M. Buchanan criticized Barro for not mentioning that the equivalence theorem had been put forward by David Ricardo in his *Principles* more than 100 years ago.[63] As Gerald P. O'Driscoll pointed out a year after Buchanan's article was published, Ricardo finally rejected the equivalence theorem as unrealistic. O'Driscoll states, "It was precisely because Ricardo perceived taxation and debt issuance as nonequivalent that he was of the opinion that 'preference should be given to the first.'"[64] Ricardo puts it as follows: "In point of the economy" there is no real difference "between financing the war by taxes or by debt."[65] "For twenty million in one year, one million per annum for ever, or 1,200,000 £ for 41 years are precisely of the same value; but the people who pay the taxes" never see it that way. "The war taxes are more economical; for when they are paid an effort is made to save the amount of the whole expenditure of the war, leaving the national capital undiminished." If the war is financed by debt, people "would have some vague idea that [the interest on the debt] will be paid by posterity." There would be little saving, and "therefore the national capital is diminished."[66] We may conclude that Ricardo was more realistic than his modern, unwitting followers.

Walter Salant drew my attention to the fact that James Tobin and Richard Goode have subjected the Ricardian theorem as restated by Barro to a searching criticism.[67] Tobin patiently and convincingly demonstrates why Barro's equivalence theorem, especially the inter-generational part of it, does not work. Tobin's detailed analysis fully confirms the view expressed above that it is hopelessly unrealistic to assume that the discounted future tax liabilities govern people's behavior in such a way that the increased supply of bonds resulting from government borrowing is fully matched by additional saving, so that interest rates remain unchanged.[68]

The Keynesian Position. While supply-siders and rational expectations theorists deny that large budget deficits boost interest rates, and supply-siders claim credit for the good recovery of the U.S. economy in 1983-1984 (a claim that in my opinion is unjustified), Keynesians reject the conclusions of both schools and regard the good performance of the U.S. economy as the result of the Keynesian policy of deficit spending, unwittingly pursued by the Reagan administration. Some of them feel that there has been too much of a good thing, that the budget deficits have become too large and should be trimmed by raising taxes.

Government borrowing does not crowd out private investment or drive up interest rates in another economic situation. I have in mind what may be described as a "classical" Keynesian world, that is, a state of the economy with mass unemployment, stable or falling prices, constant marginal cost, and a Keynesian liquidity trap. This was approximately the state of the economy during the Great Depression in the early 1930s when Keynes wrote *The General Theory*. There is widespread agreement that if the government in such a world engages in deficit spending financed by borrowing from the banking system, output and employment would expand at stable prices, and interest rates would not rise. Private investment would not be crowded out; on the contrary, rising output would stimulate private investment.

The trouble is that we no longer live in a Keynesian world. True, we are not in a classical full-employment situation either. We are somewhere between the two extremes, the Keynesian of perfectly elastic supply and the classical of totally inelastic supply.[69] There is a good deal of unemployment and slack now, and there is some elasticity of aggregate output with respect to an expansion in effective demand. Inflationary expectations have been sensitized by a long period of inflationary abuse, and numerous bottlenecks exist. Hence, inflation would quickly accelerate when aggregate demand expands.[70]

What are the implications for the problems of the budget and its effect on interest rates? First, a word on what would be the situation under classical full employment. If full employment is taken literally as implying totally inelastic supply, government deficit spending and borrowing would crowd out private investment, and interest rates both nominal and real would rise, accompanied by more or less inflation, depending on monetary factors.

What about the intermediate positions? Are we close enough to full employment so that government borrowing will drive up interest rates? This is a matter of judgment. My own guess is that we are indeed much closer to full employment than to the Keynesian extreme. In other words, the bulk of unemployment is not Keynesian but classical.

The general conclusion of our analysis so far is that what might be called the common sense view is correct: government deficits do raise interest rates.

The Decline in Productivity Growth[71]

The trend of national productivity has faltered during the past decade.[72] While output per man-hour grew at an average annual rate of over 3 percent from 1947 to 1967, it has since then increased at only half the rate. Investment in plant and equipment in the private sector has played a much smaller role in the current business cycle upswing than in earlier upswings since World War II.

It stands to reason that the decline of productivity growth had an unfavorable effect on inflation and unemployment. With a higher productivity growth wages could rise faster without causing unemployment or inflation. To put it the other way around, a given wage push causes more inflation or more unemployment with a slower productivity growth than with a faster one.

Evidently both declining productivity growth and lagging investments are pervasive and exceedingly complex phenomena whose causes, too, are pervasive and complex. Fortunately, no exhaustive study is required for the present purposes; it will suffice to identify a few factors that are surely very important.

The causal factors to which the decline in rate of productivity growth is usually attributed are: (1) the increased share in the labor force of women and teenagers whose productivity is much less than that of prime-age males; (2) the lagging volume of investment; and (3) the enormous growth of the public sector, the sharp increase in government employment, and the exploding propensity of the government to control and regulate the economy. Arthur Burns aptly refers to this last factor as a veritable "regulatory frenzy, with members of Congress and officials of the executive agencies vying with one another in devising new economic controls." He described the growth of regulations as follows:

> At the federal level alone, at least ninety agencies are now involved in this activity. The *Federal Register*, which records new regulations, ran to 3,400 pages in 1937, but swelled to about 10,000 pages in 1953 and to 65,000 pages in 1977. In this year's federal budget the amount allocated to regulation is . . . more than twice the expenditure in 1974. To this figure must be added not only the corresponding expenditures by state and local governments, but also the huge costs of compliance imposed on private industry. The Center for the Study of American Business at Washington University [St. Louis] estimates that these compliance costs amounted to over $60 billion in 1976 and that they may come to over $90 billion this year.[73]

Burns points out that to the financial cost of government regulations must be added the fact that many business executives find so much of their time and energy absorbed by coping with regulatory problems that they cannot sufficiently attend to their proper entrepreneurial functions such as developing new products and better technologies.

For the lag of productive private investment, too, government policies are clearly responsible to a very large extent. There is, on the one hand, the regulatory explosion and, on the other hand, the mounting tax burden resulting from rapidly increasing government expenditures, including mushrooming transfer payments. It is now widely recognized that, partly as a consequence of prolonged inflation, the decline of investment is largely attributable to high marginal tax rates, the double taxation of dividends, and the taxation of over-estimated or nonexistent profits resulting from faulty accounting rules that fail to take account of inflation.[74]

It follows that the disappointing productivity growth and investment lag are to a very large extent the consequences of excessive government interventions and faulty tax policies. But even if it were possible to identify other causes--or if the slow productivity growth is accepted as the price we have to pay for a better environment, or a more acceptable income distribution, or for any other worthy objective--in a competitive, free enterprise economy a lower productivity growth would not lead to inflation or unemployment. In a fully competitive economy, given an appropriate noninflationary monetary policy, the growth of money wages and other money incomes would adjust to the slower productivity growth. Only government policies that foster or tolerate union power and wage push and yield to other pressure groups make inflation or unemployment, or both, the inevitable consequence of lagging productivity growth and low investment.

Notes

1. Reprinted in abridged form from "Some Currently Suggested Explanations and Cures for Inflation," *Institutional Arrangements and the Inflation Problem.* Carnegie-Rochester Conference Series on Public Policy, edited by Karl Brunner and Allan H. Meltzer, vol. 3 (Amsterdam: North-Holland Publishing Company, 1976), pp. 143-177, and reprinted as American Enterprise Institute, Reprint No. 55, November 1976.

2. The magnitude of this rise depends on the precise definition of M. It is pronounced for M_1 but not for M_2 because the latter comprises interest bearing financial assets.

3. As is well known, such a rare case was the hyperinflation in Germany after World War I when V rose to fantastic heights and real balances--expressed in gold or general purchasing power--fell to a small fraction of their normal level. I have discussed that case in some length in my *Theory of International Trade,* (London-New York, 1936). First German edition Berlin 1933.

4. Differential impact on different sectors conceivably could have different secondary effects on overall activity through precipitating the collapse of some large firms. It is the task of the monetary authorities to contain the consequences on overall activity of such accidents.

5. The theory of the differential impact of monetary and fiscal measures on prices and quantities has been more clearly spelled out for the problem of fighting recession (deflation) than for counteracting inflation. R. Mantel, ("The Dollar and the Policy Mix: 1971," *Princeton Essays in International Finance No. 85*, May 1971) has argued that an easy money policy for stimulating a stagnating economy merely drives up prices while an expansionary fiscal policy will result in higher output and employment. Presumably he would apply his theory also to the case of cooling an inflationary economy. Mantel's theory seems to be based entirely on the assumption that easy money engenders inflationary expectations. Even if one is prepared to put so much store in assumptions on how price expectations will be influenced, it is difficult to see why a large budget deficit too should not stimulate inflationary price expectations.

6. "Some Neglected Aspects of Inflation in the World Economy" in *Public Finance*, Vol. 28, The Hague: 1973, esp. pp. 204-208.

7. These things have been analyzed at great length in the modern theory of the *Micro-Economic Foundations of Employment and Inflation*, edited by E.S. Phelps, New York, 1970. This analytical work is very useful and has greatly enriched our understanding of the workings of the labor market. But in my opinion it has gone much too far in obliterating the distinction between (a) a free, competitive labor market and a union-dominated one, and between (b) frictional unemployment and unemployment due to deficient demand combined with wage rigidity ("Keynesian unemployment"). Furthermore I find the reinterpretation of Keynes's theory of involuntary unemployment (Leijonhufvud, Tobin) quite unconvincing. (See my *Economic Growth and Stability*: Appendix B, "Some Recent Developments in the Theory of Unemployment" pp. 205-210.)

8. See Friedman, "The Role of Monetary Policy," 1969.

9. See, Gottfried Haberler, *Economic Growth and Stability* (Los Angeles: Nash, 1974), pp. 114-116.

10. This particular measure resembles a monopsony because it keeps the price below the competitive level in the interest of some consumers. But since it restricts output and distorts the efficient distribution of gas--intrastate sales are not subject to federal regulation--the effect is in the end inflationary.

11. H. Houthakker, "A Positive Way to Fight Inflation," *Wall Street Journal*, July 30, 1974. T. G. Moore, *Flexible Transportation Regulation and The Interstate Commerce Commission*, (Washington, D.C.: American Enterprise Institute, 1972). Murray L. Weidenbaum, *Government Mandated Price Increases: A Neglected Aspect of Inflation*, (Washington, D.C.: American Enterprise Institute, 1972).

12. The next stage in the evolution of the inflationary process would be that an increase in the rate of inflation, by adversely affecting inflationary expectations and creating uncertainties, ceases to be a stimulant and becomes a depressant. Some analysts, for example Alan Greenspan, believe that we have

already reached that stage. That is probably too pessimistic in the short-run, but if inflation is not stopped soon we probably shall reach this stage. (See also Postscript to this paper.)

13. It is, of course, not necessary that the various pressure groups actually think in these terms, although one encounters more and more frequently policy statements of labor organizations and other pressure groups which couch their demands in terms of a larger share.

14. See his presidential address, "Inflation and Unemployment," *American Economic Review*, March 1973, p. 13.

15. There have been cases where an inflation has been stopped without any prolonged recession. The German hyperinflation after World War I (1923) and the repressed inflation after World War II (1948) were followed by rapid expansion. But both were very different from our present inflation. The hyperinflation was an uncontrolled profit inflation, prices running ahead of wages. (The same was true of the other less-than-hyperinflations in France, Italy and elsewhere.) And the inflation after World War II was a repressed inflation; the symptoms of inflation were suppressed by tight controls and economic activity was strangled in the process. When the money overhang was removed by the currency reform in 1948, Ludwig Erhard abolished all controls at one stroke. Naturally the economy responded with sustained expansion. Our present inflation is very different and it is therefore unconvincing to argue (e.g., J. K. Galbraith, "Inflation: A Presidential Catechism," *The New York Times Magazine*, September 15, 1974) that it can be stopped quickly without recessions as were the inflations in Germany and in France after World Wars I and II. In recent years, the country that has been most successful in containing inflation, West Germany, has consistently refused to use either price or wage controls, even under a social-democratic government.

16. "Zwölf Thesen zur Inflationsbekämpfung," *Frankfurter Allgemeine Zeitung*, August 19, 1974.

17. Friedrich Lutz, "Dilemmasituationen Nationaler Antünflationspolitik," in *25 Jahre Mrktwirtachaft in der Bundesrepublik Deutschland*, Stuttgart: 1972. Other pessimists are George Terborgh, *Control of Home-Grown Inflation*, Washington, D.C.: 1972 (mimeographed), W. Hutt, *The Strike Threat System--The Economic Consequences of Collective Bargaining*, New Rochelle, N.Y.: 1973 and Emerson P. Schmidt, *Union Power and the Public Interest*, Los Angeles: 1973.

18. Reprinted in abridged form from "The Problem of Stagflation" *Contemporary Economic Problems*, William Fellner, ed. (Washington, D.C.: American Enterprise Institute, 1976), pp. 225-272. Especially pp. 264-268.

19. See especially a volume of essays under that title edited by Edward S. Phelps (New York: W. W. Norton, 1970). See also the interesting article by Arthur Okun, "Inflation: Its Mechanics and Welfare Costs," in *Brookings Papers on Economic Activity*, 1975 (2), pp. 351-90.

20. Okun, "Inflation: Its Mechanics and Welfare Costs." Sir John Hicks, too, has stressed the difference between what he calls the "fixprice" and "flexprice" sectors of the economy. See his booklet *The Crisis of Keynesian Economics* (Oxford: Clarendon Press, 1974), passim.

21. Axel Leijonhufvud, *On Keynesian Economics and the Economics of Keynes* (London and New York: Oxford University Press, 1968), p. 38.

22. Armen A. Alchian, "Information Costs, Pricing and Resource Unemployment," in *Microeconomic Foundations of Employment and Inflation Theory*, ed. E. Phelps, p. 44.

23. James Tobin, "Inflation and Unemployment," *American Economic Review*, March 1972, p. 5.

24. It is true, there can be found passages in *The General Theory* which suggest that Keynes held the theory criticized here. On p. 264 for example he wrote: "since there is, as a rule, no means of securing a simultaneous and equal reduction of money wages in all industries, it is in the interest of all workers to resist a reduction in their own particular case." This could be interpreted to mean that workers were primarily interested in relative wages. True, no one wants to be discriminated against, and the invisible hand of free competition would bring about equal pay for equal work and eliminate any discrimination. But the process of competition requires that the price be bid down when there is excess supply. To say that despite the heavy unemployment, wage reductions are refused because workers are primarily concerned with relative wages--in other words, because they are unwilling to work at a lower wage than that of workers in some other industries--implies that the individual workers who become unemployed (as distinguished from their unions) prefer a zero-wage to a positive wage. That is not a plausible behavior assumption and it is difficult to believe that Keynes meant to make it. The situation is, however, quite different if we drop the assumption of competition and instead assume collective bargaining through a union. For a union it is perfectly rational to accept a certain amount of unemployment, provided the total wage (of those employed and those unemployed) is greater than under full employment. Obviously, generous unemployment benefits will make it much easier for the unions to solve the difficult problem of sharing the burden of unemployment among their members and thus will induce the unions to accept a larger amount of unemployment than they would otherwise accept.

In the next sentence after the one quoted above, Keynes makes it clear that he was thinking of a general wage cutting: "In fact, a movement by employers to revise money-wage bargains downward will be much more strongly resisted, than a gradual and automatic lowering of real wages as a result of rising prices." There can hardly be a quarrel with that proposition up to the point where money illusion has been fully eroded by prolonged inflation and real wage resistance and real wage push have developed. That point marks *The Crisis of Keynesian Economics* of which Hicks speaks. As was noted earlier,

Keynes favored changes in relative "wages of particular industries so as to expedite transfers from those which are relatively declining to those which are relatively expanding." (*The General Theory*, p. 270.)

25. F. H. Knight, "The Business Cycle, Interest and Money," reprinted from *Review of Economics and Statistics*, vol. 23, no. 2 (May 1941), in F. H. Knight, *On the History and Methods of Economics* (Chicago: University of Chicago Press, 1956), p. 335.

26. This ominous development has gone farthest in Great Britain. *The Economist* of London recently (November 15, 1975, p. 18) reported about a study by two Oxford economists (Robert Bacon and Walter Eltis) which reaches the conclusion that "Britain's [economic] disaster in the past decade . . . has been that . . . in 1961-1973 the numbers of men employed in industry fell by 14% . . . The emigration has been into the public sector employment, where the marginal productivity of labor is often tiny or nil, with a . . . 53% increase in local government employment . . . and a 14% increase in central government employment." The study by Bacon and Eltis was summarized in three articles in the *Sunday Times* (London), November 2, 9, and 16, 1975, and will be published in full by Macmillan (London) later this year.

The same alarming development threatens Italy. Guido Carli, the former governor of the Italian National Bank, has warned that the government deficits in Italy have now grown beyond the capacity of the economy to absorb them, crushing the economy and cutting living standards. These deficits result from the growth of the bureaucracy, generous social security and health insurance payments, liberal unemployment benefits, and the massive cost of what Carli calls "concealed unemployment"--that is, in many industries workers produce goods, at public expense, for which there is no demand. (See *New York Times*, December 9, 1975.) The United States is rapidly moving in the same direction. See Warren Nutter, *Where Are We Headed?*, AEI Reprint No. 34 (Washington, D.C.: American Enterprise Institute, 1976).

27. William Fellner, "Lessons from the Failure of Demand-Management Policies: A Look at the Theoretical Foundations," *Journal of Economic Literature*, vol. 14, no. 1 (March 1976), pp. 34-53; Herbert Giersch, "Some Neglected Aspects of Inflation in the World Economy," *Public Finance* (The Hague, 1973), esp. pp. 104-08; F. A. Hayek, "Unions, Inflation and Profits," in *Studies in Philosophy, Politics and Economics* (Chicago: University of Chicago Press, 1967), and "Inflation, the Path to Unemployment," in *Inflation: Causes, Consequences, and Cures* (London: Institute of Economic Affairs, 1974), "Zwölf Thesen zur Inflationsbekämpfung," in *Frankfurter Allgemeine Zeitung*, August 19, 1974; Hendrik S. Houthakker, "Incomes Policies as a Supplementary Tool" in *Answers to Inflation and Recession: Economic Policies for a Modern Society* (New York: The Conference Board, 1975). The title of Houthakker's speech is misleading. He argues that price and wage controls and incomes policies (in the conventional sense) can make

only an "extremely modest contribution." His thesis is that macroeconomic policies must be supplemented by "structural reform."

28. From "The Problem of Stagflation," *Contemporary Economic Problems*, William Fellner, ed. (Washington, D.C.: American Enterprise Institute, 1976), pp. 225-272. This selection pp. 264-268.

29. See for example Hendrik S. Houthakker, "Specific Reform Measures for the United States," in *Answers to Inflation*, pp. 83-85; Murray L. Weidenbaum, *Government-Mandated Price Increases: A Neglected Aspect of Inflation* (Washington, D.C.: American Enterprise Institute, 1975), and numerous other AEI publications; and *Annual Report of the Council of Economic Advisers, 1975*, Chapter 5, "Government Regulations."

30. See especially the CEA report for 1975, Chapter 5, and numerous AEI publications.

31. See, for example, Gottfried Haberler, *Economic Growth and Stability* (Los Angeles: Nash, 1974), p. 107.

32. Houthakker, "Specific Reform Measures for the United States," pp. 83-85.

33. Speech at the University of Georgia, Athens, Georgia, September 19, 1975 (reproduced from typescript). Britain's economic disaster in the past decade, should serve as a warning not to expand government employment without proper safeguards.

34. Ibid.

35. Actually there is a strong movement in Congress to raise the minimum wage from $2.30 to $3.00 an hour and henceforth to adjust it automatically for any rise in the consumer price index (indexation). This measure would sharply reduce job opportunities for teenagers and other underprivileged persons, it would magnify and perpetuate, even in boom times, unemployment among such groups and would accentuate the inflation.

36. Such an agreement would not compel the two groups to forego the pleasure of continuing their quarrels, the monetarist insisting that the trade off cannot be permanent and the Keynesian objecting that the "natural" level of unemployment will never be reached.

37. From "Reflections on the U.S. Trade Deficit and the Floating Dollar." *Contemporary Economic Problems*, William Fellner, ed. (Washington, D.C.: American Enterprise Institute, 1978), pp. 211-243. Especially pp. 233-238.

38. Gottfried Haberler, "Incomes Policy and Inflation: Some Further Reflections," in *American Economic Review*, vol. 62 (May 1972), pp. 234-241, available as Reprint No. 5 (Washington, D.C.: American Enterprise Institute, 1972); and Gottfried Haberler, *Economic Growth and Stability* (Los Angeles: Nash, 1974), chapter 7.

39. This type of incomes policy (with some concessions to the first type) was recommended by Arthur Burns. For references see the publications

mentioned in the preceding footnote.

40. I briefly discussed TIP in "Tax Measures against Wage Push," in Haberler, *Economic Growth and Stability*, pp. 132-133.

41. See Okun, "The Great Stagflation Swamp"; Henry C. Wallich and Sidney Weintraub, "A Tax-Based Incomes Policy," *Journal of Economic Issues*, vol. 5 (June 1971); see also A. P. Lerner "Stagflation--Its Causes and Cures," *Challenge*, vol. 20 (September-October 1977), for still another version of TIP.

42. See, for example, a letter to the *New York Times*, March 12, 1978, signed by Walter Heller, Arthur Okun, Robert Solow, James Tobin, Henry Wallich, and Sidney Weintraub.

43. See Gardner Ackley, "Okun's New Tax Based Incomes Policy Proposal," *Economic Outlook*, Winter 1978 (Ann Arbor: Survey Research Center, University of Michigan), pp. 8-9.

44. Wage guidelines, if strictly enforced, freeze the wage structure, which leads to increasing distortions when the underlying situation changes. The excess-wage tax does the same, although to a lesser extent. The higher the tax the more closely its effects approximate the effect of enforced guideposts.

45. Arthur Okun has proposed a moratorium on new cost raising measures. He evidently regards it as hopeless to try to change existing cost raising policies. See "The Great Stagflation Swamp," p. 12.

46. See the essays by Phillip Cagan and William Fellner in the volume from this essay was drawn.

47. From "Notes on Rational and Irrational Expectations," Chapter 27 (pp. 603-617) of Koo, *Selected Essays of Gottfried Haberler*, reprinted from AEI Reprint No. 11 (Washington, D.C.: American Enterprise Institute, 1980), which is translated from "Wandlungen in Wirtschaft und Gesellschaft: Die Wirtschaft-sund die Sozialwissenschaften vor neuen Aufgaben," Enril Kung, ed., J.C.B. Mohr (Paul Siebeck), Tübingen, 1980. This selection pp. 607-611; 615-616.

48. There exist several attempts at summarizing the literature, with extensive bibliographies. See, for example, Poole, William: "Rational Expectations in the Macro Model," in *Brookings Papers in Economic Activity*, 1976, pp. 463-514; Santomero, A. M. and Seater, John J.: "The Inflation-Unemployment Trade-off: A Critique of the Literature," *Journal of Economic Literature*, Vol. XVI, No. 2, June 1978, pp. 499-544; and Shiller, Robert J.: "Rational Expectations and the Dynamic Structure of Macroeconomic Models, A Critical Review," *Journal of Monetary Economics*, Vol. 4, No. 1, January 1978, pp. 1-44. The latest macroeconomic textbooks have short references to the rational expectations theory. See, for example, Wonnacott, Paul: *Macroeconomics* (2nd edition, Homewood, Illinois, 1978) and Dornbusch, Rüdiger and Fischer, Stanley: *Macro-Economics* (New York: McGraw-Hill Book Co., 1978).

Paul Samuelson has announced that the 11th edition of his famous text *Economics* will present "an understandable survey" of the rational expectations theory which "offers a serious challenge to both monetarism and simple Keynesianism." The new edition will be published by McGraw-Hill, New York, early in 1980.

A good non-mathematical summary has been presented by Herschel I. Grossman, "Rational Expectations, Business Cycles and Government Behavior," in *Rational Expectations, Business Cycles, and Government Behavior*, Stanley Fischer, ed. (Chicago: University of Chicago Press, 1980). For a searching but not unsympathetic criticism see Arrow, Kenneth J.: "The Future and the Present in Economic Life," *Economic Inquiry, Vol. 16*, April, 1978, pp. 157-169.

For a good popular presentation of arguments for and against the rational expectations approach see, "How Expectations Defeat Economic Policy," *Business Week*, November 8, 1976, and Guzzardi, W.: "The New Down-to-Earth Economics," *Fortune*, December, 1978.

49. Lucas, Robert E.: "An Equilibrium Model of the Business Cycle," *Journal of Political Economy, Vol. 83* (December 1975) p. 1113.

50. On the last point see Grossman, *op. cit.*

51. *Op. cit.*, p. 160.

52. *Op. cit.*, p. 165.

53. If one endows the private agents with so much foresight as the rational expectations theory does, should one not go one step further and assume that the private agents will take into consideration that their reaction to the government's policy will induce some policy reactions on the part of the government? Moreover, should one not concede some rationality even to the government? Perhaps the authorities, too, try to take into consideration the likely reactions of the private agents to the government's actions. There is work to do for the model builders to incorporate these actions and reactions into their scheme! Something like Oskar Morgenstern's Sherlock Holmes-Moriarty impasse may emerge. See Morgenstern, Oskar: *Wirtschaftsprognose*, p. 98 and, "The Collaboration Between Oskar Morgenstern and John von Neumann on the Theory of Games" *The Journal of Economic Literature*, Vol 14, Sept. 1976, p. 806. Attention should also be given to what Karl Popper calls the "Oedipus effect," the effect that a prediction may have on the predicted events. In everyday language: A prophecy may be self-fulfilling or self-frustrating. (See Popper, Karl, *The Poverty of Historicism*, 2nd ed., London, 1960.)

54. *Op. cit.*, p. 113. Italics in the original. Competitive, market-clearing prices effectively rule out involuntary unemployment.

55. The assumption of perfect competition greatly facilitates the mathematical analysis. It is comparatively easy to introduce minor qualifications (e.g., deviations from the pure model such as Chamberlin's monopolistic competition, oligopolistic pricing and sluggish price adjustments in certain parts of the economy) without changing the main results. (See, for example, Bennett T. McCallum's interesting paper, "Monetarism, Rational Expectation, Oligo-

polistic Pricing and the MPS Econometric Model" *Journal of Political Economy*, Vol. 87 No. 1, 1979, pp. 57-73.) But the almost total downward rigidity of money wages and growing "real wage resistance" (Hicks) is a different matter that changes the picture profoundly.

56. *Op. cit.*, p. 167. Arrow adds that this is "very much in the spirit of textbook neoclassical theory." But when neoclassical writers turn their attention to unemployment, money and the business cycle, they usually do pay attention to rigidities, failure of markets to clear and similar complications. Pigou, the arch-neoclassicist, attributes about a third of the amplitude of industrial fluctuations to wage and price rigidities. Pigou, *op. cit.* Chapter XX.

57. *Journal of Monetary Economics*, No. 2 (1976). pp. 1-37.

58. This is how Arthur Burns argued when he was chairman of the Federal Reserve Board. He told a Congressional Committee that the Federal Reserve could have kept the price level steady, but it would have meant that prices other than those of oil would go down, which would have created much unemployment. I have analyzed the oil shock along similar lines in my paper. "Oil, Inflation, Recession and the International Monetary System" (*The Journal of Energy and Development*, Vol. 1, No. 2, Spring, 1976, available as American Enterprise Institute Reprint No. 45, Washington, D.C. 1976.) [Chapter 14 in the volume from which this chapter was drawn.]

In a footnote Barro says that if the monetary authority announced, "that there had been an oil crisis" and told "people that this crisis meant lower output and higher prices, [it] would be equivalent to the appropriate active response of money." (*op. cit.*, p. 26) Realistically, that would mean persuading the labor unions to accept a lower *real* wage either in the form of higher prices or of lower money wage rates. Appeals to unions to behave reasonably or rationally have rarely been successful. But the crucial problems posed by powerful labor unions, other pressure groups, government regulations, fixed contracts, etc., are completely ignored in the rational expectations literature and minimized by monetarists in general.

59. Lucas, Robert E.: "Expectations and Neutrality of Money," *Journal of Economic Theory*, Vol. 4, 1972, p. 103.

60. Moreover, it seems to be capable of being revived, at least to some extent, by spells of comparative price stability.

61. From "International Issues Raised by Criticisms of the U.S. Budget Deficits." *Essays in Contemporary Economic Problems-The Economy in Deficit, 1985*. Phillip Cagan, editor. (Washington, D.C.: American Enterprise Institute, 1985), pp. 124-145. This selection is drawn from pp. 125-129; 141-142.

62. Robert J. Barro, "Are Government Bonds Net Wealth?" *Journal of Political Economy*, vol. 82 (November/December 1974), pp. 1095-117. See also Robert J. Barro, *Macroeconomics* (New York: Wiley, 1984), pp. 380-93.

63. James M. Buchanan, "Barro on the Ricardo Equivalence Theorem," *Journal of Political Economy*, vol. 84 (April 1976), pp. 337-41.

Buchanan had discussed the equivalence theorem in his *Public Principles of Public Debt*, 1958. Barro acknowledged he was unaware of Ricardo's theory.

64. Gerald P. O'Driscoll, "The Ricardian Nonequivalence Theorem," *Journal of Political Economy*, vol. 85 (February 1977), pp. 207-10.

Vito Tanzi drew my attention to the fact that Vilfredo Pareto referred to the Ricardian equivalence theorem. According to Tanzi, "While not contesting the Ricardian argument of the equivalence . . . Pareto observed that no taxpayer makes the Ricardian calculations." He concluded that "deficit financing is one way of inducing the citizens to accept what they would not accept with taxes. For example, if during the war the governments had tried to collect through taxes a much as they collected through loans, it is very likely that they would not have succeeded." (Letter written by Pareto to Benvenuto Griziotti. Cited in Griziotti's "Fatti e teorie delle finanze in Vilfredo Pareto," *Rivista di Scienza delle Finanze* [1944], pp. 136-40. The citation is on p. 137.)

Tanzi points out that the Ricardian theorem is an example of "fiscal illusion." Another example is a theorem put forward by John Stuart Mill that people in general resent paying direct taxes but "let themselves be fleeced" by indirect taxes (ibid.).

65. The phrase "in point of the economy" is puzzling; "ideally" is perhaps the right word.

66. The quotations come from Ricardo's paper "Funding System," which was written after the *Principles*, but the gist of the theory can be found already in the *Principles*. See *The Works and Correspondence of David Ricardo*, Piero Sraffa, ed. (Cambridge: Cambridge University Press, 1951), vol. 1, *The Principles*, pp. 244-49, and vol. 4, "Funding System," pp. 186-88. The problem of budget deficits and interest rates, including Ricardo's equivalence or rather nonequivalence theorem, was thoroughly discussed by William Fellner in his paper "Monetary and Fiscal Policy in a Disinflationary Process: Justified and Unjustified Misgivings about Budget Deficits," in *Essays in Contemporary Economic Problems: Disinflation*, p. 70.

67. See James Tobin, *Asset Accumulation and Economic Activity: Reflections on Contemporary Macroeconomic Theory*, Yrjö Jahnnson Lectures (Chicago: University of Chicago Press, 1980), pp. 31, 50, 54-57; and Richard Goode, *Government Finance in Developing Countries* (Washington, D.C.: Brookings Institution, 1984).

68. Richard Goode, too, takes a dim view of the equivalence theory, which he says is put forward by "adherents to an extreme version of rationalistic theory. . . On the face the theory seems implausible. It implies that people can predict the future tax system, economic conditions and their own position" (Goode, *Government Finance*, p. 196).

69. Strictly speaking, even the depressed period of the early 1930s did not quite correspond to the Keynesian model. Keynes himself was fully aware of this. There were some bottlenecks, and prices rose after the cyclical turning

point in 1933 with expanding demand. In fact, the U.S. prices rose at what was then regarded as an alarming rate, although unemployment was still very high-- an early case of stagflation. Those price increases were due, however, to deliberate price- and cost-boosting measures of the New Deal.

70. Keynesians have been slow to recognize the changed world. Keynes, himself, however, recognized the changed economic climate already in 1937, one year after the appearance of *The General Theory*; and in three famous articles in the *Times*, he urged a shift in policy to curb inflation, although at that time inflation in Britain was not very high by postwar standards and unemployment was still about 10 percent. We have to distinguish between Keynesian economics and the economics of Keynes. Keynes's articles are reprinted in T. W. Hutchison, *Keynes versus the 'Keynesians' . . .? An Essay in the Thinking of J. M. Keynes and the Accuracy of Its Interpretation by His Followers*, Hobart Paperback No. 11 (London: Institute of Economic Affairs, 1977). See also *The Collected Writings of John Maynard Keynes*, vol. 21 (Cambridge: Cambridge University Press, 1982), pp. 384-95.

71. From "The Present Economic Malaise." *Contemporary Economic Problems*, William Fellner, ed. (Washington, D.C.: American Enterprise Institute, 1979), pp. 261-290. This selection is drawn from pp. 278-280.

72. For present purposes only the broad facts need be recalled; for details see the contributions of Denison, Fellner, Kendrick, and Perlman to the volume from which this chapter is drawn.

73. See Arthur F. Burns, *The Condition of the American Economy* (Washington, D.C.: American Enterprise Institute, 1978), pp. 7-8. The role of government policies in causing the virtual collapse of productivity growth is brought out forcefully in William Fellner's contribution to the volume from which this is drawn, "The Declining American Productivity Growth: An Introductory Note," pp. 3-12.

74. Two important papers by Martin Feldstein show how inflation and the existing tax system interact to discourage saving and investment and so reduce the level of productivity growth. See Martin Feldstein, *The Stagflation Problem*, Testimony of the Joint Economic Committee of the U.S. Congress, April 30, 1979, processed; and Martin Feldstein and Lawrence Summers, "Inflation and the Taxation of Capital Income in the Corporate Sector," National Bureau of Economic Research Working Paper no. 312 (New York, 1979), processed.

4

International Dimensions of Macroeconomic Policy

International Macro Policy Coordination

A Critique of the Locomotive and Convoy Strategies[1]

The dollar is still the world's foremost official and private reserve and transactions currency. The emergence of potential rivals in that role, the German mark, Swiss franc, and Japanese yen, has brought with it the danger of shifts out of the huge foreign-held dollar balances. The basic factor inducing attempts at diversification of international (and domestic) dollar reserves is the large inflation differential between the United States and the three strong currency countries. The market realizes that the currencies of the low-inflation countries have a long-run tendency to appreciate. The incentive to diversify would quickly diminish if the U.S. inflation rate were reduced close to the rate in the rival currency countries by a credible U.S. anti-inflation policy. The so-called locomotive strategy of pressuring the strong currency countries to expand faster is tantamount to an attempt to eliminate the inflation differential by inflating the low-inflation countries rather than disinflating the high-inflation countries. This approach and its latest version, the "convoy" strategy, are criticized on the ground that they would intensify worldwide inflationary tendencies, which would sooner or later lead to another worldwide recession. It is pointed out that the locomotive and convoy strategy is especially ill-advised from the point of view of the policy's strongest advocate--Britain--because simultaneous inflationary expansion in all industrial countries would lead to an unsustainable commodity boom, as in 1972-1973, which would turn the terms of trade sharply against Britain.

The so-called locomotive policy pushed by Britain, the United States, and the OECD secretariat can be regarded as an attempt to eliminate the inflation differential, not by reducing the rate of inflation in the weak currency countries, but by raising it in the strong currency countries. This can be described as a policy of curing the healthy rather than the sick,[2] but it could be an effective cure of the U.S. balance of payments disequilibrium.

Of course, the advocates of the locomotive policy do not put it that way. They point to unemployment, slack, and slow growth in Germany and Japan, and assert that these countries can apply an expansionary monetary-fiscal stimulus without accelerating inflation.

The argument is, however, unconvincing. In the first place it ignores the stagflation dilemma or assumes that Germany and Japan are exceptions. Up to now Germany has been more successful than the United States and the United Kingdom in limiting the stagflation syndrome. But for fairly obvious reasons its past comparative immunity to the stagflation disease has become weaker and will probably further diminish. And for well-known reasons sensitivity to inflation is much greater in Germany than in the United States and Britain. Germany may be willing to pay a somewhat higher price in terms of temporary unemployment and slack for greater price stability. The difference is not large. Actually there exists no government in the present day world that is not terribly afraid of unemployment.

Second, if Germany succeeded in reducing unemployment and accelerating growth without faster inflation, the inflation differential between the United States and Germany would persist, and the mark would still have a long-run tendency to appreciate.

Third and most important, Germany and Japan can make the same contribution to reducing their surpluses and the U.S. deficit, and thereby to stimulating the world economy, by letting their exchange rate float up as by expanding internally. The difference is that the continuous appreciation of the mark exerts a continuous pull on the outstanding dollar balance, a continuing incentive to diversify. However, this aspect of the problem has not been mentioned by the locomotive drivers.[3]

Much has been made of the fact that in Germany the appreciation of the mark (as in the case of the Swiss franc and the yen) is a depressing as well as an anti-inflationary factor which, if not counteracted by expansionary measures, could impede the reduction of the trade surplus and thus reduce the stimulus to other countries. It has been said that this factor has been overlooked by the governments concerned. This is obviously not the case. The three governments fully realize that the appreciation of their currencies is a hard blow to their export industries, which account for a very high percentage of total output and employment.

The problem should be viewed in the context of the overall stance of monetary policy, which in Germany is still aimed at further reducing the rate of inflation. Otmar Emminger, President of the German Bundesbank, has stated on several occasions that German monetary policy has been shaded in the direction of greater monetary ease to allow for the depressing effect of a possible further appreciation of the mark.[4] Like the U.S. government, the governments of the other locomotive countries are confronted with the difficult task of winding down inflation without creating too much unemployment. The stagflation dilemma afflicts all industrial countries although the intensity of the dilemma and the relative weight attached to price stability and full employment vary somewhat from country to country.

An important aspect of the locomotive policy which has not received any attention on the part of the policy's proponents, is its impact on the terms of trade.[5] A rapid simultaneous inflationary expansion in all important industrial countries would almost certainly lead to a commodity boom, as in the early 1970s, shifting the terms of trade sharply in favor of the raw material exporting countries. This would be a matter of great importance for Britain. It makes the British insistence that Germany, Japan, and the United States expand faster look decidedly ill-advised.[6] As Max Corden pointed out, there is "in this world of flexible exchange rates . . . no need . . . to wait for an American or German boom before inflating the British economy, if that is what the British government wants."[7] Britain would be much better off if it alone expanded, because in that case it would enjoy much better terms of trade.

The locomotive policy makes more sense for the less developed countries (LDCS). But before somebody replies that the locomotive policy has been proposed mainly to help the LDCS and not the weaker industrial countries,[8] he should ask himself the question how much good an inflationary boom would do to the LDCS if the boom is again followed, as it surely would be, by a severe recession. At the Economic Summit in London in May 1977, the assembled heads of state declared: "Inflation does not reduce unemployment. On the contrary, it is one of its major causes." The Germans evidently still believe that a nation cannot inflate itself into a stable full employment equilibrium, while the proponents of the locomotive theory have retreated to the Keynesian position, which assumes that money illusion is substantially intact and that inflationary expectations present no serious problems. However, it has become more and more difficult to ignore the fact that many years of inflation have eroded money illusion, have sensitized inflationary expectations, and have made Keynesian policies increasingly ineffective except in the very short run.

According to newspaper reports, the locomotive theory has recently been expanded by the OECD secretariat and by key U.S. officials into the convoy theory, a proposal for coordinated fiscal-monetary expansion in a large number of countries led by, but not confined to, the three largest (locomotive) countries--the United States, Germany, and Japan. The main advantage claimed for the new approach seems to be that if many countries expand at the same time, there is less danger that some of them will run into serious balance of payments problems.

The convoy strategy seems to me subject to even more serious objections than the locomotive theory. First, if in addition to the strong locomotive countries with low-inflation rates other weaker countries with high-inflation rates expand, the overall inflationary effect of the new approach becomes stronger. Accelerating worldwide inflation does not improve the chances for sustained world prosperity. Second, the emphasis on an improved pattern of current account balances is out of place in a world of floating exchange rates. Moreover it is not clear why current account deficits should decline if simultaneously with the surplus countries the deficit countries take expansionary measures. This would make the current account imbalance under the convoy policy larger, and not smaller, than under the locomotive policy.[9]

To summarize briefly: So long as the United States has a much higher rate of inflation than other potential reserve currency countries, the market will conclude that the dollar has a long-run tendency to depreciate vis-à-vis the mark, Swiss franc, and yen, providing a strong incentive for official and private dollar holders to diversify their currency holdings and thus putting heavy pressure on the dollar. This would change if the United States adopted a credible anti-inflation policy to bring the inflation rate down close to the level of the strong currency countries. The so-called locomotive policy pushed by the United States and Britain would reduce the inflation differential not by reducing inflation in the weak currency countries but by raising it in the strong currency countries. This would lead to higher world inflation, which is not likely to restore stability in the world currency markets.

The locomotive strategy, the attempt to persuade the surplus countries to inflate and thus to reduce the inflation differential, is bound to fail, or if it succeeded, it would heat up world inflation. It might reduce the pressure on the dollar, but it would not provide a solid basis for world prosperity.

The locomotive strategy is objectionable also from the political point of view. There is no government in the modern world that is not deeply committed to full employment and growth, although there are differences in the relative weight they attach to price stability, employment, and growth. Some countries are prepared to tolerate a little more slack than others to bring down inflation. But there is no government in the modern world that will accept mass unemployment without fighting back with expansionary measures. To continue an acrimonious debate in order to induce others to change their policy mix a little bit is not conducive to international harmony and cooperation. International negotiations should concentrate on exchange rate management and commercial policy. The legitimate subjects for complaints are the manipulation of exchange rates and protectionist measures, not the attempts of some countries to maintain price stability by allowing a little more slack than others would prefer. In a highly inflationary world, putting pressure on the few oases of stability to join the inflationary convoy is a perverse policy.

International Policy Coordination: Do We Need It?[10]

In the past two years international policy coordination has once again been all the rage, with the United States in the driver's seat. In practice the principal concrete manifestation of the new drive for policy coordination has been the increasingly urgent and impatient American demand that Germany and Japan stimulate their economies in order to reduce their trade surpluses and the U.S. trade deficits. More on that presently. First it will be well to review very briefly the historical roots of international policy coordination or cooperation--the two terms are often used interchangeably.

Barry Eichengreen recently reminded us that early in the interwar period--not to go further back--proposals were made to improve the working of the international monetary system by policy coordination.[11]

One of the resolutions of the Genoa Conference (1922) says, for example:

> Measures of currency reform will be facilitated if the practice of continuous cooperation among central banks . . . can be developed. Such cooperation AMONG central banks . . . would provide opportunities of coordinating their policy, without hampering the freedom of the several banks.[12]

Later in the 1920s the Bank for International Settlements (BIS) was established in Basle, Switzerland. Its original purpose was to manage the transfer of German reparations to the victors in World War I. It survived the Great Depression of the 1930s and even the Second World War--a monument to the staying power of international bureaucracies. It developed into an international institution for consultation, cooperation, and coordination of monetary policy. Formally it is a European institution, the club of the major European central banks, but its monthly meetings are regularly attended by a governor of the Federal Reserve System and by a high official of the Bank of Japan.

After the end of World War II, European economic cooperation and coordination received a strong push from the Marshall Plan. A large international bureaucracy was set up in Paris. This, too, managed to enlarge and to perpetuate itself. After several metamorphoses it became the OECD (Organization of Economic Cooperation and Development), representing the industrial countries, including the United States, Canada, and Japan.

It would lead too far to discuss all the other international agencies that are directly or tangentially involved in policy coordination; they include the International Monetary Fund, the United Nations and its numerous offshoots, the European Economic Commission, the Economic Commission for Latin American (ECLA), the United Nations Conference on Trade and Development (UNCTAD), etc.

The drive for international coordination of policies again went into high gear with the Tokyo economic summit of May 1986. The heads of state instructed the ministers of finance of the Group of Seven to meet "at least once a year" to review "the mutual compatibility" of their policy objectives and forecasts, "taking into account indicators such as GNP growth rates, inflation rates, interest rates, unemployment rates, fiscal deficit ratios, current account and trade balances, monetary growth rates, reserves, and exchange rates."

The ball has been picked up by the Interim Committee of the IMF. The April 1986 Interim Committee communiqué refers to "the possible usefulness of indicators in implementing Fund surveillance" (paragraph 6). The committee asked the executive board to explore "the formulation of a set of objective indicators related to policy actions and economic performance, which might help to identify a need for discussion of countries' policies."[13]

On September 27, 1986, just before the annual meeting of the IMF and the World Bank, the ministers of finance of the Group of Seven met in Washington, D.C. "to conduct the first exercise of multilateral surveillance pursuant to the Tokyo Economic Summit Declaration of the heads of State of May 6, 1986."[14] The one-page statement is a bland document, evidently a compromise which, according to press reports, was reached after spirited and somewhat acrimonious discussions:

The Ministers reviewed recent economic objectives and forecasts collectively, using a range of economic indicators, with a particular view to examining their mutual compatibility. The Ministers noted that progress had been made in promoting steady, noninflationary growth. The Ministers also noted, however, that the present scale of some current-account imbalances cannot be sustained. The exchange rate changes since last year are making an important contribution toward redressing these imbalances. The Ministers agreed that cooperative efforts need to be intensified in order to reduce the imbalances in the context of an open, growing world economy. They noted, in this connection, that economic growth in surplus countries was improving, but that such growth will need to be sustained. Countries with major deficits must follow policies that will foster significant reductions in their external deficits; those countries committed themselves, among other things, to make further progress in reducing their budget deficits in order to free resources to the external sector. The Ministers agreed that the policies of all countries would be formulated with the following objectives in mind: To follow sound monetary policies supporting noninflationary growth; to continue the process of removing structural rigidities in order to increase the long-term production potential of their economies; and to continue efforts to resist protectionist pressures.

The vagueness of this statement underscores what was said above--that so far the only concrete attempt at international policy coordination has been the insistent U.S. pressure on Germany and Japan to stimulate their economies.

The current drive for international policy coordination, including U.S. pressure on Germany and Japan, is a replay of what happened in the late 1970s. The surrounding circumstances were somewhat different, but then as now the United States had what were considered enormous and intolerable trade deficits--$31 billion in 1977, $34 billion in 1978-- and the policy response was the same: The surplus countries, mainly Germany and Japan, were urged by the United States to stimulate their economies. This was called the "locomotive theory," which was later expanded to the "convoy theory," a proposal for coordinated fiscal- monetary expansion in a large number of countries.[15] In an extreme form this approach was put forward by H. J. Witteveen.[16] This scenario called for real growth in the United States to average 4 percent a year from 1978 to 1980, compared with 4.5 percent in 1978; 7.5 percent real growth a year in Japan from 1978 to 1980, compared with 5.7 percent in 1978; and 4.5 percent in Germany from 1978 to 1980, compared with 3.1 percent in 1978. The consequence of these changes in the relative growth rates of the three countries, and of other changes of similar magnitude for other industrial countries, would have been to reduce the U.S. trade deficit by $1.8 billion, the Japanese surplus by $5.7 billion, and the German surplus by $4.8 billion. Herbert Stein very aptly called this approach "international fine tuning." It is not surprising that it was not implemented. I will, therefore, confine myself to a discussion of the special case--U.S. pressure on Germany and Japan to stimulate their economies.

In one important respect the economic situation in the late 1970s was very different from what it is in the 1980s. It will be recalled that an inflationary boom escalated consumer price increases from about 5 percent per year in 1976 to almost 20 percent in 1980, because the Carter Administration immediately embarked on an expansionary policy. No wonder that the dollar was weak despite large interventions in the foreign exchange market. Under these circumstances if Germany and Japan had acceded to American demands for stimulation of their economies by monetary fiscal expansion, the result would have been more rapid worldwide inflation followed by a more severe worldwide recession.

In the 1980s the U.S. economy took a different course. After the stabilization crisis of 1981-1982 the economy took off on a vigorous expansion, which passed its fourth anniversary in November 1986. Unlike earlier cyclical expansions, the current one has been marked by declining rather than rising rates of inflation. But the huge trade deficits still dominate the scene, and the United States continues to press Germany and Japan to stimulate their economies. Addressing the annual meeting of the IMF and the world Bank on September 30, 1986, in Washington, President Reagan said faster growth "is the key" to the major problems of the world economy. The United States has done its part. U.S. economic recovery has pulled the world out of the recession; now "other industrial nations must also contribute their share for world recovery and adopt more growth oriented policies." Secretary Baker still insists that their are only two solutions to the global trade imbalance. Either the other industrial countries must grow faster or the dollar has to decline further to make U.S. industries competitive. Since the famous U.S.-Japanese agreement in the Baker-Miyazawa accord of October 31, 1986, U.S. criticism is now addressed mainly to Germany. The official criticism has been echoed in sharper forms in the media. Anthony M. Solomon, former president of the New York Federal Reserve Bank, wrote in early 1986,

> Now that exchange rates are on a more reasonable course and oil prices are declining, there is every likelihood the inflation rate in Germany will be negative in 1986. Clearly, that ought to offer immense opportunity for German authorities to provide stimulus to lower the current-account surplus, to lower unemployment and to contribute to a better balance in the world economy without threatening any outbreak of inflation. Instead, from German officials we get stonewalling because the economic thinking that pervades is every bit as ideological, every bit as divorced from the realities of the time, as we have seen on occasions in the United States in the past five years. That ideology is constructing a seemingly impenetrable intellectual roadblock to the execution of necessary policy changes.[17]

All this is hardly convincing. The conservative German government of Helmut Kohl would like nothing better than to approach the 1987 election with rising output and employment--all the more so since they are criticized by the left-wing opposition and the labor unions with the same largely Keynesian arguments that the conservative U.S. Administration uses. They are afraid, however, of giving the impression that they have caved in to American pressures.

The American policy suffers from two weaknesses: first, reproaching Germany and Japan for their large export surpluses ignores the fact that the U.S. external deficits represent an inflow of foreign capital, which the U.S. economy still needs because domestic savings are insufficient to finance both private investments and huge budget deficits. Second, several econometric studies have concluded that the effects of even a substantial increase in the rate of growth in Germany and Japan on the U.S. external deficit would be minimal. The *IMF World Economic Outlook* concludes:

> Unfortunately, the effects on the U.S. current account of shifts in growth rates abroad appear to be relatively small. It is unlikely that a 1 percentage point increase in domestic growth in Japan and the Federal Republic of Germany (maintained over a three-year period and with allowance for induced effects on growth in other countries) would alter the U.S. trade balance by more than $5-10 billion.[18]

Note that the study makes allowance for indirect effects and that a rise of real growth by one percentage point, say from 3-1/2 to 4-1/2 percent, over three years is quite substantial.

This does not deny that faster noninflationary growth would be desirable or that in the short run pressure on the United States would be alleviated if the Germans and Japanese embarked on a highly inflationary expansion. What it does mean is that in order to bring down the external deficit the U.S. budget deficit must be reduced. This is an American responsibility, which cannot be shifted to other countries.

Now let us assume that the dollar has declined far enough to shrink the external deficit sharply; or assume that expansion abroad has reduced the U.S. deficit, which implies that capital inflow from abroad has stopped. Interest rates will rise and, if the budget deficit has not been sharply reduced and domestic savings have not increased, public sector borrowing will crowd out private sector investment. This underscores the decisive importance of the budget deficits. The September 1986 statement of the Group of Seven put it succinctly: "Countries with major deficits committed themselves to make further progress in reducing their budget deficits, *in order to free resources to the external sector*." Of course, how to reduce the budget deficit sufficiently fast without causing a recession is a difficult problem.

There is another aspect of the dollar problem that also underscores the importance of speedy action on the budget deficit. The U.S. economy is in its fifth year of expansion--one of the longest in the history of business cycles. Naturally, it shows signs of slowing down. The Federal Reserve has been under increasing pressure to reduce interest rates to prevent a slide into a recession. The Fed has insisted that it cannot go much further unless Germany and Japan go along, because there is danger that when the interest differential between the United States on the one hand and Germany and Japan on the other shrinks, capital inflow will stop or a net outflow will develop, causing a sharp decline of the dollar.

I think that the possibility of such a development cannot be excluded. But I still believe that an irrational stampede of investors at home and abroad out of dollars, as some experts have been predicting for the past three years, is unlikely, because the market understands that in such a case central banks, the Fed, and foreign central banks would intervene, organizing a dollar rescue operation as they did in 1978. It surely would be better, however, not to let it come to that, but to attack the evil at its root by reducing the budget deficit. For two reasons, the United States cannot go on forever importing capital from abroad: first, sooner or later investors at home and abroad will become nervous if they see no change in policy, and a run on the dollar may develop; second, the service charge on the foreign debt rises rapidly. The economy will have to do without new capital from aborad and will have to develop an export surplus to service the foreign debt, implying a sizable squeeze on what is called "domestic absorption"--that is, on consumption and investment. In other words, the standard of living will be reduced below what it otherwise would be. If the trade deficit and the associated inflow of foreign capital continue for, say, two or three more years, it has been estimated that the service charge on the foreign debt may near 1 percent of GNP. This surely would not be a crushing burden, but in a sluggish economy could well trigger a recession.

Some Policy Conclusions. No modern government is indifferent to unemployment--all of them want full employment and rapid growth. Germany and Japan are no exception. But it is also true that tolerance and fear of inflation vary somewhat from country to country. Germany, for example, with its history of destructive inflation, hyperinflation after World War I, and equally damaging repressed inflation after World War II, is more fearful of inflation than the United States is.

If this is granted, it follows, I believe, that all countries should be allowed to pursue their policies as well as they can, provided they observe the rules of the game as laid down by the IMF and the GATT. Currencies should be freely convertible at fixed or flexible exchange rates; there should be no manipulation of exchange rates, no import restrictions on balance-of-payments grounds, and the like. Let the Europeans struggle with their structural unemployment; if the Germans, the Dutch, or the Belgians think that they need two-digit unemployment to keep inflation at bay, it is their problem, not ours.

This does not mean, however, that countries should never criticize each other or should refrain from giving advice. Far from it. All governments make mistakes, all can learn from the failures and successes of others, and they should welcome friendly criticism and advice. But this is best done quietly in organizations such as the OECD, the IMF, and the BIS, or in bilateral negotiations. The superiority of quiet diplomacy has been strikingly demonstrated by the famous U.S.-Japanese agreement reached by Secretary Baker and Japanese Minister of Finance Miyazawa.

This approach is surely much better than criticizing each other publicly. Threatening other countries with a further decline of the dollar--"using the dollar as a weapon," as it was put in the press--may serve domestic political objectives but is internationally counter-productive, because no country likes doing things under pressure from abroad. The politicization of exchange rates is a dangerous game. It has caused much turbulence in the foreign exchange markets. Free markets do a better job of setting exchange rates than governments do.

International Criticism of the
U.S. Budget Deficit[19]

Criticism of U.S. Fiscal Policy in Other Industrial Countries. To begin with, the criticism of the U.S. budget deficits has been blunted by the unexpectedly vigorous recovery of the U.S. economy despite high interest rates, large trade deficits, and a strong dollar. The cyclical recovery since 1982 has been not only the most vigorous but also the least inflationary since 1960.

Furthermore, part of the trade deficit is due to a cyclical discrepancy, the U.S. economy expanding fast while the rest of the world, developed as well as less developed, lags behind. To the extent to which this is true, the U.S. trade deficit is a natural and beneficial phenomenon because it means that the United States is performing the highly desirable function of a locomotive pulling the world economy out of the recession. Moreover, the criticism one often hears that the richest country in the world should not import capital from poor countries is beside the point, and the process is self-correcting; the U.S. trade deficit will decline when the rest of the world catches up with the U.S. recovery.

In sharp contrast to earlier recoveries from world recession, the current one has been much less vigorous in Europe than in the United States. Some of the reasons of the poor performance of Western Europe have been authoritatively stated by Stephen Marris, the former chief economist of the Organization for Economic Cooperation and Development. I quote some salient facts noted by Marris:

> European economies are in important respects less flexible than the American economy . . . European workers are generally better protected against economic misfortune than their American counterparts. Collective agreements and government regulations give them more job security. But this makes it more difficult and expensive for European employers to lay off workers when demand weakens. And, they are more reluctant to take on new workers when demand picks up, preferring instead to work overtime. Provisions for unemployment are also more generous in Europe. Laid-off workers have more time to look around for a new job. But, by the same token, this slows down the movement of labor from declining to expanding industries.

Labor mobility is also inhibited in Europe by the greater rigidity of the *relative* wage structure between industries, occupations, and regions. It is more difficult for employers in expanding industries to bid up wages to attract labor, or for laid-off workers in declining industries to bid down wages to get their jobs back.

The main culprit is the downward rigidity of real wages, coupled with the high taxes . . . Between 1960 and 1983 the ratio of general government expenditures to gross national product (GNP) in the European Community rose from 32 percent to 52 percent.

In America the overall burden of taxation is lower, and real incomes seem to have adjusted more flexibly to the shocks of the 1970s. 20 million new jobs have been created in America since 1973 . . . Against this, there was a net *loss* of around 2.5 million jobs in the European Community over the same period. Compared with Europeans, Americans coming into the labor force have been more willing to accept whatever level of real wages was necessary to induce employers to hire them; in other words, to "price themselves" into jobs.[20]

The contrast between Europe and the United States was highlighted in 1983 by the crippling strikes in the United Kingdom and West Germany. In Britain the coal miners' strike (which is still not settled at this writing, November 1984) is threatening the recovery after the recession. In Germany the strike of metal workers for a thirty-five-hour week at the same pay as the forty-hour week was settled by a costly compromise. In the United States, however, wage settlements have been surprisingly moderate in the recovery, so far at least.

To Marris's list of handicaps of the European economies compared with that of the United States, I would add the following: The U.S. economy enjoys the tremendous advantage of a large free trade area and of private competitive enterprise in transportation, communications, and electric power, which is partly due to the large size of the market.[21]

Over the years the importance of a large internal free trade area has increased and is likely to increase further because of the rapid technological advances that have occurred and are still occurring in transportation and communications. True, the European Common market was supposed to establish free trade among the members of the European Community (EC). Tariffs and quotas have indeed largely been abolished on trade between the members of the EC, but many impediments to the free movement of commodities still exist. Some member countries tend to substitute more or less subtle administrative restrictions for tariffs and quotas, and the Common Market hardly applies to the growing trade in services.[22] Furthermore, some members, particularly France, have tight exchange control, which is a major obstacle to free trade, though its ostensible purpose is "merely" to restrict capital flows. Exchange control makes it impossible to integrate financial markets--a very serious handicap. Customs formalities and inspection at the borders between the members are still in place, and controllers and customs officials are very active to justify their existence.

Equally important, the European countries, unlike the United States, are burdened by the existence of national public monopolies in transportation, communications, and electric power. These public monopolies suffer from bureaucratic inefficiencies and are impervious to international competition. In addition, numerous nationalized industries suffer from the same handicaps. Unlike private industries, state enterprises are under strong pressure to buy their inputs (raw materials, intermediate goods, machinery, etc.) from domestic sources, even if the cost is much higher than imports would be.

Marris is not satisfied with the structural explanation of the contrast between Europe and the United States. He insists that a basic difference between European and American macropolicies is at least equally responsible. While the United States is running huge budget deficits, Europe's recovery is being held back by low structural deficits. In other words, European policies are not sufficiently expansionary ("Keynesian").

I find this conclusion entirely unconvincing for two reasons, First, European macropolicies have not been uniform. There is, for example, a sharp contrast between the two largest economies--those of France and West Germany.

France, on the one hand, under the socialist government of Francois Mitterrand, has pursued Keynesian policy as recommended by Marris, running large budget deficits and, as a consequence ,has experienced huge trade deficits and high inflation. Last year France was forced to switch course toward an "austerity" program. How far it will go remains to be seen. The rate of growth has declined, and unemployment has increased. France still bears the albatross of nationalized banks and industries.

West Germany, on the other hand, has pursued a much more cautious policy. The German economy has staged an export-led cyclical recovery. Although quite modest compared with the recent U.S. recovery and with earlier German ones, it was remarkable in that the inflation rate has been brought down to below two percent at this writing (November 1984). Unemployment, however, is still high, about ten percent, and the metal workers' strike of summer 1984 has slowed the recovery. I will discuss further the nature and causes of high unemployment later in the chapter.

The second reason why Marris's theory is unconvincing is that, given the structural rigidities and immobility of labor he describes, an expansionary (Keynesian) macropolicy would quickly reignite inflation as exemplified by France. Helmut Schlesinger made this point. He made it clear that the Bundesbank would stick to its cautious policy, because accelerated inflation would soon be followed by recession.

I have stressed the long-run structural advantages of the U.S. economy compared with European economies as the main reason for the great strength of the dollar. It will be well to look back and to ask why fewer than ten years ago the dollar was so weak it had to be devalued sharply against other major currencies, especially the German mark, the Swiss franc, and the Japanese yen.

The answer is that in the short run the favorable effect of the long-run structural factors can be swamped by exogenous inflationary shocks or by cyclical factors.[23] About 1964, for reasons that need not be further discussed here, the United States entered an inflationary period. The crucial fact was that the U.S. inflation rate was much higher than that of

Germany, Switzerland, and Japan. These countries refused to accept the inflation that they would have had to endure if they had maintained a fixed exchange rate with the dollar. The dollar therefore came under pressure and in the end had to be sharply devalued. Even after its spectacular rise in the past two years, the dollar is still below its value vis-à-vis the three strong currency countries of the 1970s.[24]

The GATT Report. After the other sections of this essay were written, the first chapter of the annual report of GATT, *International Trade 1983/84*, became available in fall 1984. As usual, it stands out among reports of international institutions, because it is not a negotiated document, trying to accommodate different, often divergent, viewpoints. The GATT document is a staff report that develops a consistent liberal stance--liberal in the classical sense of laissez faire, *laissez-passer*, not in the perverted modern sense.[25]

The report dwells upon the superior performance of the U.S. economy compared with that of the Western European economies in the current cyclical recovery. It points out that this contrast did not exist in other recoveries since 1960. The report described this change by saying that "the U.S. locomotive no longer pulls," making reference to the "locomotive" theory that was popular in the 1970s. The United States was then admonished by the European critics to play its role of locomotive, that is to say, to expand fast to pull the rest of the Western world out of the recession.

Actually, the U.S. locomotive pulled much harder in the current recovery; specifically U.S. imports rose twice as much as in earlier recoveries. The European economies, however, did not respond as in earlier recoveries. Why? The GATT report mentions roughly the same structural impediments and inflexibilities to adjustment that are more pronounced in Europe than in the United States, which were mentioned above. Rigid and excessively high wages, overgenerous welfare measures, and intra-European fragmentation of markets despite the existence of a "Common Market" are the principal trouble spots.

In contrast to Marris and to other Keynesians, the authors of the GATT report do not think that the way to speed up growth in the European economies is through government deficit spending and concerted reflation. They believe that recurrent stimulations of economies, whether or not they work in the short run, are likely to increase fluctuations in the long run. In other words, a policy of fine tuning minor recessions would be counterproductive. The authors suggest that modest upswings and downswings are a natural and probably beneficial feature of market systems.

The U.S. Locomotive Pulls. The U.S. locomotive has pulled hard in the current recovery. *The Economist* has taken up this theme and, in an article titled "The Mighty Borrower," says, "Other countries have had reason to thank the American boom. In 1982 they all urgently needed an economic recovery, and they all wanted theirs to be export-led. . . . America has pump-primed the world out of the 1980-82 recession."[26]

The response of the European economies has, however, been weak. This is not the fault of the United States. The Europeans have to blame themselves for their structural handicaps. It should be kept in mind, first, that the strength of the pull of the U.S. locomotive is measured by the size of the U.S. trade deficit and, second, that the U.S. trade deficit has a cyclical component. When the European economies respond, U.S. exports will increase, and the trade deficit will shrink.

High interest rates, large capital imports, the overvalued, strong dollar, and the large U.S. budget and trade deficits are the targets of European criticism. High U.S. interest rates are due partly to heavy government borrowing, partly to strong investment demands. It is difficult to estimate the comparative strength of the two factors, but it is certain that in the current U.S. recovery, private investment has gone up much more sharply than is generally recognized.[27] The strong investment demand for funds is due to tax incentives and the rapid expansion of the economy.

The strong dollar is due not only to high U.S. interest rates but also to the fact that the United States has again become the safe haven for foreign investors from Europe and elsewhere because of unsettled economic and political conditions abroad. This is not the fault of the United States.

High interest rates, large capital imports, the strong dollar, and the trade deficits are part and parcel of the pull of the U.S. locomotive that the Europeans wanted.

The critics of U.S. policies cannot have it both ways. They cannot have a rapid U.S. expansion and at the same time stable, low interest rates. They cannot have a strong pull of the U.S. locomotive and low trade deficits. They cannot have U.S. trade deficits and no capital flowing into the United States. The dollar cannot come down without the foreign countries putting their house in order to stop capital flight.

Instead of blaming the United States for all their troubles, the Europeans should put their own house in order. That would take care of most of their problems.

This view is now gaining support in Europe. Otmar Emminger, the former president of the German Bundesbank, has cautiously endorsed this view in an important paper, saying that the European complaints of the high U.S. interest rates overlook the fact that the high rates are "the unavoidable consequence of the U.S. expansion." He expressed the view that "up to now the effect of the U.S. expansion on the rest of the world has been predominately positive."[28] In a later paper Emminger reiterated his opinion "that if one weighs the positive and negative elements [of the strong dollar and the huge U.S. trade deficits] against each other, the balance for most other countries, and for the world economy in general, is positive--at least in the short run."[29]

Professor Herbert Giersch has argued for some time that high unemployment in Germany and elsewhere in Europe is not Keynesian but structural; it is specifically a result of wages being rigid and too high in two senses. First, the overall wage level is too high, and profits are too low. Second, relative wages between regions and sectors of the economy are rigid and out of line. The policy conclusions are straight-forward. What is required is not a more expansive monetary and fiscal policy (reflation), but structural reforms.

Giersch has recently restated his views in an impressive paper, "Perspective for the World Economy."[30] He concluded that for Germany and other European countries to catch up with the United States, they must reduce taxes substantially, improve depreciation allowances, abolish regulations in many areas, and make wages more flexible. In other words, what holds back German investment and growth is not a tight or expensive supply of investible funds due to high U.S. interest rates, but slacked demand for investment funds due to structural weaknesses, institutional rigidities, and faulty policies.

France, as so often in the past, has been a special case. As Herbert Lüthy has said, "French clocks show a different time."[31] France has bucked the liberal trend--liberal in the classical sense of laissez faire. It has gone Socialist. The Keynesian policies and wholesale nationalization of the Mitterrand government have triggered massive capital flight. To stem the outflow of funds, France has established tight exchange control with searches at the border and censorship of the mail, reminiscent of the Schachtian system under the Nazi regime.[32] Members of Mitterand's cabinet have, nonetheless, been in the forefront of criticism of U.S. fiscal policy.

Criticism of U.S. Fiscal Policies in the Less Developed Countries. The third world countries are the chief beneficiaries of the U.S. recovery and of the strong dollar. Nonetheless, they are among the sharpest critics of U.S. policies in general and of the U.S. budget deficits in particular. This should not surprise us, for the less-developed countries have been habitual complainers. Their representatives in the United Nations and other international organizations have been blaming the industrial countries in general and the United States in particular for all their economic troubles. It is said, for example, that the strong dollar has put a heavy burden on them because prices of many commodities, such as crude oil, are usually expressed in terms of dollars and thus automatically increase when the dollar goes up in the foreign exchange market. This argument, which is also used in industrial countries, overlooks the fact that the prices of these commodities are determined in competitive markets. Even the price of crude oil has *not* gone up with the strong dollar. On the contrary, it has sharply dropped in terms of dollars, despite the Organization of Petroleum Exporting Countries (OPEC).

There is, however, some truth in the contention that the burden of their huge foreign debt is increased by the appreciation of the dollar, though this charge refers only to the structural component of the rise in interest rates, not to the cyclical part.

The less-developed countries do have legitimate grievances about the protectionist policies of the industrial countries. Unfortunately, most less-developed countries make things much worse through highly protectionist measures of their own. They should understand that a further reduction in the volume of trade caused by their protectionist measures will not alleviate the loss caused by protection in the industrial countries. On the contrary, it means a further deterioration of their economic welfare.

The LDCs of the third world are a very heterogeneous group, much more so than the industrial countries. In Southeast Asia, Taiwan, South Korea, Malaysia, Singapore, Thailand, and Hong Kong are doing very well despite high interest rates and protectionist policies in the industrial countries. The countries on the Arabian peninsula, Saudi Arabia, Kuwait, the United Arab Emirates--the core of OPEC--float on nearly half of the free world's oil reserve. Other oil-rich countries, like Nigeria, have squandered their newly discovered riches by gross mismanagement. There are the really poor and backward countries, the "fourth world," mainly in Africa.

There are, finally, some potentially very rich countries with excellent human and material resources, which have no business being less developed. Argentina is the outstanding example. Although its situation is extreme, it is by no means entirely atypical.

In the past Argentina has often been compared with Australia. Years ago Colin Clark, in his celebrated pioneering study *Conditions of Economic Progress*, predicted confidently that Argentina's real per capital GNP would soon approach that of the United States and Canada.[33] This was not an unreasonable prediction, but it did not work out that way. Why? A brief description is in order.[34]

The source of Argentina's plight is uncontrolled and wasteful spending by the government, especially by a great variety of state enterprises. This spending started under the first Peron regime, which forced industrialization and coddled trade unions--all at the expense of agriculture, the natural backbone of the Argentine economy. The successive military governments that followed the ouster of Peron failed to bring about a radical change in policy. On the contrary, the state enterprises, many of them run by top officers of the armed forces, continued their inefficient, wasteful projects and pushed ahead with often grotesquely ill-considered projects. Road bridges were built with no traffic to cross them; nuclear power plants were built when the capacity for generating electricity already exceeded demand, and petrochemical plants were completed long before there was any use for their products. Military expenditures skyrocketed. The result was huge government deficits and galloping inflation. Thus Argentina's economy languished when countries like Mexico and Brazil had respectable growth. When the world recession struck, Argentina tried to keep its economy going by borrowing abroad and by printing money at home.

Unfortunately, the democratic government of President Alfonsin, which came to power in 1983, has not brought about a radical reversal of past policies. In some respects it has made things even worse. A populist regime is not in a good position to resist excessive wage demands and protectionist pressures.

Countries like Argentina should restore their creditworthiness by accepting and carrying out the austerity program recommended by the IMF. They should restrain monetary growth to curb inflation and establish a realistic exchange rate by floating. The "classical medicine" (to use Keynes's expression) will not work, however, unless the major structural impediments are removed. Specifically, public spending, which has skyrocketed in the past ten years, should be sharply cut; and government budget deficits, including those of public enterprises, must be sharply trimmed. As many of the state enterprises as possible should be denationalized and turned over to private hands. For that, help of foreign corporations would be indispensable. Foreign direct investment should, therefore, be encouraged. A similar point has been made by Anne Krueger, vice-president of the World Bank. In a wide-ranging speech she argued for a shift from "debt financing" to "equity financing."[35] Equity financing, direct investment from abroad, provides not only capital but also entrepreneurship and management know-how. Furthermore, it will be necessary to phase out the very expensive policy pursued in many of these countries of keeping down food prices by high subsidies.[36] These policies, along with excessive indexation of wages, are the driving force of inflation. With these cost trends unchanged, monetary-fiscal disinflation would bring the economy to a grinding halt. A policy of pure monetarism, relying exclusively on monetary-fiscal restraint, makes no sense.

Without a drastic change in policies a default on the outstanding debt will be unavoidable. To postpone the default by new credits would be throwing away good money after bad and would make the final adjustment even more difficult. Reform along the lines indicated would, after a painful transition, start a beneficial circle and restore credit-worthiness.

Exchange Rates and Inflation

The Vicious Circle Argument Against Floating[37]

The claim that floating enables each country to pursue its internal policy objectives, be it more rapid expansion to promote full employment or tighter money to combat inflation, unhampered by what is going on outside the country's boundaries, is now often challenged on the ground that a "vicious circle" prevents the exercise of the new freedom. In other words, the alleged autonomy provided by floating is merely nominal, not real. John Williamson puts it very clearly this way:

> Monetary policy has not in fact furnished [under floating] the extra degree of freedom in achieving internal objectives that was promised.

On the contrary, a monetary policy, markedly more expansionary than that in the rest of the world, is quickly translated into depreciation and sets off a vicious circle.[38]

Since the theory of the vicious circle has been accepted, for example, by the Bank for International Settlements in several of its annual reports, it is worth examining in some detail.

During the Great Depression of the 1930s floating (or its equivalent in terms of open or disguised devaluation) enabled some countries to pursue an independent policy of expansion and so to extricate themselves from the spiral of world deflation. They were not bothered by vicious inflationary circles.

In the 1970s the situation is, of course, very different. There has been world inflation, not deflation or mass unemployment. Floating, as we have seen, has given "the extra degree of freedom" to countries willing to use it to extricate themselves from world inflation.

But how about countries on the other side of the fence who wish to pursue "a monetary policy markedly more expansionary than that in the rest of the world"? Have they been hampered by a vicious circle? A more expansionary policy in an inflationary environment means more inflation. Unfortunately, there are many countries that have used (or misused) the "extra degree of freedom" provided by floating to pursue highly inflationary policies.

There is, however, a kernel of truth in the vicious circle theory, in fact, every inflation acquires sooner or later properties of a vicious circle, and this tendency may be strengthened by foreign exchange developments. Advocates of floating have been aware of this. In 1974, I wrote:

Several economists have pointed out that a falling exchange value of a currency under floating is likely to provide a stronger inducement for the central bank to curb inflation than a declining reserve [under fixed rates]. For one thing a slump of the value of the currency in the foreign exchange market is a much clearer danger signal than a declining reserve which can be more easily hidden from the public eye. For another, a country with an ample reserve can alleviate its inflation by "exporting" some of it to other countries, i.e., by increasing domestic supplies through larger imports and smaller exports, financing the deficit by reserve losses. Under floating, on the other hand, each country has to swallow the inflation which it generates. This provides a strong inducement to curb inflation. These conjectures of theorists have recently been confirmed [by the Chairman of the Federal Reserve Board]. Arthur Burns, not an ardent advocate of floating, pointed out that under floating 'faster inflation in the United States than abroad would tend to induce a depreciation of the dollar, which in turn would exacerbate our inflation problem.' He drew the conclusion that 'under the present regime of floating it is *more necessary than ever* to proceed cautiously in executing an expansionary policy.' Burns also noted that 'no such intensification can take place under a regime of fixed exchange rates as long as international reserves remain sufficient to obviate the need for devaluation.'[39]

A further comment seems to be in order. The fact that floating provides an inducement for the monetary authorities to step on the brakes does not guarantee that inflation will in fact be curbed. A strong inducement to disinflate can always be overwhelmed by an even stronger propensity to inflate.[40]

Actually, the U.S. authorities learned their lesson. As we have seen, the inflation rate after it had reached the level of over 12 percent in July 1974 was brought down to below five percent at the end of 1976. The dollar rescue operations of November 1, 1978, and October 6, 1979, again demonstrated the disciplinary power of floating rates.

There remains the question of overshooting. The definition and measurement of overshooting presents formidable conceptual and statistical problems, which cannot be fully explored here. I confine myself to a few comments.

Let me start by saying that under floating relatively inflationary countries will have to accept a declining exchange value of their currencies. Suppose the rate of decline of the exchange value of the currency does not exceed the relative inflation rate. In that case one can hardly speak of a vicious circle started by floating, although it is true that such a country will have a higher inflation rate under floating than it might have had under a fixed rate regime. For under a fixed rate system it could alleviate its inflation for some time by running a current account deficit, *provided* the country had a large international reserve or credit line, as the United States had when the world was on the dollar standard.

Now suppose the exchange rate overshoots, and the currency depreciates in excess of the relative inflation rate; in other words, the *real* effective exchange rate declines, perhaps because of attempts at diversification of foreign-held balances on the part of official or private holders of such balances. Could that not start a vicious circle--import prices rising, the cost of living going up, and indexed wages increasing? Perhaps it could, but if so it could be started just as well by some domestic shock. Suppose there is a crop failure: Then food prices rise, the cost of living goes up, indexed wages and salaries are adjusted, and inflationary expectations gain strength. This clearly demonstrates that the roots of the vicious circle, if it exists, are to be sought in domestic arrangements--monetary policy and wage indexation.[41] But we usually do not assume that a modern economy is in such an unstable equilibrium. At any rate, no vicious circle, whether its cause is domestic or foreign, could go far without monetary accommodation.

It will perhaps be argued that, in order to make sure that no vicious circle is started, any overshooting of the exchange rate should be counteracted by skillful interventions in the foreign exchange market. But that is easier said than done. True, policy makers and economists frequently make statements that the exchange market has overreacted, that this or that currency is overvalued or undervalued. And there is now a strong tendency to speak of overshooting, if the exchange rate has moved beyond the level indicated by the relative inflation rate--in other words, if the *real* effective exchange rate has moved significantly or if the nominal exchange rate has deviated significantly from some purchasing power parity.

But it is very hard to make such statements operational. There exist many different measures of purchasing power parity and of real exchange rate changes--different types of price and cost levels (consumer prices, wholesale prices, unit labor cost, etc.) and different methods of weighting (bilateral, multilateral trade weights). The different methods yield often conflicting and always quantitatively divergent results.

Surely not every change in the real exchange rates is a symptom of disequilibrium (overshooting). As Otmar Emminger has pointed out in a forceful defense of the present international monetary system,[42] a decrease in the real exchange rate may be necessary to restore equilibrium in the balance of payments. Suppose a country has a large current account deficit that is financed by public sector foreign borrowing. The elimination of such a deficit will usually require a drop of the exchange rate in excess of the inflation differential. Emminger also observed that a decline in the real exchange rate, that is, some overshooting, may be necessary and desirable to jolt the authorities into taking energetic inflationary measures.

To sum up, the attempt to counteract every alleged overshooting of the exchange rate by skillful intervention in the foreign exchange market is a very risky business. It is likely to do more harm than good if it goes beyond smoothing strictly short-run fluctuations in the exchange rate, that is, correcting "disorderly market conditions" as the phrase goes. The underlying theory of vicious circles spoiling the functioning of the system of floating exchange rates is based on the erroneous, or at any rate vastly exaggerated, notion of a basic instability of the market economy.

Flexible Exchange Rates and Inflation[43]

If I say things which should be obvious and have been said many times before, my excuse is that they are so often forgotten, as many speeches in Manila have demonstrated once again.

The annual meeting of the Fund and its Bretton Woods twin, the World Bank, in Manila (October 4-8, 1976) was, as usual, a huge gathering of many thousand high-priced experts, ministers of finance, central bankers, and other high officials from all 130-odd member countries; international officials from the innumerable international agencies; and the usual army of hangers-on--bankers, economists, journalists, et cetera. There were no important decisions made in Manila. But some of the many speeches were interesting in revealing the current thinking of the leading financial officials about some of the current economic problems, for example about world inflation and recession and about the way in which the now legalized system of widespread floating operates.

Recent Criticism of Floating. At Manila many complaints were voiced about the working of the floating system. Floating was defended by Canada, West Germany, and the United States, but most other comments were in a critical or plaintive mood.

A frequent charge was that floating has had inflationary effects. The governor for Italy said: "The high rate of inflation [in Italy] is due in no small part to the sharp depreciation of the lira in the first months of the year. The high degree of indexation of the Italian economy has blunted the usefulness of exchange rate depreciation since it leads rapidly to higher domestic inflation."[44] Similarly the governor of the Banque de France declared:

> Speculative anticipations by economic agents amplify the size of exchange rate movements . . . A fall in the exchange rate in the market is reflected, even before the slightest impact is felt on export

> volume, in an immediate rise in the cost of imports. Thus, in the first
> phase, the external depreciation of the currency aggravates the internal
> inflation rate . . . setting in motion a cumulative process at the end of
> which the currency's exchange value continues to fall.

Such remarks have been amplified and sensationalized by financial journalists. There has been talk of vicious and virtuous circles: Weak currency countries with high inflation rates such as Britain and Italy are said to be "trapped in a vicious circle," while strong currency countries with little or no inflation such as West Germany, Switzerland, and the United States (and also the Netherlands, despite an almost 10 percent inflation rate) are said to enjoy a "virtuous circle." Thus floating is said to "drive a wedge between industrial nations."[45]

A large part of the serious economic literature on floating and inflation has been carefully reviewed by Andrew D. Crockett and Morris Goldstein of the IMF. Their "overall conclusion [is] that the type of exchange rate system has little influence . . . on world inflation." But they find "a certain intuitive appeal" in the notion that in a world in which prices have become "rather inflexible, especially in the downward direction . . . devaluations will produce . . . a larger . . . effect on domestic prices than appreciations."[46]

What is true is that, under floating, an inflationary country will feel the consequences of inflation more quickly than under fixed exchange rates, because under the latter regime countries have the possibility of alleviating their inflation by running a deficit--*provided* they have an ample reserve or credit line to finance their deficit. In other words, under fixed exchanges a country can export some of its inflation, while under floating it has to swallow the inflation which it generates.[47] In that sense it can be said that floating has an inflationary effect on deficit countries. But by the same token it protects surplus countries from imported inflation. This is sometimes denied or played down on the ground that in the modern world, prices and wages are rigid downward. It is true that wage rigidity gives rise to the well-known Hayek-Schultze ratchet effect: every shift in demand raises that price where demand has increased, and these price increases are not offset by price declines where demand has decreased.[48] (Needless to add, this kind of ratchet inflation, too, requires a permissive monetary policy to occur.) It follows that wage rigidity *reduces* the anti-inflationary effect of an appreciation of the currency, but it does not *eliminate* it for two reasons: First, wage or price rigidity obviously will not prevent the decline of prices of noncompetitive imports (that is, of commodities that are not produced domestically) in terms of the *appreciated currency*. Second, as far as competitive imports (imports of commodities that are produced in the appreciating country) are concerned, additional supplies from abroad will at least slow down the ongoing inflation, although under a regime of rigid wages to a lesser extent and at a higher cost of unemployment than would be the case, if wages and prices were more flexible. West Germany and Switzerland provide dramatic proof, if proof is needed. Switzerland has been able to reduce the inflation rate practically to zero, and West Germany has reduced it to below 4 percent by letting their currencies sharply float up.

The fact that under floating the consequences of inflationary policies are felt immediately, because they cannot be alleviated by "exporting" part of the inflation to other countries, constitutes a strong incentive for financial discipline. Academic advocates of floating have often made that point. It has been recently supported in official statements. For example, Arthur Burns, not an ardent supporter of floating, told a congressional committee that:

> . . . under the present regime of floating it is more necessary than ever to proceed cautiously in executing our expansionary policy. For faster inflation in the United States than abroad would tend to induce a depreciation of the dollar, which in turn would exacerbate our inflation problem.[49]

Emile van Lennep, secretary general of OECD, said in his speech at the Manila meeting:

> It is, I think, now evident that the fears that more flexibility would ease the external discipline of deficit countries have proved unfounded. After a transitional period, governments have learned that because of the close interaction between domestic policies, exchange rates and inflation rates, a continuing tendency for their currencies to depreciate can be even more dangerous than a continuing loss of reserves.

It should be noted that van Lennep speaks of a "transitional period." Some countries may, indeed, have mistaken floating as a license to let down their guard against inflation. If so, they have been quickly taught a lesson.

It should perhaps be added that the fact that floating provides its own inducement to curb inflation does not guarantee that inflation will in fact be curbed. A strong inducement to disinflate can be overwhelmed by an even stronger propensity to inflate.

It is true that every long drawn-out inflation develops vicious circle properties and is apt to set "in motion a cumulative process" as the governor of the Banque de France said at Manila.[50] Inflation "feeds on itself," because people will try to reduce their cash balances by spending money faster on commodities and foreign money, and it cannot be excluded that on some occasions the exchange rate in the market may overshoot the long-run equilibrium. But the "cumulative" process could not go on without a permissive monetary policy, and the vicious circle can be broken by tight money, although not without causing temporary unemployment. Both Italy and Britain had plenty of opportunity to get out of the vicious circle, and they could have softened the transition to less inflation with the help of their huge foreign borrowing. Unfortunately, they did not utilize the breathing spell. This was not the fault of floating but was due to a failure to curb inflation by appropriate monetary policies.

It should be observed that import restrictions, whether in the form of tariffs, quotas, import deposit schemes, or a tax on the purchase of foreign exchange, do *not* alleviate the inflation. Financing a deficit by drawing down reserves or by borrowing abroad does reduce inflationary pressure because this policy permits an increase of the supply of goods in the home market. Import restrictions, in contrast, do not reduce inflationary pressures. On the contrary, they are counterproductive because of their protectionist effects which imply a misallocation of resources and thus reduce aggregate supply.[51] While devaluation and floating stimulate exports and discourage imports, import restrictions operate only on imports.

It could be argued that an import deposit scheme, unlike tariffs and quotas, may have a slight deflationary (anti-inflationary) side effect if the deposits are effectively sterilized for some time. But the same anti-inflationary effect can be achieved by monetary policy without the distortions caused by import restrictions. In summary, anything import restrictions can do, devaluation or floating plus an appropriate monetary policy can do more cheaply and efficiently.[52]

The main advantage that has been claimed for flexible exchange rates since Keynes is that it enables each country to pursue independently the demand-management policy which it prefers. Floating can protect a country from inflation or deflation, which under fixed exchanges is imposed on it by a balance of payments surplus or deficit. Keynes stressed the threat of having to submit to deflationary pressures from abroad; today inflationary pressures from abroad are the danger uppermost in one's mind. Doubts have been raised again recently about these claims for floating. For floating has not prevented a worldwide inflationary explosion, nor an equally worldwide stagflation and recession in 1973 and 1974, succeeded by an almost worldwide rapid recovery in 1975, which in turn was followed by a "pause" in 1976. A fairly large literature has sprung up under the heading of international transmission of economic disturbances, which investigates whether, under floating, there really was a greater divergence among different countries with respect to business cycles, price stability, monetary growth, et cetera, than there was under the par value system.[53]

As often happens, intensive econometric-statistical investigations have tended to obscure or lose sight of broad, basic facts and insights. One such fact is that, broadly speaking, in the intermediate and long run, exchange rate changes reflect divergent inflation trends.[54]But in the era of stagflation *divergent* inflation rates between countries do not necessarily preclude *convergence* of real business cycles, that is, of cyclical fluctuations in output and employment. Thus, it is not surprising that floating did not immediately change the worldwide nature of inflation, although some countries managed to reduce their inflation rate drastically (West Germany, Switzerland). The inflation explosion of 1973 had, after all, originated during the fixed rate system and was intensified in all countries by the oil price rise and the policy reactions to it. Nor is it surprising that attempts in all industrial countries to curb inflation produced, despite floating, a worldwide recession. It is practically impossible to reverse an inflationary trend without a transitional recession. Floating shields a country from *monetary* influences from abroad, in the sense that, under floating, countries cannot be forced (as they are under fixed rates) by inflationary neighbors to expand their money supply, or by deflationary neighbors to contract their money supply. But floating does not protect against *real* influences from abroad. Among such real influences, including those caused by monetary factors (by inflation or deflation), are changes in the terms of trade, the oil price rise, protectionist measures taken by foreign countries, recession abroad which reduces real demand for imports and implies a deterioration of the terms of trade, and foreign competition for particular industries.[55] All this follows from generally accepted economic principles which do not require any further econometric confirmation.

The upshot of this discussion is to confirm our conclusion that floating is here to stay for the foreseeable future. As Edward Bernstein put it, "the system of fluctuating exchange rates has worked reasonably well, much better than would have been possible if attempts had been made to perpetuate the Bretton Woods system of fixed parities by patchwork here and there."[56] We can take it for granted, however, that in most countries the float will be a managed one, although much can be said in favor of free unmanaged floating. The question remains how floating should be managed.

Notes

1. From "Reflections on the U.S. Trade Deficit and the Floating Dollar." *Contemporary Economic Problems*, William Fellner, ed. (Washington, D.C.: American Enterprise Institute, 1978), pp. 211-243. This selection is drawn from pp. 212, 227-231, 238 and 239.

2. It will be recalled that this was the favorite phrase used by German officials--inappropriately--when they resisted appreciation of the mark and asked for depreciation of the dollar instead under the Bretton Woods system, before it became generally accepted that, in an inflationary world, price stability cannot be achieved without floating.

3. This follows from the fact that they assume that the locomotive countries can expand without accelerating inflation, which would leave the inflation differential unchanged and would not eliminate the pull it exerts on the dollar balances.

4. See, for example, *Ausszüge aus Presseartikeln* (Frankfurt: Deutsche Bundesbank), no. 10, January 30, 1978; no. 12, February 2, 1978; no. 18, February 28, 1978; and no. 24, April 4, 1978.

5. It has been mentioned, however, in Max Corden's article "Expansion of the World Economy and the Duties of the Surplus Countries," *The World Economy*, vol. 1, no. 2 (January 1978), p. 126.

6. The strange notion and morbid fear of deflation among British economists is illustrated in a letter to the *London Times*, February 15, 1978 by Nicholas Kaldor (answering a letter by F. A. Hayek of February 11, 1978) in which he characterizes Chancellor Brüning's policy in 1930-1932 of severe deflation (sharp contraction of the money supply causing a large decline of the price level) and stubborn refusal to devalue or float the mark as "monetarist policies" and says that "the economics of Chancellor Schmidt and his advisors are very similar to those of Dr. Brüning and in this country [Britain], too, there is a return to the views prevailing at the time of Montague Norman and Philip Snowden."

7. W. M. Corden, *Inflation, Exchange Rates and the World Economy* (Chicago: Chicago University Press, 1977), p. 132.

8. Actually, the proponents of the locomotive policy usually mention the weak industrial countries along with the LDCs as the beneficiaries of the policy. It has even been said that German expansion was important to check communism in France and Italy!

9. If the locomotive countries expand internally, or alternatively if they let their currency appreciate, the deficit countries will be stimulated and their deficits will decline. It will perhaps be argued that they will have to support this increase of real demand from abroad by expansionary monetary-fiscal measures and that this supporting expansion is the real meaning of the convoy policy. But this argument would ignore the fact that the deficit countries still suffer from high inflation.

10. From "The International Monetary System and Proposals for International Policy Coordination." *Deficits, Taxes, and Economic Adjustments*, Phillip Cagan, editor. (Washington, D.C., 1987), pp. 63-96. This selection pp. 86-92; 95-96.

11. See Barry Eichengreen, "International Policy Coordination in Historic Perspective: A View from the Interwar Years," in Willem H. Buiter and Richard C. Marston, eds., *International Economic Policy Coordination* (Cambridge, England: Cambridge University Press, for the National Bureau of Economic Research, 1985), pp. 139-83.

12. From Resolution 3 of the Report of the Financial Commission of the Genoa Conference, 1922.

13. The proposed use of "indicators" has been hailed as a new approach and a major advance of policy making in general and of international coordination of policies in particular. In my opinion there is nothing new in this "approach"; not even the term "indicators" is new. In 1973 a report for the Committee of Twenty on Reform of the International Monetary System and Related Issues by "The Technical Group on Indicators" (under the chairmanship of Robert Solomon) discussed the use of indicators in the adjustment process (see *International Monetary Reform*, IMF, Washington, D.C., 1974), pp. 51-76. Any discussion of the state, performance, and prospects of a particular economy cannot help using economic variables.

14. Quotations from the official statement of the meeting.

15. This episode was discussed in my chapter, "Reflections on the U.S. Trade Deficit and the Floating Dollar," in William Fellner, Project Director, *Contemporary Economic Problems, 1978* (Washington, D.C.: American Enterprise Institute, 1978). See especially pp. 227-30 and the Postscript, pp. 240-43. See also Herbert Stein's trenchant analysis of the whole approach in "International Coordination of Domestic Economic Policies," *The AEI Economist*, June 1978, American Enterprise Institute, Washington, D.C.

16. H. J. Witteveen, "Scenario for Coordinated Growth and Payments Adjustment," presented at the IMF meeting in Mexico, May 24, 1978.

17. Anthony M. Solomon, "Germany Puts Savings Over Jobs," *Wall Street Journal*, March 24, 1986.

18. *IMF World Economic Outlook* (Washington, D.C.: International Monetary Fund, October 1986), p. 24. Several other econometric studies, too, have reached the conclusion that faster growth in Germany and Japan has little effect on the U.S. current account. See, for example, unpublished studies by the staff of the Federal Reserve Board. See also Filles Oudiz and Jeffrey Sachs, "Macroeconomic Policy Coordination among the Industrial Economies," *Brookings Papers on Economic Activity 1*, William C. Brainard and George L. Perry, eds., The Brookings Institution, Washington, D.C., 1984; and Jeffrey A. Frankel, "The Sources of Disagreement among the International Macro Models and Implications for Policy Coordination," Working Paper No. 1925, National Bureau of Economic Research, Cambridge, Massachusetts, May 1986.

19. From "International Issues Raised by Criticisms of the U.S. Budget Deficits." *Essays in Contemporary Economic Problems--The Economy in Deficit*, 1985. Phillip Cagan, editor. (Washington, D.C.: American Enterprise Institute, 1985), pp. 124-145. This selection excerpted from pp. 129-145.

20. Stephen Marris, "Why Europe's Recovery Is Lagging Behind: With an Unconventional View of What Should Be Done about It," *Europe, Magazine of the European Community*, March/April 1984.

Since this was written an important, wide-ranging paper by Ambassador Arthur F. Burns, "The Economic Sluggishness of Western Europe" (delivered at the Dunlap Distinguished American Lecture, University of Dubuque, Iowa, September 5, 1984, to be published), has become available. Burns presents a thorough analysis of the structural handicaps of Europe as compared with the United States and vividly describes the excesses of the welfare state and the oppressive regulatory climate in many European countries.

21. Since this was written, *The Economist* of London has taken up the subject (issue of November 24, 1984, "Why Europe Has Failed," p. 13, and "Europe's Technology Gap," pp. 93-98). The articles describe in considerable detail the enormous benefits the United States derives from the fact that its economy is a real free trade area of continental size with no restrictions or formalities at the state borders; that public utilities, airlines, railroads, and so on are in private hands, which ensures efficient competitive large-scale production; and that safety, health, and other regulations are uniform throughout the country.

In stark contrast, Europe is sorely handicapped because the "common market" has failed dismally to establish real free trade; public utilities, airlines, and so on are in public hands, which means that levels of output are way below the optimum; and safety, health, and other regulations vary from country to country. The article points out that these impediments explain why Europe lags badly behind the United States and Japan in the development of high-technology industries. Thus Europe has been prevented from fully participating in ". . . the biggest market-driven wave of economic development [the world] has known, detonated by an explosion of knowledge. By one estimate, nine times as much scientific knowledge has been generated since the Second World War as mankind was able to produce in all its previous history. The amount of information in the world now doubles every eight years. Prosperity goes to countries that have a mechanism to put it to use." ("How Europe Has Failed," *The Economist*, London, November 24, 1984, p. 13).

22. For details see *The Economist*, London, June 23, 1984, p. 29.

23. These two factors are not always separable. Both the OECD and the EC routinely publish cyclically adjusted budget deficits for their members.

24. For details, see my contribution in *Essays in Contemporary Economic Problems: Disinflation*.

25. The GATT report has received hardly any attention in the media. A notable exception is an excellent article by Samuel Brittan, "The U.S. Loco No Longer Pulls," *Financial Times*, September 13, 1984. Mr. Brittan pays high tribute to the principal author of the report, Jan Tumlir, executive director of GATT. I wish to associate myself with that tribute.

26. "The Mighty Borrower," *The Economist*, London, September 22, 1984, p. 15.

27. On this point see the testimony of William A. Niskanen before U.S. Congress, Joint Economic Committee, August 8, 1984, in Council of Economic Advisers, *The Midyear Economic Outlook*.

28. See Otmar Emminger, "Der Währungspolitik stehen unruhige Zeiten bevor. Trendwende des Dollars/Rückkehr zur Normalität oder neue Turbulenzen?" in Deutsche Bundesbank, *Auszüge aus Presseartikeln*, Frankfurt am Main, April 6, 1984.

29. Otmar Emminger, "Adjustments in World Payments: An Evaluation," draft of a paper for the conference sponsored by the Federal Reserve Bank of Boston, May 20-21, 1984.

30. "Perspektiven der Weltwirtschaft" [Perspective for the World Economy], preliminary version, Kiel, 1984 (mimeographed).

After this was written, I learned through an article in the *Wall Street Journal* (November 19, 1984, front page) under the title "Machines Blamed for Europe's Joblessness," that Professor Giersch's theory about wages being too high has recently been confirmed by an expert report to the European Commission (EC) in Brussels. The report finds that European industries have invested too much in labor-saving machines. In fact, "the EC countries spent some 20 percent of their gross domestic product on fixed investment in the past 10 years, compared with 16 percent in the United States. But the EC managed to increase GDP by only 1.7 percent a year compared with 2.3 percent in the United States." The report concludes "that prosperity might be better served by employing human beings even if there is a machine that can do the same job [more cheaply]. Europe has actually gotten a poor return from heavy capital spending over the past decade."

According to the report, the main reason is that wages are too high and too rigid. I would add that interest rates are too low. High wages and low interest rates induce excessive substitution of capital for labor and high unemployment. I further conclude that there was after all some merit in the much maligned U.S. high-interest policy. It is needless to add that U.S. interest rates will have to come down when the economy slows down or goes into recession, as it will sooner or later.

(The quotations come from the article in the *Wall Street Journal*. The title of the report is "Some Aspects of Industrial Productive Performance in the European Community: An Appraisal," in *European Economy*, no. 20, Commission of the European Communities, Belgium, July 1984.)

The assertion that in some European countries real wages are too high has received its most thorough econometric test in an article by Jacques R. Artus, "The Disequilibrium Real Wage Hypothesis: An Empirical Evaluation" (International Monetary Fund *Staff Papers*, vol. 31, no. 2, June 1984, pp. 249-302). The author concludes: "As far as the manufacturing sector is concerned, there are indeed strong reasons to believe that in France, the Federal Republic of Germany, and the United Kingdom the real wage rate is too high, in the sense of being incompatible with high employment. In particular, in these three countries we did not find any evidence that a large part of the actual increase in the share of labor costs in value added is warranted by long-run changes in production techniques, in the price of energy, or in the relative availability of labor and capital."

31. *Frankreich's Uhren gehen anders* [French clocks show a different time] is the title of a famous book by the Swiss historian Herbert Lüthy.

32. *The Economist*, London, May 13, 1984, reported from Switzerland that French customs officers have increased their "harassment" of people heading for Switzerland, giving "unjustified rough treatment to aged travellers." Things became so bad that the Swiss ambassador to France warned that if it did not stop "the relations between the two countries would be damaged."

33. Colin Clark, *Conditions of Economic Progress* (London, 1951).

34. The following analysis is partly based on a very interesting article: "Flag Day for Argentina," *The Economist*, London, April 1984, pp. 11-12. *The Economist* lays its finger on the right spot, but it goes too far in blaming all the trouble on the successive military regimes. The trouble started earlier with the Peron regime (1946 to 1953).

35. Anne Krueger, "Aspects of Capital Flows between Developing and Developed Countries" (paper presented at the Pinhas Sapir Conference on Development, Tel Aviv, Israel, May 28-31, 1984, mimeographed).

36. In agricultural exporting countries, like Argentina, the food subsidies take the form of restrictions on exports of agricultural products to keep food prices down. The results are huge losses of output and lower tax revenues.

37. From "The Dollar in the World Economy: Recent Developments in Perspective." *Contemporary Economic Problems*, William Fellner, Project Director. (Washington, D.C.: American Enterprise Institute, 1980), pp. 135-165. This selection pp. 151-154.

38. Williamson, "World Stagflation," p. 33.

39. Statement before the U.S. House of Representatives, Subcommittee on International Finance of the Committee on Banking and Currency, April 4, 1974. Emphasis added.

40. Gottfried Haberler, "The Future of the International Monetary System," *Zeitschrift für Nationalökonomie*, vol. 34 (1974), pp. 391-392. Available as Reprint No. 30 (Washington, D.C.: American Enterprise Institute, 1975).

41. The literature on balance of payments adjustments abounds with cases where troubles caused by internal policy failures and dilemmas (especially the stagflation dilemma) are misinterpreted as being due to stubborn inelasticities of international demand or to failures of the adjustment mechanism to work under floating. A typical example: Suppose a country has a large external deficit that is financed by reserve losses and public sector borrowing. If that deficit is to be eliminated, under full employment, some belt tightening (reduction of "absorption") is unavoidable. Since money wages are rigid downward, the necessary reduction of absorption has to be brought about by a depreciation of the currency or a downward float jacking up the price level. If real wages, too, are rigid because of widespread indexation of incomes, union pressure, and assorted government policies protecting the standard of living of different groups, the only method left to adjust the balance of payments is to reduce import demand by permitting a sufficient amount of unemployment and slack to develop by refusing to expand monetary circulation. If, on the other hand, expansionary monetary and fiscal measures are taken to combat the incipient unemployment, a "vicious circle is set off," and this is then misinterpreted as a failure of the adjustment mechanism to work under floating.

I have called attention to this misinterpretation on several occasions. See for example the section "Limits of Effectiveness of Floating" (p. 186), and especially footnote 37 (pp. 271-273) in Gottfried Haberler, *Economic Growth and Stability, An Analysis of Economic Change and Policies* (Los Angeles: 1974).

42. See Emminger, "The International Monetary System Under Stress."

43. From "The International Monetary System after Jamaica and Manila." *Contemporary Economic Problems*, William Fellner, editor. (Washington, D.C.: American Enterprise Institute, 1977), pp. 239-288. This

selection excerpted from pp. 243; 250-256.

44. A high degree of indexation of wages and other incomes is a major roadblock for a stabilization policy whenever real wages have gotten out of line. For example, when an external deficit has to be eliminated because reserves are running out, the level of real wages ("absorption") has to be reduced if unemployment is to be avoided. In such a case indexation becomes a serious hurdle for adjustment, irrespective of whether the adjustment is attempted by internal deflation, depreciation, or downward float. If real wage rates cannot be reduced, unemployment becomes the only method to bring about the unavoidable reduction of absorption and the adjustment of the balance of payments.

45. Paul Lewis, *New York Times* (October 10, 1976).

46. Andrew D. Crockett and Morris Goldstein, "Inflation Under Fixed and Flexible Exchange Rates," International Monetary Fund *Staff Papers*, vol. 23, no. 3 (Washington, D.C., November 1976), pp. 509-44. This paper has been incorrectly quoted in the above-mentioned article in the *New York Times* as supporting the vicious-circle theory. In their letter to the *Times* of October 13, 1976, the authors called attention to the mistake.

47. In modern economic jargon this simple proposition has been expressed by saying that there is a feedback from a depreciating currency on domestic prices and costs which in turn worsens the short-run trade-off between inflation and unemployment, that is, steepens the short-run Phillips curve. See for example Rudiger Dornbusch and Paul Krugman, "Flexible Exchange Rates in the Short Run," *Brookings Papers on Economic Activity*, 1976 (3), as quoted by Richard N. Cooper, "Five Years Since Smithsonian," *Economist* (December 18, 1976), p. 34. As D. H. Robertson once said: "Well, that is just fine. We all have our funny little ways of putting things." (*Utility and All That and Other Essays* [London: Allen and Unwin, 1952], p. 40.)

48. It has been objected that the ratchet mechanism--which explains inflation as the result of demand shifts raising prices where demand has increased, while failing to reduce prices where demand has decreased--does not operate in an inflationary environment for the following reason: In such an environment, industries where demand has decreased can make their contributions to keeping down the overall rate of inflation by reducing the rate of price and money wage rise without making the change negative. (See, for example, W. M. Corden, *Inflation, Exchange Rates, and the World Economy: Lectures on International Monetary Economics* [Oxford: Clarendon Press, 1977], p. 70.) This would be true if it were not a fact that in an inflationary environment *real* wages, too, tend to become rigid downward. Why do workers and their unions resist money wage restrictions in a stable price environment? Because they wish to protect their living standard. It follows that in an inflationary environment they resist a reduction in their real wage. Indexation is the collective expression of real wage resistance. Actually unions often go

beyond real wage maintenance and insist on the customary real wage increase.

49. Statement before the Subcommittee on International Finance of the Committee on Banking and Currency, House of Representatives, April 4, 1974. Burns also noted that "no such intensification [of inflation] can take place under a regime of fixed exchange rates as long as international reserves remain sufficient to obviate the need for devaluation." This is often regarded as an advantage of the system of fixed rates. But the other side of the coin should not be forgotten. If country A alleviates its inflation by "exporting" some of it, inflation is intensified abroad. True, situations are thinkable in which deficit *and* surplus countries both would profit from the reserve flow under fixed exchanges. This would be the case if the surplus countries suffered from unemployment (recession) while the deficit countries are under inflationary pressure. But these are exceptional circumstances which, if they happen to exist at any moment, are not likely to last for any length of time. (For details and references to the literature see my *Money in the International Market*, 2nd ed. [Cambridge, Mass.: Harvard University Press, 1969], pp. 16-17, and my contribution "The International Monetary System: Some Recent Developments and Discussions" in *Approaches to Greater Flexibility of Exchange Rates: The Bürgenstock Papers*, ed. George N. Halm [Princeton, N.J.: Princeton University Press, 1970], pp. 113-23.) See also my "Comments" to Arthur B. Laffer's paper "Two Arguments for Fixed Exchange Rates," *The Economics of Common Currencies*, ed. H. G. Johnson and Alexander Swoboda (London: Allen and Unwin, 1973), pp. 35-39.

50. Bernard Clappier, "Statement by the Governor of the Bank for France," *Summary Proceedings Annual Meeting 1976* (Washington, D.C.: International Monetary Fund, 1976), p. 74.

51. Here the usual marginal qualifications to the proposition that import restrictions reduce GNP should be mentioned: The terms of trade could conceivably be improved or, if there is a lot of unemployment in particular industries in the short run, a tariff can increase employment and production. Obviously, some of these qualifications do not apply to general import restrictions on balance of payments grounds imposed by any single country.

52. The case against import controls for balance of payments reasons has been stated convincingly by W. M. Corden, I. M. D. Little, and M. F. G. Scott, *Import Controls versus Devaluation and Britain's Economic Prospects*, Trade Policy Research Center Guest Paper, no. 2 (London, 1975). This paper presents a devastating criticism of the protectionist proposals for Britain that have been put forward in *The Economic Policy Review*, no. 1. (Cambridge: University of Cambridge, Department of Applied Economics, 1975). The *Review* is the organ of the so-called new school of the split group of Keynesian economists.

53. This literature has been well reviewed by Marina v. N. Whitman in her contribution "International Interdependence and the U.S. Economy" in

William Fellner, ed., *Contemporary Economic Problems, 1976* (Washington, D.C.: American Enterprise Institute, 1976). See especially pp. 194-208.

54. See for example IMF *Annual Reports*, especially the one for 1975. There are, of course, short-run deviations between inflation rates and exchange rate changes. It is, furthermore, well known from the theory of the purchasing parity that occasionally fairly large, long-run deviations of exchange rates from the purchasing-power parity occur, if the latter is defined in terms of consumer price levels. These deviations are due to differences in productivity growth between countries. For details and references to the literature see Gottfried Haberler, "International Aspects of U.S. Inflation" in *A New Look at Inflation* (Washington, D.C.: American Enterprise Institute, 1973), especially pp. 91-93 and "Inflation As a Worldwide Phenomenon--An Overview" in *The Phenomenon of Worldwide Inflation*, ed. D. Meiselman and A. Laffer (Washington, D.C.: American Enterprise Institute, 1975), pp. 24-25.

55. The literature on the problem of, and insulation from, different types of external disturbances under a regime of floating exchange rates has been well reviewed by Edward Tower and Thomas D. Willett in *Theory of Optimum Currency Areas and Exchange-Rate Flexibility*, Special Paper in International Economics, no. 11 (Princeton, N.J.: Princeton University Press, 1976).

56. Edward M. Bernstein, "The Monetary Authorities and the Free Exchange Market," Speech at Foreign Exchange Conference of American Bankers Association, New York, November 4, 1976 (mimeo).

5

International Monetary Issues

The International Monetary System

*The Present International Monetary System
in Historical Perspective*[1]

From the Gold Standard to Bretton Woods. It is important to recognize the present system as the last stage of a continuous, or perhaps discontinuous, evolution from the gold standard to widespread managed floating via the Bretton Woods par value system. Under the gold standard, exchange rates were fixed and could be changed only in extreme circumstances--a rigidity which had disastrous consequences in the 1930s.[2] The major functional innovation of Bretton Woods was that the par value system provided for orderly changes of exchange rates in case of a "fundamental disequilibrium." The new system worked well during the first twenty years or so. During this period there were many exchange rate changes, almost all of them depreciations vis-à-vis gold and the dollar. The world recovered rapidly from the ravages of the war, trade barriers and payment restrictions were gradually reduced, and more and more currencies became convertible into each other. As a consequence, world trade grew by leaps and bounds, and the whole world, developed as well as developing countries, enjoyed a period of almost unprecedented growth and prosperity.

From Bretton Woods to Widespread Floating. In the mid-1960s the par value system developed troubles. Currency crises became more numerous and violent and followed each other at shorter intervals. The British pound was the first major currency that was involved. Later the dollar came under suspicion and unwanted dollar balances piled up abroad. Convertibility of the dollar into gold was "suspended" on

August 15, 1971. The dollar floated down until it was devalued in terms of most currencies in the Smithsonian Agreement in December 1971. After another devaluation of the dollar early in 1973, widespread though managed floating of all major currencies began in march 1973.

The main reason for the breakdown of the Bretton Woods par value system was a basic defect in the IMF charter which made the system unfit to cope with the exceptional strains and stresses that developed in the late 1960s and early 1970s.[3] This defect was that the method of occasional, discontinuous, and therefore large changes in exchange rates, the adjustable or jumping peg, opened the floodgate for disruptive speculation. Under this system, the speculators speculated against the central banks whose hands were tied because they had to support the par value of the currency. This makes speculation easy and almost riskless. Under the system of continuous floating, on the other hand, speculators speculate against each other and against the market which is a much more risky business.[4]

But why did this basic defect not show up earlier? In retrospect the explanation is not difficult. During the early years after the war, when the economies of Europe and Japan were prostrate from war destruction and exhaustion, U.S. industries enjoyed a quasi-monopoly position, and, later, foreign countries eagerly accumulated dollar balances to rebuild their international reserves. Generous U.S. foreign aid financed large deficits, and tight controls in many countries suppressed remaining imbalances. Domestic supply shortages and extensive rationing in many countries made exchange rate adjustments appear of little use.

In the 1960s the dollar got into trouble for several reasons. Because of the rapid recovery of Europe and Japan, U.S. industries lost their quasi-monopoly position. Numerous currency depreciations strengthened the competitive position of rival industrial countries. The strength of the dollar was finally undermined by the inflation in the U.S. that followed the period of price stability from 1958-1964, which the Eisenhower Administration had bequeathed to its successors. When the Johnson Administration delayed raising taxes sufficiently to finance the escalating war in Vietnam as well as the equally expensive "great society" programs and engaged in inflationary deficit financing, the dollar became hopelessly overvalued.

There is an alternative, though not necessarily contradictory, explanation of the decline of the dollar. For years, Jacques Rueff and Robert Triffin had predicted that, for reasons so well known that they need not be repeated, the gold dollar exchange standard could not have lasted even if the United States had succeeded in keeping its inflation to a tolerable level. It is a moot question what would have happened if the United States had kept the price level substantially stable after 1965. The fact that the role of the dollar as reserve and intervention currency and its function as *numéraire* have been well preserved in recent years of *comparative* price stability in the United States, despite floating and suspension of gold convertibility, suggests that the alleged instability of the dollar standard may have been exaggerated.[5]

Be that as it may, the worldwide wave of inflation after 1965 culminating in the price explosion of 1973-1974 made widespread floating inevitable. It is inconceivable that the industrial countries could agree on a common inflation rate, if the average rate of inflation is in the neighborhood of 10 percent, because tolerance for inflation and unemployment differs greatly from country to country. Differential inflation, the differential impact of the oil price rise, and differential recession experience finally convinced most advocates of fixed exchange rates that floating is here to stay for the foreseeable future. The oil shock, which intensified the inflation although it did not start it, had the effect of moving the IMF Committee on Reform of the International Monetary System (Committee of Twenty) off dead center. Even after floating had become widespread, the committee had said again and again that "the reformed" system would be one of "stable but adjustable exchange rates" and that floating would be permitted only in "particular situations." According to Tom de Vries, "this made the work of the Committee look increasing unreal . . . The Committee was saved . . . by the quadrupling of the price of oil in the fourth quarter of 1973."[6]

It is interesting to reflect that the very success of the first twenty years of the Bretton Woods era has helped to expose the defect of the IMF Charter. The enormous growth of world trade, not only in nominal but also in real terms and in proportion to GNP, has increased the magnitude (if not the volatility) of cyclical and other swings in the trade and current-account balances. Similarly, increased capital mobility, a necessary ingredient of the rapid growth of the world economy, which was made possible by the gradual dismantling of exchange control, produced larger swings in the capital balance. Most important perhaps, frequent exchange rate changes have alerted more and more people, not only professional speculators, to watch for danger signals and to take quick actions to protect themselves from losses or to profit from anticipating parity changes.

There is another defect, in fact an internal contradiction, in the Articles of Agreement, which has become increasingly troublesome and will remain so in the future. What I have in mind is the fact that the charter looks favorably at capital controls; it not only permits them, but in certain circumstances requires their imposition.[7] It is still not recognized widely enough that capital controls and the absence of restrictions on current transactions are incompatible. It is often possible to suppress imbalances temporarily and to prop up overvalued currencies by means of capital controls, but only at the high cost of increasingly severe distortions and restrictions of trade and other current transactions.[8] "Avoidance of restrictions on current payments" is perhaps the most basic objective of the Fund.[9] The reason for the incompatibility of capital controls and freedom of current payments is that it is very easy to camouflage capital transactions as current-account transactions. There exist legal and illegal methods of disguising capital movements. An illegal method is, for example, over- or under-invoicing of exports and imports. A perfectly legal bypass of capital controls results from the fact that trade flows can become a substitute for capital flows: Suppose it is illegal to acquire claims abroad (securities of any kind) in anticipation of an expected depreciation of the home currency. The next best method of anticipating a substantial depreciation of the currency is to accumulate export and import commodities. Only very tight controls of current transactions could prevent this sort of disguised capital flow. Given the large volume of international trade, such speculative transactions and the well-known "leads and lags" can and often do move many billions of dollars in a short time across national boundaries. The international commodity boom of 1972-1973 may have been significantly intensified by such transactions--one way in which the par value system has contributed to worldwide inflation.

The conclusion is that widespread floating is here to stay. If in the future the world economy or at least its core, the industrial countries, are spared the great turbulences of the last few years, exchange rate fluctuations would become milder. But even in that case a return to the par value system is most unlikely. True, theoretically a system of fixed rates would be the ideal arrangement for most countries--provided it could be achieved without severe restrictions of international trade and payments and without imposing too much unemployment or inflation on any country. A necessary though not sufficient condition would be that inflation be substantially eliminated in all countries with fixed rates.

Unfortunately these conditions are rarely fulfilled in our modern world of sovereign states. Experience has shown again and again that a very high degree of harmonization of basic policy objectives (full employment, price stability, et cetera) and tight coordination of national policies are required to forestall the frequent emergence of large balance of payments disequilibria that cannot be handled by the par value system without disruptive speculation and currency crises. Such coordination or rather centralization of policy exists inside each country. Even the closely knit countries of the European Common Market have so far been unable to achieve the required degree of coordination of their national policies.

To avoid misunderstanding, a further remark is in order. Widespread floating does not mean that the currencies of all 130-odd members of the Fund fluctuate independently. There are many countries, especially small ones, that attach their currencies to that of some large country and are willing to accept the inflation that the policy of pegging may imply. According to Fund statistics, 81 currencies of the 122 currencies listed on June 30, 1975, were pegged to a single currency, 54 of them to the dollar. Only 11 currencies floated independently, but among the floaters were--and still are--most of the leading currencies of the world, the U.S. and Canadian dollars, the yen, the British pound, the French franc, the West German mark with its retinue of currencies ("snake" currencies and the Austrian schilling), and others. These countries accounted for 46.4 percent of the trade of Fund members, and the 81 currencies pegged to a single currency accounted for only 14.4 percent.[10]

If I say things which should be obvious and have been said many times before, my excuse is that they are so often forgotten.

The Present International Monetary System in Perspective[11]

The present disenchantment with the international monetary system is part of the general economic malaise of the 1970s that has followed the euphoria and optimism of the 1950s and 1960s.[12] The fiftieth anniversary in 1979 of the outbreak of the Great Depression has added to the present gloom.

The Evolution of the International Monetary System. It will be well to go back for a moment to the 1930s and consider the role that the international monetary system then in operation, the gold standard with fixed exchange rates, played in the catastrophic world slump.

The U.S. economy was in the center of the storm, but there were some epicenters, in Britain and in Germany for example. The U.S. depression was almost entirely homemade, although on some occasions it was aggravated by disturbances from abroad, such as the abandonment of the gold standard by Britain and the depreciation of sterling in September 1931, which induced the Federal Reserve to take deflationary measures in the midst of a deep depression.[13] In most other countries, in contrast, the depression was largely dominated by international developments.

It stands to reason that under the system of fixed exchanges (gold standard) the deep depression in major countries, and in the United States in particular, would spread rapidly to the rest of the world. Contrary to what is often said, it was not flexible exchange rates, but excessive rigidity that propagated and enormously aggravated the world depression. True, eventually exchange rates were changed, and between 1931 and 1936, literally all currencies were devalued in terms of gold. But the slowness and discontinuous nature of the process maximized the pains of adjustment: Each devaluation--sterling in 1931, the dollar in 1933-1934, the currencies of the so-called gold bloc (France, Switzerland, and the Netherlands) in 1936, etc.--served to some extent their purpose of stimulating the economy of the devaluating country, but put deflationary pressure on other countries which responded by imposing exchange control and import restrictions. Thus world trade shrank by about two-thirds in nominal terms (gold dollars) and by about one-half in real terms, the difference reflecting the catastrophic drop in prices.

To say that fixed exchange rates under the gold standard aggravated the depression and made it worldwide does not mean that the gold standard as such was a bad system; rather, it means that the gold standard cannot work in a highly deflationary environment.

The question may be asked whether exchange-rate flexibility would have worked better. Politically, psychologically, and ideologically, floating was probably out of the question. But I would point out that in the end a number of countries--Australia, the Scandinavian countries, and Nazi Germany--managed to extricate themselves from the world depression under the cover of open or disguised devaluation of the currency long before the United States, France, and some other countries were able to return to full employment. In the United States this did not happen, it will be recalled, before World War II. (The general question whether floating insulates a country from disturbances and shocks from abroad, and if so, to what extent, will be discussed later in the chapter.)

The Bretton Woods regime was a great improvement over the gold standard of the interwar period. For almost a quarter century it worked quite well and helped to make the period one of great prosperity and rapid growth for the whole Western world, including the less developed countries. World trade flourished, and only in one year, the recession year of 1975, was there a mild decline of 3 percent in the volume of world exports.[14] The main achievement of the Bretton Woods regime was the ease and smoothness with which necessary exchange-rate changes could be made, as compared with the gold standard of the interwar period.

But it must not be forgotten that the Bretton Woods regime--unlike the gold standard of the interwar period--operated in a favorable environment. After World War II, the major countries managed their affairs better than they had during the interwar period, and the result was world prosperity. There was no deep depression, no monetary contraction in the United States, and generous U.S. aid immediately after the war, to war allies and enemy countries alike, made the various economic miracles in Western Europe and Japan possible.

The Bretton Woods system broke down in the early 1970s because its method of changing exchange rates, the method of the adjustable or jumping peg, could not cope with the stresses caused by the rising tide of world inflation and increased capital mobility. What might be called the Graham effect,[15] that is, the tendency of the adjustable peg system to open the floodgates to disruptive, almost riskless speculation, made the system increasingly unworkable. Since under that system a currency under pressure cannot go up but can only go down, it is easy to speculate against the central banks whose hands are tied by the obligation to maintain the par value of the currency. Thus in the last years of the Bretton Woods regime successive changes in exchange rates were preceded and accompanied by increasingly massive flows of speculative capital, which entailed an enormous increase in international reserves and thus fed the flames of worldwide inflation.

To sum up, it was the rising tide of world inflation after 1965, especially in the United States, that killed Bretton Woods and forced the adoption of widespread floating on reluctant governments. It was not the other way around, even though it has been often said that floating exchange rates caused world inflation.

Notes on the Working of the Floating System. In an inflationary world a regime of fixed exchanges would require an agreement, tacit or explicit, on a common rate of inflation. Among the industrial countries, as things stand now, a common inflation rate of at least 10 percent to 15 percent would be required. Such an agreement is inconceivable and would be undesirable. That is the reason Bretton Woods broke down. Concretely, what caused the adoption of floating was the unwillingness of Germany, Switzerland, Japan, and some other countries to accept the high inflation rate that, in view of the U.S. inflation since 1965, a fixed exchange rate with the dollar would have imposed on them. That implies that floating enabled these countries to have a lower inflation rate than the United States and, in other words, that floating insulated these countries from imported inflation and restored monetary autonomy. Under floating no country can be forced, as is often the case under fixed rates, to expand the money supply in an inflationary manner. Nor can a country be forced in a deflationary environment to accept a contraction of the money supply, as countries were forced to do under the gold standard during the Great Depression on the 1930s.

It is necessary to restate these rather simple truths because they are often denied. For example, John Williamson in an interesting paper says: "Floating does virtually nothing to insulate output in one country from demand in the rest of the world."[16] It is not quite clear what this means. If it means that floating does not insulate a country from general inflationary increases of demand from abroad or from general deflationary decreases in demand, it is not true, as the examples mentioned above demonstrate. If it means that changes in foreign demand for particular commodities or groups of commodities cannot be warded off by floating (or more generally by monetary measures), it is, of course, true. But no one has claimed that floating can ward off changes in the demand for particular commodities. Floating can protect only against *monetary* disturbances from abroad, not against *real* ones.

Real disturbances are not only exogenous shocks, such as the oil price rise, but also changes in the terms of trade that often are associated with monetary changes. An example is the changes in relative prices that usually occur in the business cycle. Thus, in the Great Depression of the 1930s the terms of trade deteriorated sharply for the less developed countries, or more precisely the raw material exporting countries. Against such real changes floating is of no help.[17]

Another real disturbance from abroad that is often associated with or caused by monetary or business cycle developments is protectionist measures adopted by foreign governments. That happened, as we have seen, on a huge scale during the Great Depression of the 1930s. For example, the Smoot-Hawley tariff imposed by the United States in 1930 was a reaction to the depression. Against such real disturbances from abroad floating is of no help.[18]

But floating obviates or at least sharply reduces the temptation to use import restriction and exchange control for balance of payments adjustment. Critics of floating often deny the validity of that assertion.[19] Actually such denials suffer from a lack of historical perspective. They cannot be reconciled with the fact that in the 1930s the unavailability of the option of floating or devaluation was responsible for a protectionist explosion. In case someone argues that the 1930 experience is not relevant for the postwar period, let me recall an episode that clearly shows what in all probability would have been the U.S. reaction to the large balance of payments deficits in recent years.

In the last quarter of 1967 confidence in the dollar was badly shaken by the 14.3 percent devaluation of sterling on November 18, and by a mounting balance of payments deficit that led to a current account deficit of $1.4 billion in 1968 following a surplus of $1.2 billion in 1967. This induced President Johnson on January 1, 1968, in a dramatic television speech to announce a new program consisting of several highly illiberal and protectionist measures. Among them was an import surcharge and severe restraints on "nonessential" foreign travel by Americans. Legislation was introduced for a heavy tax on tourist expenditures outside the Western Hemisphere, graduated according to the amount spent a day (15 percent on expenditures between eight dollars and fifteen dollars a day, and 30 percent on expenditures exceeding fifteen dollars a day). Fortunately, this fantastic proposal was rejected by the House Ways and Means Committee.[20]

One can imagine what under a fixed-rate regime the U.S. reaction to the much larger deficits of recent years would have been. As Otmar Emminger recently said, "No other system but floating could have coped with the enormous short-term swings in the U.S. balance on current account--from a surplus of $18 billion in 1975 to deficits of some $14 billion in 1977 and 1978."[21]

Gold, the European Monetary System, and the Need to Float[22]

It is hardly necessary to explain at great length why a restoration of the gold standard is impossible. Who would want to entrust the future of the international monetary system to the mercies of South Africa and the Soviet Union, the two largest gold producers? A system of stable but adjustable exchange rates à la Bretton Woods is, as we have seen, very vulnerable to destabilizing speculation. The basic difficulty of any fixed-rate system is that it requires a high degree of mutual policy adjustment or international policy coordination, which in the present-day world can be achieved only in exceptional cases. The vaunted European monetary system (EMS) is not exception. It is a Bretton Woods-type system of stable but adjustable exchange rates, very vulnerable to disruptive capital flows. Frequent realignments of exchange rates are preceded and accompanied by destabilizing speculation, which requires tight exchange control in some participating countries--in France, for example.

Early in 1987, the EMS was shaken by a severe crisis, which underscores the conclusion that markets do a better job than governments in setting exchange rates. The row between two members of the EMS, France and West Germany, has provided a striking example of the dangers of politicizing exchange rates and of the unworkability of a Bretton Woods-type international monetary system.

It was not surprising that the French franc came under intense pressure after Prime Minister Jacques Chirac capitulated to student demonstrations, thereby effectively telling trade unions and other pressure groups that street demonstrations and violence pay. When the franc fell, Chirac attacked the German authorities. "This is a mark crisis," he said, "not a franc crisis. Let the German authorities do what is necessary."[23] What is regarded as necessary is a realignment of exchange rates and a little inflation in Germany. The realignment was achieved after hectic negotiations and a thirteen-hour emergency meeting of the ministers of finance on January 11, 1987. The value of the German mark and the Dutch guilder increased by 3 percent and that of the Belgian franc by 2 percent against the other members of the EMS. This can only be described as a token realignment, which will make hardly a dent in the underlying disequilibrium.

The other requirement, a little inflation in Germany, was called for in an editorial of the *Wall Street Journal*, "Waiting for Bonn," "What Germany needs is strong, domestic-led growth, which it's not going to get until it stops fixating on its inflation rate--near zero--and starts feeding some marks to its economy and advancing its tax cuts." The German Socialist party, the left-wing opposition to Chancellor Helmut Kohl's conservative government, ought to be grateful for the support it gets from conservative governments and newspapers abroad.

All this caused confusion and much turbulence in the foreign exchange markets. The dollar depreciated sharply against the mark and the yen despite the Baker-Miyazawa agreement. Foreign central banks bought many billion dollars to hold the line. According to rumors and press reports (which gained credibility through belated and half-hearted official denials), the administration wanted the dollar to decline in order to bring pressure on Germany and Japan to stimulate their economies. It is true that sufficient inflation in the strong currency surplus countries, especially Germany and Japan, would let the deficit countries, the United States and France, off the hook. But it would be like infecting the healthy instead of curing the sick. Worldwide inflation is not a sound basis for the world economy.

It is instructive to reflect for a moment on why we never hear about balance-of-payments problems of different regions of large countries, say the United States, despite the occurrence from time to time of serious regional disturbances. The most important reason is that monetary policy is the same throughout the United States, ruling out the significant differential inflation that often occurs between sovereign states. Also very important are perfect mobility of capital and much higher interregional mobility of labor than can be found between sovereign states anywhere in the world, even in the European Common Market. Still another factor, which has been mentioned in the literature, is the common fiscal system. If a region in the United States is experiencing a serious disturbance, it automatically gets some relief from the reduction of its tax liabilities to the federal government and possibly some contribution from the government through unemployment benefits and the like.

I conclude from all this that floating should continue, and I am convinced that it will, for the following reason: a return to fixed exchange rates would require international agreement on the rates that should be fixed. It is not inconceivable, but it is practically impossible that a meaningful agreement on the pattern of exchange rates could be reached in the Group of Seven or even in the Group of Five. By "meaningful," I mean a set of exchange rates that the participants undertake to defend.

International Liquidity in a World of Floating Exchange Rates[24] [25]

In the 1950s and 1960s it became customary to discuss the problems of international monetary reform under the three headings of adjustment, liquidity, and confidence.[26] The adjustment problem is the problem of how to maintain or restore equilibrium in the balance of payments by some suitable automatic mechanism and/or policy measures under fixed, stable but adjustable, or floating exchange rates. To this point, the present paper has been concerned with adjustment problems, with special emphasis on floating.

Confidence and liquidity problems arise primarily under fixed or stable but adjustable exchange rates. Whether these problems arise also under floating, and if they do in what form, will be discussed presently. In the international monetary area, the confidence problem relates to reserve currencies, notably, the most important one, the dollar. The possibility that lack of confidence could lead to large, sudden switches between different reserve media, specifically from dollars into gold, was regarded as a major weakness of the international monetary system in the 1950s and 1960s. The theory of Rueff and Triffin that the dollar-gold standard and the pure dollar standard are inherently unstable because they would sooner or later lead to violent and disruptive confidence crises has already been mentioned.

Since the suspension of gold convertibility and the advent of widespread floating, little has been said or heard of the confidence problem. Does that mean that under floating there is no confidence problem? If the confidence problem is defined as it usually was in the 1950s and 1960s (for example by the Machlup study group mentioned in footnote 2) as the possibility of "sudden switches between different reserve media," there is no confidence problem any more under the present system of floating because the convertibility of currencies including the dollar into a "primary" reserve asset such as gold has been abolished.[27] In a wider sense confidence in a currency, a reserve currency or any other currency, is still and always will be a problem. Confidence in the dollar could conceivably be impaired. For example if the United States again experienced high inflation, the very large foreign dollar holdings--a legacy of the fixed rate system but now held voluntarily--could become a problem, threatening a depreciation of the dollar in terms of some other currencies.

I shall not, however, pursue that subject any further. Let me simply say that the conventional confidence problem as it was discussed in the 1950s and 1960s does not exist any more. Confidence in the stability of individual currencies is still important and if the currency in question is a widely held reserve currency, as the dollar, confidence in it becomes a matter of world concern. In Britain the problem of foreign sterling balances has been acute when confidence in the future of the pound waned.

International Liquidity. The problem of international liquidity, or better, of the adequacy or inadequacy of international monetary reserves, has received a lot of attention in the discussions on international monetary reform before the advent of widespread floating--in fact too much attention compared with the adjustment problem in the opinion of many observers, including the present writer. Innumerable plans for monetary reform aimed at assuring an adequate but not excessive supply of reserves have been put forward.[28] In the whole postwar period until the late 1960s the emphasis was on the alleged dangers of a *shortage* of international liquidity. British economists almost unanimously (with the notable exception of Sir Ralph Hawtrey) predicted dire consequences, deflation and depression, unless the perceived growing inadequacy of international reserves was counteracted by the adoption of one of the numerous plans for reserve creation ranging from doubling the gold price to setting up the IMF as a real world central bank, a lender of last resort, with broad money-creating powers. When the predicted deflation failed to materialize, and it became clear in the late 1960s and early 1970s that inflation and not deflation was the threat, the emphasis shifted from the danger of inadequacy of reserves to that of excessive reserve growth. In the closing years of the Bretton Woods era international reserves grew, indeed, by leaps and bounds, from SDR 93 billion in 1970 to SDR 180 billion in 1974, according to IMF statistics.[29] Through the mechanism of fixed exchanges, the U.S. inflation which got under way in 1965 spread swiftly through the whole world.[30] After the advent of widespread floating, the growth of reserves slowed sharply, and the largest part accrued to the oil-exporting countries. OPEC countries are, however, a very special case, because as is fairly generally agreed, additional reserves of the oil countries should be regarded as part of their long-term foreign investments and not as the basis of increased money supply.

In view of all this, it is not surprising that the excitement and worry about international liquidity, which previously had dominated the discussions about monetary reform, have greatly abated. Does that mean that international liquidity is no problem any more? Almost but not quite. Indeed, under a free, unmanaged float there would be no liquidity problem. Under managed floating, on the other hand, countries need reserves to intervene in the market. But there are several reasons why the need for reserves is much less urgent under floating, even if it is managed, than under the adjustable peg.

The liquidity problem is intertwined with the adjustment and confidence problems. If the adjustment mechanism does not work well and stubborn balance of payments disequilibria occur frequently, large reserves are required; and if there is a confidence problem in the sense that large sudden switches between different reserve media cannot be ruled out, countries, especially reserve currency countries, need large reserves. On both grounds reserve need is sharply reduced under managed floating. On the one hand, the adjustment mechanism becomes much more efficient when exchange rates are allowed to float and, on the other hand, the confidence problem has all but vanished when currencies are no longer convertible at a fixed rate into some ultimate reserve medium such as gold.[31] As we have seen, disruptive speculation is greatly encouraged and facilitated by the adjustable peg ("stable but adjustable rates") and is discouraged and made hazardous by floating.

The present international monetary system of widespread floating as legalized by the amended charter of the Fund--or nonsystem as those whose blueprints were not followed like to call it--has been criticized on the ground that it failed to put any limit or control on global monetary reserves or liquidity. To come to grips with this criticism let us consider how, under floating, global reserves should be defined and measured and how important the control of global reserves, however defined, still is.

Under fixed and even semifixed exchange rates these questions permit a fairly unambiguous and straightforward answer. Under the gold standard, global reserves were defined as the world stock of monetary gold. Later, under the gold exchange standard, balances of reserve currencies held by central banks of nonreserve countries should be added. Under the Bretton Woods system, reserve positions in the Fund and SDRs were further additions. Large changes in these world aggregates undoubtedly had something to do with fluctuations in the world price level, with waves of world inflation and deflation. I say, "large changes," because one would surely not expect a close parallelism between minor fluctuations in these two very broad and even then (under the gold standard) somewhat hazy aggregates.[32]

Under widespread floating, the two aggregates, global reserves on the one hand and the world price level and its changes on the other hand, have become highly fragmented magnitudes. Moreover, close substitutes for monetary reserves, namely official and semiofficial borrowing, have grown by leaps and bounds in many countries. To be sure, the Fund dutifully publishes every month the percentage change in consumer prices for the whole world. This is some sort of an average of changes of consumer prices in all member countries. For example, in August 1976, the change in consumer prices for the world as a whole over the previous

twelve months was 10.5 percent. This figure is a weighted average of
5.6 percent for the United States, 1.5 percent for Switzerland, 396
percent for Argentina, 200 percent for Chile (down from 400 percent a
year ago), et cetera. The Fund also publishes global reserves, of which
foreign exchange is by far the largest component. These figures do not
make allowance for the growth of reserve substitutes, that is, official and
semiofficial borrowing. It is possible to correlate the two series, or
rather, jumbles of figures. But who would be bold enough to attribute
any causal significance to such an operation and derive policy conclusions concerning the adequacy of world reserves?

How would the Fund exercise control over global reserves? SDR
creation and utilization of Fund quotas are under international control.
But as mentioned, by far the largest component of world reserves
consists of foreign exchange, mostly dollar balances. One can, of
course, dream of a monetary reform that would concentrate all reserves
including gold and foreign exchange in the Fund in exchange for SDRs.[33]
That such a reform would be politically utterly impossible is perhaps not
the main objection. It may not even be a nice dream. Given the
present-day drift in international politics and power struggle, such a
concentration of power in the hands of an international organization
could become very dangerous. It would be bound to become an issue in
the international class struggle that is now going on under the slogan of
a "New International Economic Order."

My conclusion is that, in the present world of widespread floating,
it is impossible to give a meaningful definition of global reserves, let
alone to define an optimal or desirable level of global reserves or of
reserve growth. It is the adjustment and not the liquidity problem that
is of paramount importance, now more than ever. The Fund's main task
should be "surveillance" of exchange rate policies, especially prevention
of dirty floating and dirty fixing of exchange rates.

However, to say that control of global reserves is not an important
or meaningful task for the Fund any more does not mean that for
individual countries the size of their reserves and their external
borrowing potential are unimportant, nor that the use countries make of
their reserves and borrowing power cannot become a matter of international concern. It is possible that in the last few years there has been
much international overborrowing and excessive lending by banks to
shore up shaky balance of payments positions. Another development that
may cause legitimate worries is the rapidly growing volume of lending
by Western banks to Communist countries. All this may, indeed, cause

serious troubles in the future. But if so, it has nothing to do with a lack of international control over the volume of *global* reserves in the conventional sense, and it could not have been prevented by such controls unless Fund control over global reserves were unconventionally interpreted to include control over money supply as well as over monetary policy in at least the major countries and perhaps Fund supervision over the lending policies of large banks.

Furthermore, discounting the importance of global reserves and their control does not mean that inflation is no problem. On the contrary, inflation is a major world problem. But it no longer has anything to do with a lack of control over *global* reserves. It has its roots in the *national* monetary, fiscal, and exchange rate policies of the major countries. The primary responsibility for curbing world inflation obviously falls on the leading industrial countries, especially the United States. This is so because, as noted above, the majority of smaller countries peg their currencies either to the currency of one of the leading industrial countries, most of them to the dollar, or to a basket of important currencies or SDRs. It is true that national monetary policies, inflation or deflation, in the many countries that peg their currencies to the dollar are profoundly influenced, if not fully determined, by the inflation, or absence of inflation, in the United States. If there is inflation in the United States, dollar balances are likely to pile up in countries that peg to the dollar, and inflation will spread. It follows that if the Fund could control inflation in the United States and in a few other key countries, it would substantially control world inflation. If control of *global* monetary reserves is unconventionally interpreted to include control of money supply, monetary policy, and inflation in the major countries then, and only then, could it be said that control of global reserves is necessary to prevent world inflation.

Actually the Fund can do nothing about inflation in the United States and only in exceptional cases about inflation in other major countries. (The British and Italian borrowing from the Fund may be such exceptional cases.) If the United States again lapsed into high inflation, the only effective measure to prevent the piling up of dollar reserves in countries that peg to the dollar and the spread of the U.S. inflation, would be to stop pegging to the dollar. In other words, if there is inflation in the United States, floating is the only effective policy to avoid both an excessive growth of international liquidity in the form of dollar balances and the spread of inflation.

The upshot is that the Fund can do very little about world inflation. It is easier, in fact, to think of Fund policies that would add, marginally though under realistic assumptions, to world inflation, than to identify measures that would help to curb inflation. Steps that would add to inflationary pressures are a general increase in the Fund's quotas and additional distribution of SDRs, especially if linked to foreign aid. Similarly adding to inflation would be a further proliferation and expansion of special lending facilities--such as the Oil Facility, the Buffer Stock Facility, the Extended Fund Facility, and the Compensatory Financing of Export Fluctuations.[34]

But by no means does this imply that such measures should not be taken under any circumstances. On the contrary, emergencies must be expected to occur from time to time which justify even large-scale credit operations by the Fund to forestall some major or minor disturbances of the world economy, including inflationary and protectionist reactions in some countries. What it does mean is that the inflationary implications of such lending should not be overlooked, just as a fire brigade when throwing water on an attic fire should not be oblivious to the damage that flooding can do to the rest of the house. The two dangers--the threatening disturbance and the inflationary side effect of the monetary measures taken--should be weighed against each other. Overreactions should be avoided, and the operations should be of the proper size and pinpointed[35] so as to minimize the danger of intensifying inflation.

To pursue this highly important problem any further would burst the frame of the present study. However, one more observation may be permitted: *Conditional* lending by the Fund--"provision of conditional liquidity"--can be used as an inducement for countries to put their financial house in order and to curb inflation. *Unconditional* lending is likely to be counterproductive because it is likely to tempt countries to delay needed structural reform and anti-inflationary measures and to postpone changes in exchange rates or floating that may be required.

Exchange-Rate and Balance of Payments Policy

Managed Floating[36]

The amended Articles of Agreement of the International Monetary Fund permit each country to adopt the exchange rate system it prefers but enjoins them to "avoid manipulating exchange rates or the international monetary system in order to prevent effective balance of payments adjustment or to gain an unfair competitive advantage over other members" (Article IV, Section 1). The Fund is directed to "oversee the compliance of each member with its obligations," to "exercise firm surveillance of the exchange rate policies of members," and to "adopt specific principles for the guidance of all members with respect to these policies" (Article IV, Section 3).

The Fund has already tried its hand at surveillance of floating. Based on the work of the Committee of Twenty, the executive directors adopted in June 1974 "Guidelines for the Management of Floating Exchange Rates."[37] These guidelines are supposed to form the basis of the Fund's annual "consultations with members with floating currencies," and observance of the guidelines will presumably be required when such countries borrow from the Fund.

The guidelines deal with the mode of interventions in the exchange market, in order to prevent "competitive alterations of exchange rates." The difference between "competitive alteration" and what formerly was called "competitive depreciation" is, presumably, that alteration is the wider concept which covers also the case of "competitive appreciation" (as it is sometimes called)--a policy of keeping the exchange rate higher than the market-clearing level and financing the resulting deficit by running down reserves or by official borrowing abroad.[38] Such a policy can also be described as deliberate exportation of inflation to keep down the country's own rate of inflation.

The new Article IV in the amended charter uses an even more comprehensive term than competitive alteration of exchange rates. It speaks of "manipulating exchange rates or the international monetary system" and enjoins countries to avoid such manipulations for the purpose of gaining "an unfair competitive advantage over other members."

It is important to adhere to the wider concept, "manipulation of the international monetary system," because it covers abuses of managed floating as well as those of par value changes. The 1974 guidelines deal only with manipulations by interventions in the exchange market under floating. But actually there seems to have been very little competitive depressing of floating exchange rates by interventions in the exchange market. True, Japan has been accused of depressing the yen by buying dollars and managing capital flows. But the case is not at all clear. (See Section 5 below for further discussion.)

Probably more important than interventions for the purpose of gaining "an unfair competitive advantage" is "dirty floating." It is important in my opinion to distinguish between dirty floating and merely managed floating. By dirty floating I mean such policies as split exchange markets, multiple exchange rates, import deposit schemes, "taxes" on the purchase of foreign currencies differentiated according to the prospective use of the foreign currency, and the like. These policies shade off into a policy of comprehensive exchange control and thus violate one of the basic objectives of the Fund, to avoid "restrictions for balance of payments purposes on current account transactions," to use the language of the guidelines for floating.[39] As was shown earlier, the policy of having a separate exchange market for capital transactions unavoidably leads to restrictions and distortions of current transactions.

By merely managed floating, I mean a policy that confines itself to influencing the exchange rates by buying and selling of foreign exchange in a free exchange market in order to "prevent or moderate sharp and disruptive fluctuations from day to day and from week to week,"[40] as well as to moderate, though not suppress or reverse, longer-run movements.

The 1974 guidelines, although they reiterate, as just mentioned, the basic objective of unrestricted current transactions, do not rule out dirty floating. On the contrary, the system of "separate capital exchange markets," in other words the system of dual exchange rates, one for current the other for capital transactions, is expressly mentioned in the official commentary on the guidelines, along with exchange market interventions and other policies, as an acceptable "action to influence an exchange rate."[41] This is unfortunate because the system of split exchange markets and dual exchange rates is the most widely used form of dirty floating.

There have been, in recent years, many cases of dirty floating of varying degrees of "dirtyness." Furthermore, there were last year two conspicuous cases of grossly mismanaged alterations (depreciations) of exchange rates--the Mexican peso and the Australian dollar. On November 28, 1976, the Australian dollar was devalued by 17.5 percent. It was probably the first case of outright competitive depreciation since floating has become widespread, as the *Economist* of London of December 4, 1976, pointed out. This judgment was reinforced by the fact that shortly after the devaluation, the Australian dollar was again revalued by a few percent in small steps. Clearly, a clean unmanaged or managed float would have been much better. Guidance by the Fund was either absent or was not heeded.

While the depreciation of the Australian dollar was not a float, but an old fashioned par value change preceded and accompanied by the usual disrupting concomitants--speculative capital flows and over-shooting--the long overdue and equally mismanaged depreciation of the Mexican peso was first officially described as a float. Actually it, too, was a case of bungled depreciation combined with export taxes and other measures which violate basic objectives of the Fund, a case of dirty fixing rather than dirty floating. Guidance by the Fund has been either lacking or was spurned.

Now, let us consider the rules of exchange market interventions for managed, but not dirty, floating.[42] There is fairly general agreement that there are no objections to interventions to iron out short-term fluctuations.[43] Guideline (1) says that "members with a floating exchange rate should intervene on the foreign exchange market as necessary to prevent or moderate sharp fluctuations from day to day and from week to week." The guidelines draw the line separating short from medium run between the week and the month.[44]

In regard to fluctuations in the intermediate run, say from one to twelve months,[45] the situation is not so clear. Many experts who are, in principle, in favor of floating (for example, E. M. Bernstein) feel strongly that since 1973, in many important cases, the fluctuations have been much larger than can be justified and that such excessive fluctuations should be moderated, though not suppressed, by official interventions in the exchange market. What the advocates of intervention have in mind primarily is fluctuations of the dollar exchange rate, in particular the dollar-deutsche mark (DM) rate.

The dollar-DM rate has indeed fluctuated sharply. For example from May 7, 1973, to July 6, 1973, the dollar fell vis-à-vis the DM by 21 percent; from July 6, 1973, to January 7, 1974, it rose by 28 percent; and it had fallen again by 16 percent by May 10, 1974. The currencies in the European snake and the Swiss franc exhibited similar fluctuations vis-à-vis the dollar. Later the fluctuations became much milder, and it should be pointed out that fluctuations of the trade-weighted effective exchange rate of the dollar were much smaller than those of the dollar-DM rate. For example from May 15, 1973, to July 16, 1973, the trade-weighted depreciation of the dollar was 1.7 percent, and from July 16, 1973, to January 15, 1974, the trade-weighted appreciation was 5.1 percent.[46]

It should be kept in mind, furthermore, that the years of 1973 to 1975 were a period of extreme turbulence and uncertainty in the world economy as well as in the U.S. economy. It was the period of the two-digit inflation followed by worldwide recession and stagflation, the period of the oil shock. Inflation rates in different countries diverged sharply and so did the impact of the oil shock and of the recession. There were special disturbing factors shaking the confidence in the dollar: the Watergate affair and the forced resignation of President Nixon had a debilitating effect on the U.S. administration's ability to pursue a consistently vigorous anti-inflation policy. There were erratic shifts in U.S. policies with respect to price and wage control and, at times, strong congressional pressure for a freeze or even a rollback of prices, wages, profits, and rents. The uncertainty associated with these events undermined the confidence in the dollar at home and abroad. Still another factor causing large fluctuations was that private operators in the marketplace had to adjust to the floating system. Speculators had become used to the easy task of speculating against the central banks whose hands were tied under the par value system (stable but adjustable exchange rates). Thus private firms--and public agencies--had to learn how to live with the much greater risks of speculating against the market under flexible exchange rates. The failures of the Herstatt Bank in West Germany and the Franklin-National Bank in the United States, and large losses of other banks from foreign exchange dealings taught their lessons, but not without considerable cost.

With this in mind, it is not at all surprising that there were sharp fluctuations in exchange rates. Ex post it is deceptively easy to conclude that some of the fluctuations turned out to be unnecessary and that a lot of money could have been made by private or official counterspeculation. However, ex ante, most of the exchange movements looked quite reasonable. Given the high degree of turmoil and uncertainty of the period, there is no reason whatever to assume that the judgment of public officials (national or international) about the "appropriate exchange rate" (to use a phrase favored by the advocates of interventions), would have been better than that of the market. The record of official judgments about exchange rates and balances of payments prospects during the Bretton Woods period was anything but encouraging.[47] Time and again exchange rates were defended stubbornly and hundreds of millions of dollars were lost by central banks in what turned out to be wrong speculations.[48] The record of official interventions in the post-Bretton Woods era has not been any better in a number of cases. In Britain, Italy, Australia, and Mexico interventions have been highly destabilizing, over-valued currencies have been propped up for a while, and the subsequent inevitable plunge was then all the more abrupt and disrupting.

Since there is no evidence that the fluctuations of the dollar-DM rate did significant damage and since the fluctuations have become milder as the turbulence in the world economy and in the American economy subsided, the case for extensive official interventions in the market, except to iron out erratic very short-run fluctuations, is not very strong.

Reference Rates and Target Zones. Ethier and Bloomfield have argued that the working of the floating system would be greatly improved if countries could be persuaded by the Fund to set what they call reference rates or reference zones for their currencies. This proposal has been endorsed by John Williamson and is widely regarded as an imaginative, novel idea. In the 1974 Fund guidelines, too, there is mention that countries may set medium-term norms or target rates (or zones), and the official commentary to the guidelines explains that the "medium-term" might be considered to refer to a period of about four years.[49]

The difference between a par value and a reference rate (or reference zone) is that unlike the par value the reference rate need not be defended by interventions. Interventions would be permitted, but they would not be mandatory, and the interventions are subject to only one rule: If the exchange rate in the market is *below* the reference rate the central bank is allowed (not obligated) to intervene by selling foreign currencies in order to push the currency up to the reference rate; if the exchange rate is *above* the reference rate the central bank is allowed (not obligated) to intervene by buying foreign currencies in order to push the currency down to the reference rate. In other words, interventions must never push the exchange rate *away* from the reference rate, but interventions are permitted to move the exchange rate *towards* the reference rates. The reference rates should be "revised at periodic prespecified intervals, by some defined international procedure."[50]

The main advantage that is claimed for the reference rate proposal is that it would deal effectively with the problem of destabilizing speculation. Since there is no obligation for the central bank to intervene in order to keep the exchange rate at (or near) the reference rate, speculators would face greater risks than they face under the par value system. I agree with this argument. The reference rate system would be less prone to engender destabilizing speculation than the par value system.

But I am not convinced by the claim that, compared with a floating system without reference rates, the reference rate system would have the advantage of eliminating or sharply reducing the alleged danger of destabilizing speculation. Williamson says that the reference rates would provide

> . . . a focus for stabilizing speculation. [If] the rate moved away from the reference rate, the market would know that future interventions could only be in the direction of pushing the rate back towards the official reference rate, thus adding to the risk [of] further destabilizing behavior.[51]

I find this unconvincing. If destabilizing speculation is not discouraged under the par value system by the *obligation* of the central bank to defend the par value, why should it be discouraged under the reference rate system by the mere *permission* to defend the reference rates? All depends on whether the market finds the reference rates credible or not. Why should reference rates be more credible than par values? Reference rates that give the impression of being out of line and are therefore liable to be changed at the next "prespecified" revision are very likely to cause heavy speculation, unless the revisions are small and are made at short intervals. But changing the reference rates at short intervals would be tantamount to replacing the reference rate system by a crawling peg system or a trotting peg system à la Brazil. The fear that changes in the reference rate may trigger speculative capital flows may well induce central banks increasingly to treat reference rates as par values.

John Williamson says that the value of having a focus for stabilizing speculation is best demonstrated by the Canadian experience, where the U.S. $1 = Can $1 parity has long played this role of inducing stabilizing speculation.[52] Some defenders of fixed rates, for example Robert Mundell, have tried to explain away the undeniable success and stability of the Canadian float by the fact that the Canadian monetary unit is called a dollar and has historically been on a par (or nearly so) with the U.S. dollar, thus serving as "a focus for stabilizing speculation." I find that explanation of the stability of the Canadian dollar unconvincing. The stability of the Canadian dollar (until now) and the absence of volatile capital flows are due to a long tradition of political stability and responsible financial and monetary policies (which probably were, in part, motivated by the wish to preserve the near-parity of the Canadian and the U.S. dollar).[53] Destroy this tradition, and the picture will change overnight. Should we assume that Mexico--not to mention Argentina or Chile--could give its currency the stability of the Canadian dollar by renaming the peso a Mexican dollar? Could the stability of the lira by promoted by calling it the "Italian mark"? A reputation of political stability and responsible economic policies once lost may take a very long time to be regained.[54]

The assumptions made in the IMF Guidelines (3)(b) that "reasonable estimates of the medium-term norm" for a country's exchange rate can be made for "a period of about four years" ahead, as the official commentary to the IMF guidelines assumes, seems to me unrealistic to the point of suggesting a typographical error. Should it be four months or four quarters?[55]

Ethier and Bloomfield stress repeatedly that their "rule is defined in terms of explicit, central-bank *behavior* rather than in terms of presumed central-bank motivations."[56]   The difficulty of implementing that prescription is highlighted by the following remarks of the authors:

> [The] Rule should be applied only to official interventions [of] the central bank. . . . [It] would [not] apply to purchases of foreign exchange by a central bank directly from state enterprises that had been encouraged [by] the government [or the central bank?] to borrow abroad as has happened in Great Britain and Italy.[57]

Since it is generally agreed that the huge British and Italian borrowings were made largely for balance of payments reasons, ignoring such transactions and restricting the rule to formal interventions by the central bank in the foreign exchange market would deprive the reference scheme of much of its relevance in the present day world.

Concluding Remarks. Our discussion of some problems concerning international surveillance of exchange rate policies has shown that it is not at all easy to formulate meaningful guidelines for floating. It would probably be best to forget about reference rates, not to mention medium-term norms or target-zones for exchange rates for several years ahead. The simpler rule contained in the IMF Guideline (2) that no country should "normally act aggressively with respect to the exchange value of its currency (i.e., should not so act [intervene in the market] as to depress that value when it is falling, or to enhance that value when it is rising)," is probably all that is needed and can reasonably be justified.

Of course, the questions remain what "normally" means, what the exceptions might be, and how one can tell whether a country has in fact observed the rule not to intervene "aggressively." Obviously it is not sufficient to look at the formal interventions of the central bank in the exchange market and to ignore completely borrowing by other public agencies abroad.[58] It is hardly possible to spell out beforehand all possible exceptions to the rule. One has to rely on continuing multilateral surveillance among major countries and on the good judgment of the Fund. It is perhaps not unreasonable to hope the Fund will be able, in its regular annual consultation with members and in negotiations about member borrowing, to reach agreement on responsible policies without condoning every violation of the letter or the spirit of the Articles of Agreement.

This is after all not a new problem. It will be recalled that the original Articles of Agreement enjoined the Fund "not [to] object to a proposed change [in an exchange rate] because of the domestic social or political policies of the member proposing the change."[59] This injunction has not prevented the Fund from exercising, more or less discreetly, strong influence on members' economic and financial policies in annual consultations or by attaching strings to borrowing agreements.

Finally, let me repeat that guiding interventions under a managed float would be less important (and conceptually though not politically more difficult) than trying to dissuade countries from engaging in dirty floating in the sense defined above, that is, in the sense of split exchange markets, dual exchange rates, import-deposit schemes, and the like.

The Case Against Capital Controls[60]

Capital Controls as Supplements to or Substitutes for Flexibility. When discussing capital controls I shall disregard such policies as official interventions in the forward exchange market, changing the "mix" of fiscal and monetary policies and "twisting" interest rates, although these measures are often classified in the literature as capital controls. The reason for this exclusion is that these policies are by and large market-oriented and in effect constitute extensions, albeit ineffective or only marginally effective ones, of general monetary policies.[61] The controls which I have in mind are the non market-oriented direct restrictions of certain types of international lending and borrowing and the introduction of split foreign-exchange markets with a dual exchange rate, an officially pegged rate for current transactions and a more or less free market rate for financial transactions, as now practiced by Belgium, France, and Italy.[62]

Direct controls on certain types of foreign lending and borrowing can take many different forms. They were first applied by capital exporting countries, for a long time by the U.K. and since the 1960s by the U.S. But in recent years they have been increasingly used by the recipients of hot money, especially France, Germany and Switzerland. Capital controls in surplus countries are usually aimed specifically at speculative capital inflows (split markets being the exception) while in deficit countries their purpose is to strengthen the overall balance of payments by reducing all types of capital exports.

A detailed description would be very difficult because these regulations differ from country to country and change continuously over time as the regulating authorities, in an unending race with evaders and circumventers, try to keep the restrictions effective by plugging leaks and loopholes and by extending more and more the scope of the restrictions. I will confine myself to giving a few examples.

For many years the U.S. has had programs of capital restrictions in operation. In their foreign lending, American banks and certain other financial institutions are subject to individual quotas based on their past volume of business. Essentially the same type of restrictions apply to direct investments in industrial countries by non-financial corporations though direct investment in less developed countries is not restricted. The third program is a tax on the purchase of foreign securities, the so-called "interest equalization tax," which has practically stopped portfolio investment abroad.[63]

In the surplus countries controls to stem the inflow of hot money have proliferated in the last few years. They range from the prohibition to pay interest on bank deposits of foreign residents, imposition of a carrying charge (negative interest) on such deposits, and differential reserve requirements, on the one hand, to prohibition of buying securities or real estate by foreigners and compulsory deposit in non-interest bearing accounts with the central banks of part or all of the proceeds of foreign borrowing by national firms ("Bardepot" in the German jargon) or outright prohibition of such borrowing on the other hand.

Superficially the French system of splitting the exchange market and establishing a different exchange rate for all capital transactions looks simpler and more elegant than the direct controls, because it is across the board and treats all types of capital and all transactors alike. But by the same token it does not even attempt to distinguish between bad, speculative capital and virtuous, legitimate capital. In practice it discriminates strongly against the latter because speculative capital is more likely to evade the net of the controls than normal, non-speculative capital. Moreover the split market has its own enormous administrative complications: all transactions must be scrutinized to decide whether they are *bona fide* current or capital transactions. French banks have to work overtime, often including Saturdays and Sundays, to keep the two markets apart and the heavy paper work has spilled over to the banks in neighboring countries which have close commercial connections with France. The controllers themselves admit that if the difference between the two exchange rates became more than 4 or 5 percent, the temptation to evade the regulations by camouflaging current transactions as capital transactions, or vice versa, would become so strong that the system would produce serious distortions or become unworkable. In order to close an easy route of evasion, tourist transactions in France are being routed via the unpegged market for capital transactions in clear violation of the Bretton Woods Agreement.[64]

Because of these enormous administrative complications, Germany and Switzerland have refused to accept the French system. Needless to add, the existence of two different types of exchange control in Germany, France and other EEC countries, which in each country have to be applied also against other Common Market countries (not only against outsiders), constitutes monetary and economic disintegration of the Common Market.

Each system of controls has its own problems and difficulties, but they all have the following in common:

(1) The controls give rise to expensive and wasteful efforts of circumvention and evasion by legal or illegal means to which the authorities react with equally expensive and wasteful measures to tighten and expand the controls.[65]

(2) It is practically impossible to restrict speculative and "illegitimate" capital without restricting and distorting normal "legitimate" or "virtuous" capital flows as well. In fact, it is much easier to restrict the latter than the former.

(3) Effective control of speculative capital requires control of current transactions, because capital transactions can easily be camouflaged as current transactions and vice versa. Again it is much easier to restrict normal long-term capital flows than short-term speculative capital movements without controlling current transactions.

If current transactions and transactions by non-financial firms remain uncontrolled, "leads and lags" (in the broad sense including leads and lags in payments as well as in the placing of orders) tend to expand and can assume very large proportions. Thus the German Bundesbank estimates that two-thirds of the enormous flows of funds into Germany in February 1973 were due to leads and lags and flows between branches of multinational firms.

A related and extremely important development is that when speculation in currencies is impeded by controls, speculation is pushed into commodity markets. If it becomes difficult and expensive to buy marks and yen to get out of the dollar or some other currency, the next best thing is to buy internationally traded commodities. Commodity speculation should be defined broadly. It comprises not only speculation by people who are not normally engaged in the production and trade of the commodities concerned--pure speculators we may call them--but also producing and trading companies. In practice speculation by the latter group is much more important and more difficult to control than that of the former.[66]

Commodity speculation as a substitute and supplement to outright currency speculation seems to have happened on a large scale this year. Thus the sharp rise of commodity prices on international markets in the first quarter of 1973 has been aggravated by the currency crisis and has been further escalated by the various capital control measures. Leads and lags, forward buying and commodity speculation can move many billions of dollars across national frontiers in a short time. Most of these evasions and circumventions of the controls are perfectly legal. To make them illegal and to restrict their volume requires detailed regulations going far beyond the financial area. Some illegal but widely practiced evasions in many countries are, among others, over- or under-invoicing of exports and imports and the shipment of bank notes abroad.

Before trying to answer the question that was formulated above--what are the merits of capital controls as substitutes for, or supplements to floating for the purpose of smoothing parity changes?--let us distinguish three types of short-term capital flows: (1) capital flows induced by interest differentials which in turn are produced by divergent cyclical movements in different countries; (2) capital flows induced by the expectation of parity changes; these are the speculative capital movements; and (3) capital flight; i.e. capital flows induced by non-economic, primarily political factors, such as fear of war, revolution, political or racial persecution and confiscation or expropriation.

Clearly the third category is the exception. Examples of politically induced capital flows are capital flights from Hitler-Europe to the U.S. during the last years before the outbreak of the Second World War,[67] the capital flight from France after the student-worker revolt in 1968, and the apparently uncontrollable capital flight from Italy during the last few years.

The bugbear of the advocates of capital controls is the danger of destabilizing, self-fulfilling speculation. Waves of speculation may start, it is said, either without any economic justification or be triggered by exaggerated and erroneous evaluation of--in reality--temporary deficits or surpluses. In other words fortuitous, cyclical and reversible troubles may be misinterpreted by the speculators as fundamental disequilibria which require exchange rate changes. With flexible exchange rates the currencies of the deficit countries may be driven down excessively; this has an inflationary impact which in turn, *ex post* justifies the depreciation. Similarly currencies of surplus countries may be driven up with deflationary effects which may, *ex post*, justify the appreciation. That inflationary and deflationary developments require permissive monetary policy is usually ignored.

I suggest that this scenario is grossly flawed and unrealistic. Capital flights never come out of the blue and even when triggered politically they usually have also a solid economic foundation. Thus in the case of the capital flight from France in 1968 the speculators foresaw correctly the wage explosion and inflation which resulted from the political upheaval and forced the devaluation of the French franc a year later. Similarly, in the Italian case mentioned above, the economic consequences of the political unrest were easy to foresee.

I now put aside the exceptional case of capital flows induced by political rather than economic events and turn to the two other categories mentioned above: cyclical, interest-induced flows which arise from differences in the phasing of the cycle--one country experiencing a cyclical upswing while another is in the doldrums of a recession--and speculative flows motivated by expected parity changes.

The advocate of controls will say the former type of flows should be checked by controls because under floating they will cause exchange rate variations which may then easily be magnified by destabilizing speculation. In fact in the case of purely cyclical or other quickly reversible movements no change in the exchange rate is justified. If quickly reversible cyclical fluctuations were the only trouble, we might just as well go back to the regime of fixed rates. Cyclical changes are indeed the show-piece of the advocates of fixed exchange rates. They point out that in this case under fixed rates the flow of reserves will dampen the boom in the surplus country and alleviate the recession in the deficit country; thus the regime of fixed exchanges will be beneficial all around.[68]

The advice to go back to fixed rates or rather to the adjustable peg is not acceptable because, for reasons explained earlier, we are clearly not merely confronted with reversible, cyclical disequilibria. We have to reckon with the frequent appearance of stubborn, fundamental disequilibria. It is occasionally possible to identify, *ex post*, episodes where the trouble was in fact temporary, but in most cases cyclical and fundamental disequilibria are intertwined. At any rate, an actual disequilibrium, surplus or deficit, cannot easily and confidently be diagnosed when it appears as definitely belonging to the one or other category. This is especially true in our inflationary period: the business cycle is not yet dead, but it is now dominated by, or superimposed on, an inflationary trend; and these price trends are apt to diverge in different countries giving rise to fundamental disequilibria.

What holds of the underlying disequilibria also holds of the resulting two categories of capital flows--the interest-induced cyclical flows and the speculative flows motivated by suspected fundamental disequilibria and expected parity changes. Usually the two types of capital flows cannot be sharply separated although sometimes episodes can be identified, *ex post*, where the one or the other clearly was dominant.

The conclusion I draw from all this is that the distinction between cyclical and fundamental disequilibria does not weaken the case for flexibility. One cannot say, as some writers would, fundamental disequilibria should be treated with flexibility, but in the case of purely cyclical troubles one should stick to fixed rates. Flexibility cannot be turned on and off according to the uncertain judgment about the cyclical or fundamental nature of a given disequilibrium. You either have flexibility or you don't have it.

But where does that leave us with respect to capital controls? On the one hand, I think that we cannot exclude *a priori* the possibility that it may happen that speculation drives the exchange rate farther in the one or the other direction than is warranted by the underlying economic situation. Speculators are, after all, not omniscient. There may be waves of excessive optimism or pessimism concerning the true value of a currency.

On the other hand, the judgments of governments about whether a given exchange rate corresponds approximately to the medium-run or long-run equilibrium level and can be held fixed by intervention have been notoriously bad in innumerable cases. On the whole, the judgment of the authorities as to whether a parity change is necessary or a disequilibrium is merely transitory has been much worse than the judgments of the speculators. There may have been some cases of unwarranted speculative attacks on some currencies, although I find it difficult to think of conspicuous examples, while it would be easy to cite many examples where the speculators were right and the authorities dead wrong.[69]

But let us assume a case arises where the government really has good reasons to believe that speculation pushes the rate too far in one direction. Instead of using the clumsy instrument of controls the government could moderate the movement in the rate by intervention in the market, in other words, by counter-speculation. As was pointed out earlier it does not seem that an occasional judicious management of a float deprives it of its effectiveness in discouraging speculation. Speculation will persist and possibly become irresistible only if the authorities insist on rigidly pegging an exchange rate that looks dubious if not downright inappropriate. A rigid defense of a specific rate makes it an easy target for speculation, while a flexible policy of moderating the market trend, without suppressing it, of counteracting excessive swings without rigidly pegging a well-defined rate, may well succeed in discouraging speculation by creating enough uncertainty as to the future movement of the rate. If the capital flows are partly or wholly due to noneconomic political factors, the situation may be different. Fortunately, these conditions--a determined urge to get one's money out of a country whatever the cost--are rare exceptions in the West. (In the communist countries the situation is, of course, entirely different.)

Conclusion. I am now ready to answer the question: should capital controls be used as a substitute for, or supplement to, floating? Controls are certainly not a substitute. Furthermore, given the economic damage and distortions caused by the controls and their high administrative costs, and realizing the effectiveness of floating in discouraging destabilizing speculation, it would be most unwise to use the heavy weapons of controls as a supplement to floating.

This advice does, however, not prejudge the question of whether floating should be managed or unmanaged. I expressed the opinion that cases of "self-fulfilling speculation" are very rare exceptions. In other

words, it does not often happen that speculation drives the exchange rate
to clearly inappropriate levels so that the monetary authorities are forced
to choose between two evils--either to "ratify" the inappropriate exchange
rate (by inflating if speculation has undervalued the currency or by
deflating if speculation has overvalued the currency) or to resist (try to
call the bluff of the speculators by counter-speculation) and risk the
possibility of deviating from the appropriate monetary policy in the
opposite direction.

If my judgment that such situations are rare is not accepted--and I
may, of course, be wrong--it does not follow that capital controls are the
answer. It only follows that there should be frequent interventions in the
exchange market; that floating should be more often and more vigorously
managed.

However, to forestall a possible misunderstanding, let me add this:
if I recommend floating, I do not want to suggest that every currency in
the world will or should float freely against every other. No doubt, even
if floating becomes very popular, many currencies will and should be
pegged against some key currency. Many currencies will continue to be
pegged to the dollar. Others will be hitched to the mark, others to
sterling, the French franc, the yen or possibly to a prospective European
(Common Market) currency. Each country will have to make up its
mind whether it wants to float independently or to stabilize its currency
in terms of some other. But any country that pegs to the currency of a
large neighbor should realize that it will have to follow not only the price
trend of that country (with the qualification mentioned earlier), but also
its major cyclical swings.

Exchange Rate Policy and the Strong Dollar of 1984[70]

The Problem of the "Overvalued" Dollar. The dramatic rise of the
dollar since 1980 can be explained by two mutually supporting factors,
high interest rates in the United States and the fact that the U.S.
economy again offers a confidence-inspiring atmosphere for foreign
investors.

The high interest rates can be traced back to large current and
projected budget deficits, in relation to the flow of private saving, and
to lingering doubt that inflation has been definitely curbed and will not
be reignited by the ongoing cyclical recovery.

The U.S. economy is a safe haven for foreign investors for several
reasons, economic as well as political ones: political and economic

stability, absence of controls on international transactions, and the existence of a large, efficient capital market.

Whatever the correct explanation, it is certainly true that the appreciation of the dollar and the large trade deficits have a significant depressive influence. This fact has disturbed some experts who say that it has cost the economy several percentage points of real growth.

This is, however, a very shortsighted argument. In the *first* place, it ignores the fact that despite the appreciation of the dollar and the large trade deficits, the U.S. economy has staged an unexpectedly vigorous expansion. Many experts believe that the expansion has been too fast to be sustainable. If that is accepted, by slowing down the pace of the expansion, the appreciation of the dollar and the trade deficit may well have a positive effect on real GNP growth in the longer run.

In the *second* place, and even more important, the argument overlooks the fact that the appreciation of the dollar and the trade deficits are also potent anti-inflationary factors. Some counterfactual theorizing will reveal the far-reaching implications of this fact.

Suppose the dollar had not gone up in the foreign exchange market because, say, market participants had lacked confidence in the future; in this case a powerful disinflationary factor would have been lost. It follows that, assuming we wish to bring down inflation, the Fed would have had to step harder on the monetary brake. Therefore, the recession would have been about the same as it actually was.[71] It is hardly necessary to point out that if the Fed had not stepped on the brake, the recession would have been merely postponed and would have later reappeared in an aggravated form.

Now let us change the scenario. Suppose the Fed or foreign central banks[72] had tried to prevent the dollar from rising by massive interventions in the foreign exchange market, as has been widely and even vociferously demanded, especially in weak-currency countries.[73]

There is no doubt it would have been easy for the Fed to prevent the dollar from rising, or to bring it down, by nonsterilized interventions, that is, by selling dollars and buying German marks, Japanese yen--and French francs--and by letting the money supply go up in the process at the high cost of reaccelerating inflation.

What remains in doubt is, *first*, whether such a policy would improve the competitive position of U.S. industries and thus reduce the trade deficit, and, *second*, whether interventions in the foreign exchange market, without an increase in the money supply--in other words, whether pure or sterilized interventions--would do any good. I discuss these two issues in turn.

The *first* question can be put as follows: The decline of the value of the dollar relative to other currencies, in other words, the decline of the trade weighted effective rate per se, undoubtedly stimulates exports and restrains imports and thus tends to improve the trade balance. But does not the inflation caused by the increase in the money supply operate in the opposite direction? Is there a reason to believe that the two opposite effects will offset each other, or that the one or the other will dominate the outcome?

Martin Feldstein, in a recent paper, reached the conclusion that "the essential impact of a change in the money stock [resulting from interventions] in the foreign exchange market is to alter only the *nominal* rate. Any decline in the real exchange value of the dollar would be only temporary." The result "therefore" would be "to leave the incentive to import and export unchanged."[74] This implies that the opposite effects mentioned above tend to offset each other exactly. This conclusion is based on the assumption that inflation would accelerate quickly, in other words, that we do not live in a Keynesian world where output could be expanded without large price increases.

Many economists would probably agree that the economy is now much closer to the "classical" extreme than to the Keynesian. The elasticity of aggregate output (real GNP) with respect to an increase in aggregate nominal demand is low, despite the relatively high unemployment rate. There are two reasons for that. First, inflationary expectations have been sensitized by a long period of inflation, and, second, much of the unemployment is structural and requires time-consuming relocation of labor. The implication is to support Feldstein's conclusion: An inflationary intervention policy to bring down the value of the dollar relative to other currencies would probably improve the competitive position of the U.S. industries only slightly and temporarily.

The Effectiveness of Sterilized Intervention. I come to the *second* open question concerning the effectiveness or ineffectiveness of pure or sterilized interventions--a question that has received a good deal of attention recently. Under this system the Fed creates money by selling dollars in the foreign exchange market and then offsets (sterilizes) the additional dollars by selling Treasury bills in the domestic security markets (or by raising the discount rate or increasing reserve requirements of the banks). This is, however, only one half of the whole transaction. The other half relates to how the Fed disposes of the foreign currency, say D-marks, which it acquires in the foreign exchange market. If the intervention is to be fully sterilized, it must be assumed that the D-marks are invested in D-mark denominated securities, for if the Fed kept the marks the German effective demand (MV) would be reduced. This becomes clear if we consider what happens if the intervention is carried out by the Bundesbank selling dollars for marks rather than by the Fed. The final outcome must be the same. But there is this difference: If the Bundesbank sells dollars for marks, the stock of marks (M) declines; if the Fed acquires marks, the velocity of circulation of money (V) declines. In both cases effective demand (MV) declines, which makes the transaction a case of nonsterilized intervention. To sterilize the effect the mark must be invested in mark-denominated securities.

There is, I believe, general agreement that sterilized interventions are much less effective, many would say totally ineffective, compared with nonsterilized interventions in influencing the exchange rates.[75] Why this is so becomes clear when we consider that, unlike nonsterilized interventions, sterilized interventions (1) do not change the money supply and (2) tend to raise interest rates in the country whose currency is sold, compared with the country whose currency is bought. In our example, when the Fed sells Treasury bills, it tends to boost U.S. interest rates. When it buys mark-denominated securities, it tends to depress German interest rates. The incipient interest differential will attract capital from abroad. These additional capital imports constitute demand for dollars. The net effect, if any, of the whole operation on the exchange rate will depend on the comparative strength of the two forces operating in *opposite* directions: Sales of dollars in the foreign exchange market weaken the dollar; sales of Treasury bills tend to strengthen the dollar.[76] If the additional demand for dollars resulting from capital inflow exceeds the additional supply of dollars resulting from the sale of dollars, the dollar will strengthen, which means that the whole operation was counterproductive. The opposite will be true if the additional demand falls short of the additional supply; in that case the whole operation has the desired effect of weakening the dollar. If the two forces are of equal strength, the intervention has no effect on the exchange rate.

Whether sterilized interventions have an effect on exchange rates depends on whether or not the public regards securities of different currency denominations as perfect substitutes. In our example, if market participants were indifferent to whether they held mark- or dollar-denominated securities, sterilized interventions would have no effect on the exchange rate, for the slightest interest differential would lead to capital shifts from marks into dollars. Hence, an additional supply of dollars resulting from sales of dollars in the foreign exchange market would be matched by increased demand resulting from capital imports.

The assumption of perfect substitutability of securities denominated in different currencies is obviously unrealistic. The reason is that there is always an exchange risk, especially under floating. This implies that sterilized interventions have some effect, as becomes clear if one considers that sterilized interventions alter the relative size of the stock of outstanding securities of different currency denominations. If the Fed intervenes, the stock of dollar-denominated securities increases. If the Bundesbank intervenes by buying mark-denominated securities to offset (sterilize) the decrease in the money supply, the stock of mark-denominated securities decreases. In either case the ratio of the stock of dollar-denominated to that of mark-denominated securities increases. To induce the market to accept the changed portfolio, an interest differential and/or a change in the actual or expected exchange rate is required. We can, then, take it for granted that sterilized interventions will have some effect.

What is still uncertain is the magnitude of the effect. It is generally assumed, rightly in my opinion, that, considering the huge volume of outstanding securities denominated in major currencies, sterilized intervention would have to be of truly massive proportions to have a significant effect--massive, that is to say, compared with the volume of interventions that have actually been made. Indirectly sterilized interventions may have an effect, for example, if they give market participants the impression that the authorities are determined to take stronger measures, if necessary, to bring about the desired change in the exchange rate--in other words, if sterilized interventions are regarded as the precursor of nonsterilized interventions.

The Recent Policy of "Coordinated Interventions" in the Foreign Exchange Market. On August 1, 1983, it was announced in Washington, with considerable fanfare, that at the urging of European countries and Japan the United States had agreed to joint "coordinated interventions" in the foreign exchange market. On the face of it, this is a sharp reversal of the present administration's policy of interventions. To describe it as a case of "correcting disorderly market conditions," as a high official put it, is rather odd. The Europeans certainly do not see it that way. They want a lower dollar. The persistent rise of the dollar may be exaggerated and undesirable, but there is nothing disorderly about it. The change in policy is better described as a gesture of good will; some would call it "appeasement." Actually, as we shall see, the U.S. concession does not amount to much.

As usual, the French were in the forefront of the critics of U.S. policy. French Minister of Finance M. Jacques Delors "sharply criticized" U.S. policy for "high interest rates and the hausse of the dollar," for "showing no concern for European interests," and for "ignoring the decisions of the Williamsburg Economic Summit." He demanded joint action and more "solidarity."[77] The minister evidently wants other countries to jump on the inflationary bandwagon to let France off the hook.

Since August 1, sizable interventions have been taken by the United States, by West Germany, and by other countries. As usual, the magnitude of interventions was not divulged, nor were the currencies involved. But according to informed sources, the total of all interventions for the first eight days or so was between $2.5 billion and $3 billion, and they have all involved sales of dollars for marks and other currencies.

Most interventions have been of the sterilized kind. When the New York Fed sells dollars, it almost simultaneously sells Treasury bills for the same amount so that the money supply is not affected. That the German interventions, too, are sterilized follows from the fact that the German minister of finance and the president of the Bundesbank have stated that interest rates will not be raised because of the fragility of the German recovery.[78] Nonsterilized interventions would do just that--raise interest rates. The Swiss National Bank, too, has intervened by selling dollars for marks; how much was not stated. The operation was officially described as "neutral with respect to Swiss monetary growth" and the president of the Swiss National Bank, Fritz Leutwiler, while expressing the view that joint action of several central banks can be useful in certain situations, has emphasized the "priority of monetary policy."[79]

Fears have been expressed that the policy of internationally coordinated interventions to stop or reverse the rise of the dollar will have inflationary effects in the United States. These fears are unfounded so long as the interventions are sterilized. Sterilized interventions have no direct inflationary effect because the money supply remains unchanged. The rise of interest rates resulting from the sale of Treasury bills may even be said to be slightly anti-inflationary. Indirectly, the policy possibly may have an inflationary effect if it succeeds in reducing the external value of the dollar, for we have seen that the high dollar is an anti-inflationary factor.

But this qualification is unimportant because, as we have seen, there is fairly general agreement that sterilized interventions have little, if any, effect on the exchange rates. True, it has been shown that if market participants are not indifferent with respect to the currency composition of their assets, sterilized interventions will have some effect on the exchange rate. It should be noted that this argument involves portfolio considerations, which makes the *stock* of assets relevant. It follows that the effect on the exchange rates is likely to be minimal in view of the enormous size of outstanding assets in relation to the magnitude of interventions.

The upshot is that the effect of the whole operation is likely to be negligible. It has been argued that it may even have a negative effect. The almost daily announcements that this or that central bank will intervene, followed as they usually are by a further rise of the dollar, may fortify bullish expectations of market participants about the future course of the dollar. Since the rise of the dollar sooner or later (probably sooner than later) will come to an end or even reverse itself somewhat, not much harm will be done.

The whole operation must look very attractive to the participating central banks. When the rise of the dollar stops, they can claim that their interventions turned the tide. And it will never be quite certain whether the intervention prolonged or shortened the rise of the dollar. These conclusions are based on the assumption that the interventions continue to be fully sterilized.

Notes

1.   From "The International Monetary System after Jamaica and Manila." *Contemporary Economic Problems*, William Fellner, editor. (Washington, D.C.: American Enterprise Institute, 1977), 239-288. This selection excerpted from pp. 243; 244-250.

2.   See Gottfried Haberler, *The World Economy, Money, and the Great Depression 1919-1939* (Washington, D.C.: American Enterprise Institute, 1976). Saying that the gold standard had disastrous consequences in a worldwide depression does not imply that the gold standard would be bad in another environment. The structural changes which made the gold standard increasingly unworkable in the twentieth century have been described many times. I have discussed them in my book *Economic Growth and Stability: An Analysis of*

Economic Change and Policies (Plainview, N.Y.: Nash Publishing Corp., 1974), chapter 8.

3. One critic of the Bretton Woods system insists that it broke down not in 1971 or 1973 but in 1947 after the premature attempt to make the pound convertible (without any correction of the exchange rate!) had collapsed and the Marshall Plan was launched. (Lord Balogh, "Keynes and the International Monetary Fund," in *Keynes and International Monetary Relations: The Second Keynes Seminar held at University of Kent at Canterbury, 1974*, ed. A. P. Tirlwall [New York: St. Martin's Press, 1976], pp. 66-87.) This is a grossly misleading statement, to put it mildly. The fact is that the Bretton Woods system did not become fully operational right after the formal establishment of the Fund in 1946. The Fund was never intended, and its resources were not large enough, to cope with the enormous capital requirements of the immediate postwar reconstruction. But the effectiveness and benefits of the system cannot be gauged *solely* by the size of its lending operations.

Equally important are the underlying principles of, and the machinery provided for, continuous cooperation and consultations, especially with respect to exchange rate changes. This represents a major advance, and the benefits for the world economy have been very large right from the Fund's inception. These benefits endure even after the demise of the par value system.

4. Probably the first to recognize the defect of a fixed rate system once the confidence in the fixity of the peg is gone was Frank D. Graham "Achilles Heels in Monetary Standards," *American Economic Review* (March 1940), pp. 16-32. Graham argued that when a serious disequilibrium has developed, the direction of any change of the exchange rate is clear, and "bear speculators are then presented with that rare and desired phenomenon a 'sure thing'" (p. 19). Thomas D. Willett has pointed out that Graham's important paper was completely ignored at the time in academic as well as in official policy discussions (*Floating Exchange Rates and International Monetary Reform*). Ten years later the sure thing criticism of the adjustable peg system was frequently made in the academic literature. See for example Milton Friedman's famous paper "The Case for Flexible Exchange Rates" written in 1950 and first published in *Essays in Positive Economics* (Chicago: University of Chicago Press, 1953) and James Meade's standard work, *The Balance of Payments* (London: Oxford University Press, 1951), chapter 17, "The Role of Speculation," pp. 218-31. It took two more decades for this insight to gain official recognition.

5. See Lawrence Officer and Thomas D. Willett, "Reserve Assets Preference and the Confidence Problem in the Crisis Zone," *Quarterly Journal of Economics* (November 1969), pp. 688-95, and "The Interaction of Adjustment and Gold Conversion Policies in a Reserve Currency System," *Western Economic Journal* (March 1970), pp. 47-60. The authors argue that the case for the inherent instability of the reserve currency system has been greatly overdone. I find the Officer-Willett theory convincing if the reserve currency

country keeps inflation sufficiently in check.

6. De Vries, "Jamaica or the Non-Reform," p. 587. Similarly, Robert Solomon says "The fatal flaw in the Committee's endeavor was the unwillingness of its members to focus on the exchange rate regime." (*The International Monetary System*, p. 323.) In 1973 Professor Xenophon Zolotas, president of the Bank of Greece, warned that the committee's terms of reference to the effect that the future international monetary system "will be based on stable but adjustable parities with the possibility of floating in particular circumstances," are no longer "appropriate"; much greater flexibility was needed, he said. (Xenophon Zolotas, "Fixed Rates or Managed Float," paper published in the *Times* [London], November 28, 1973, reprinted in Xenophon Zolotas, *International Monetary Issues and Development Policies: Selected Essays* [Athens: Bank of Greece, 1977], pp. 236-41.) J. Marcus Fleming once remarked in rueful self-criticism: "At every stage in the discussion [of the reform of the international monetary system] reform proposals have lagged behind events and have been quickly outmoded by new events." (*Reflections on the International Monetary Reform*, Essays in International Finance, no. 107 [Princeton, N.J.: Princeton University, International Finance Section, 1974], p. 17.)

7. These provisions were probably inspired by Keynes who, impressed by the weakening economic position of Britain, had become deeply distrustful of international capital movements. In his famous "Proposals for an International Clearing Union," he said: "There is no country which can, in the future allow the flight of funds for political reasons or to evade domestic taxation or in anticipation of the owner turning refugee." (Dictators and revolutionaries will heartily agree.) Keynes was, however, aware that capital controls "to be effective probably require machinery of exchange control for *all* transactions" and that controls would require "postal censorship" unless capital movements are controlled "at both ends." He therefore tried to persuade the United States to adopt the British system of tight controls. (Keynes's proposals are reprinted in *World Monetary Reform Plans and Issues*, ed. Herbert G. Grubel [Stanford, California: Stanford University Press, 1963], pp. 72-73.) Harry D. White, too, was skeptical about the desirability of free international capital flows. See his book *The French International Accounts 1880-1913* (Cambridge, Mass.: Harvard University Press, 1933), pp. 311-12. As early as 1943, Friedrich Lutz warned of the far-reaching deleterious implications of capital controls and concluded that "the only sound method of preventing short term capital movements of the speculative and political kind is to remove their causes." (*The Keynes and White Proposals*, Essays in International Finance, no. 1 [Princeton, N.J.: Princeton University, International Finance Section, 1943], p. 19.) For further discussions and references to the literature see my paper "The Case Against Capital Controls for Balance of Payments Reasons," in *Capital Movements and Their Control (Proceedings of the Second Conference of*

the International Center for Monetary and Banking Studies), ed. Alexander K. Swoboda (Leiden, Netherlands: A. W. Sijthoff, 1976). Available also as Reprint No. 62 (Washington, D.C.: American Enterprise Institute, 1976).

8. A dual exchange rate, a pegged one for current transactions and a freely floating rate for capital transactions, is a method of controlling capital movements which has been used by a number of countries, notably France, Italy, and Belgium. The Belgian dual rate system is still in operation. So long as the discount of the capital transactions rate is small and not persistent (not higher than, say, 5 percent), the method works tolerably well. But whether it is efficient is another question. See my paper "The Case against Capital Controls for Balance of Payments Reasons," cited in the preceding footnote. The Belgian case has been analyzed by Paul D. Grauwe, "The Belgian Dual Exchange Market System: An Inequitable and Ineffective System" in *Bank Credit, Money and Inflation in Open Economies*, ed. Michele Fratianni and Karl Tavernier (Berlin: Duncker & Humblot, 1976), pp. 389-402.

9. The words in quotes are the title of Section 2 of Article VIII which bears the title "General Obligations of Members" (see note 1).

10. IMF *Annual Report for 1975* (Washington, D.C.: 1975), Table 9, p. 24. The classification of currencies as floaters and peggers may be a little arbitrary in some cases, and since June 1976 the figures have changed somewhat. The basic contours of the picture are clear and have remained the same.

11. From "The Dollar in the World Economy: Recent Developments in Perspective." *Contemporary Economic Problems*, William Fellner, Project Director. (Washington, D.C.: American Enterprise Institute, 1980), pp. 135-165. This selection pp. 146-150.

12. See my contribution to *Contemporary Economic Problems 1979*.

13. Most of these disturbances from abroad were feedbacks of the U.S. depression.

14. See General Agreement on Tariffs and Trade (GATT), *International Trade 1978/79* (Geneva, 1979), p. 2.

15. Frank D. Graham was probably the first to point out that under the adjustable peg when a serious disequilibrium has developed the direction of a change in the exchange rate is clear and 'bear speculators are then presented with that rare and desired phenomenon of a sure thing." Frank D. Graham, "Achilles Heels in Monetary Standards," *American Economic Review* (March 1940), p. 19. For references to the later literature, see my paper "The International Monetary System after Jamaica and Manila," *Contemporary Economic Problems 1977*, p. 245.

16. John Williamson, "World Stagflation and International Monetary Arrangements," a paper prepared for the Consultative Group on International Economic and Monetary Affairs, mimeographed, p. 32. Williamson refers to a paper by Jacques R. Artus and John R. Young, "Fixed and Flexible Rates: A

Renewal of the Debate," *Staff Papers of the International Monetary Fund*, vol.
26, no. 4 (December 1979). These two authors, however, take a much less
extreme position.

    17. Contrary to what critics of floating often say (for example, Artus
and Young, "Fixed and Flexible Rates," p. 656), advocates of floating have
been aware of these limitations of the insulating power of floating exchange
rates. See, for example, Gottfried Haberler, "Inflation as a Worldwide
Phenomenon--An Overview," in David Meiselman and Arthur B. Laffer, eds.,
The Phenomenon of Worldwide Inflation (Washington, D.C.: American
Enterprise Institute, 1975), p. 23.

    18. There is no question that the Smoot-Hawley tariff, both through
its direct impact and as a bad example, was a highly disturbing factor that
contributed mightily to the catastrophic contraction of world trade. But that the
monetary, deflationary impact of the U.S. depression on the rest of the world
was by far the strongest depressive force is demonstrated by the fact that a
number of countries were able to extricate themselves from the deflationary
spiral and stage a vigorous recovery under the cover of floating or devaluation
long before the U.S. economy emerged from the depression, despite the fact that
the Smoot-Hawley tariff was still in force.

    19. See, for example, Artus and Young, "Fixed and Flexible Rates,"
p. 660.

    20. A whole bunch of restrictions on capital exports, foreign lending
by U.S. banks, and mandatory repatriation of part of foreign investment income
were put into effect by presidential executive order. For details, see Gottfried
Haberler and Thomas D. Willett, *U.S. Balance of Payments Policies and
International Monetary Reform: A Critical Analysis* (Washington, D.C.:
American Enterprise Institute, 1969), pp. 19-39.

    21. Otmar Emminger, "The International Monetary System Under
Stress: What Can We Learn from the Past?" a speech at a conference of the
American Enterprise Institute, February 28, 1980. Available as Reprint No.
112 (Washington, D.C.: American Enterprise Institute, 1980).

    22. From "The International Monetary System and Proposals for
International Policy Coordination." *Deficits, Taxes, and Economic Adjustments*,
Phillip Cagan, editor. (Washington, D.C., 1987), pp. 63-96. This selection pp.
83-84.

    23. The *Financial Times*, London, January 7, 1987. The recent row
between France and Germany is reminiscent of what happened in 1968 and
1969. Then, as now, France was shaken by violent student demonstrations and
strikes, the French franc was weak, and the German mark strong. President de
Gaulle's minister of finance declared, "This is not, properly speaking, a French
crisis. It is an international crisis," and President de Gaulle said devaluation
"would be the worst form of absurdity." The Germans were equally adamant.
"An official spokesman told a news conference that the decision to upvalue

the mark was 'final, unequivocal and for eternity.'" The impasse dragged on until after de Gaulle's resignation on April 28, 1969; his successor then devalued the frank by 11.1 percent on August 8, 1969. For further details see Robert Solomon, *The International Monetary System 1945-1981* (New York: Harper & Row, 1982).

24. From "The International Monetary System after Jamaica and Manila." *Contemporary Economic Problems*, William Fellner, editor. (Washington, D.C.: American Enterprise Institute, 1977), this selection pp. 266-273.

25. This section draws heavily on the author's paper "How important Is Control Over International Reserve?" presented at the Marcus Fleming Memorial Conference on the International Monetary System, November 11-12, 1976, sponsored by the International Monetary Fund. The papers presented at that conference are published in *The New International Monetary System*, Robert A. Mundell and Jacques J. Polak (eds.) (New York: Columbia University Press, 1977), pp. 116-132. In that paper I sketch the earlier history of the problems of international liquidity.

26. The problems were set out in these terms in *International Monetary Arrangements: The Problem of Choice*, Report on the Deliberations of an International Study Group of Thirty-two Economists. (Princeton, N.J.: Princeton University, International Finance Section, 1964.) The initiator and organizer of the study group was Fritz Machlup. In later years the work was continued in numerous meetings of the so-called Bellagio group under the direction of William Fellner, Fritz Machlup, and Robert Triffin. See also the excellent comprehensive discussion of the adjustment, liquidity, and confidence problem in Leland B. Yeager's impressive treatise *International Monetary Relations, Theory, History and Policy*, 2nd ed. (New York: Harper and Row, 1976), especially pp. 611-55.

27. It should be recalled that convertibility has two distinct meanings--asset convertibility (convertibility into some "primary" reserve asset) and market convertibility (convertibility into other currencies in a free, unrestricted foreign exchange market). The dollar still is and always was fully convertible in the important market sense, except that for Americans (not foreigners) capital transfers were restricted for several years. These restrictions were lifted in 1974.

28. See Fritz Machlup, *Plans for Reform of the International Monetary System*, Special Papers in International Economics, no. 3 (Princeton, N.J.: Princeton University, International Finance Section, 1964).

29. Total reserves of all IMF members, end of period in SDRs. See *International Financial Statistics*, any recent issue.

30. This does not mean, however, that the United States was the only culprit. Many countries inflated even faster than the United States, and the majority of countries followed the U.S. lead without resistance, if not with

pleasure--in some cases with the added satisfaction of being able to put all the blame on Uncle Sam.

31. Let me repeat that the much more important market convertibility of currencies is fully preserved under floating, unless convertibility is restricted or abolished by exchange control. The danger of controls being imposed is much greater under the adjustable peg than under floating.

32. On the so-called "international quantity theory" which postulates a *close* relationship between international liquidity and the world price level, and on the criticism that the international quantity theory has received from Marcus Fleming, Jacques Polak, Egon Sohmen, and Thomas Willett, see my paper, "How Important Is Control over International Reserves?" The criticism of the authors largely antedates the period of widespread floating. Floating has all but obliterated any correlation that may have existed between the two magnitudes.

33. Before the advent of widespread floating, plans for the concentration and consolidation of world monetary reserves in the Fund have in fact been put forward by the dozen. (See Machlup, *Plans for Reform of the International Monetary System*, for an early selection.) The Committee of Twenty wrestled with this problem for years.

34. Lord Robbins believes that it was a "fundamental flaw" in the Bretton Woods charter that "it contained no instruments which were capable of dealing with general inflation . . . The plain fact is that the IMF was conceived as an institution providing safeguards against general deflation . . . Moreover, what innovations have taken place since those days, the SDRs for instance . . . were conceived to be a safeguard against an alleged insufficient world liquidity." ("Domestic Goals and Financial Interdependence," Speech at International Monetary Conference, Frankfurt, April 28, 1977, published in *Auszüge aus Presseartikeln*, Deutsche Bundesbank, no. 28, Frankfurt am Main, May 6, 1977, p. 5.)

35. To illustrate: An across-the-board distribution of additional SDRs or a general increase of country quotas in the Fund would clearly be an inflationary move. But the use of international liquidity, even of ad hoc-created additional liquidity, for a loan to an inflationary country as part of a comprehensive agreement on a change in policy that enables the country to get out of the inflationary rut can be defended as an anti-inflationary move.

36. From "The International Monetary System after Jamaica and Manila." *Contemporary Economic Problems*, William Fellner, editor. (Washington, D.C.: American Enterprise Institute, 1977), pp. 239-288. This selection pp. 256-265.

37. See IMF *Annual Report for 1974* (Washington, D.C., 1974), pp. 112-16.

38. Official borrowing surely should include part of the foreign borrowing by state enterprises and in some cases even officially induced borrowing by large private firms. It stands to reason that the line between

genuinely private and official borrowing (and lending) tends to become more and more blurred in modern, highly planned, and manipulated economies, such as the British and Italian ones.

39. IMF *Annual Report for 1974*, Guideline (5), p. 114.

40. Ibid., Guideline (1), p. 115.

41. Ibid., p. 115.

42. Clean floating and dirty floating are not always clearly differentiated. Many authors use the term *clean floating* synonymously with *free, unmanaged floating*. Others deny that there is such a thing as clean floating on the ground that "the authorities affect the exchange rate through their macropolicies whether they want it or not." (June Flanders, "Some Problems of Stabilization Policy Under Floating Exchange Rates," in *Trade, Stability and Macroeconomics: Essays in Honor of Lloyd Metzler*, ed. George Horwich and Paul A. Samuelson [New York: Academic Press, 1974], p. 123.) Of course, everything depends on everything else, and everybody is free to define his terms as he wants. But it would be rather awkward and misleading to speak of a managed, "unclean" float, if, instead of intervening in the exchange market, the monetary authorities of a country took steps to slow down an ongoing inflation by reducing the rate of monetary growth to stop a decline in external value of the currency.

43. For a thorough discussion of the problems of official interventions which raises some doubts about the wisdom of trying to smooth short-run fluctuations in exchange rates, see Leland B. Yeager, *International Monetary Relations: Theory, History and Policy* (New York: Harper and Row, 1966), chapter 13, "Stabilizing Official Interventions," pp. 232-47.

44. Guideline (1) has been criticized by Ethier and Bloomfield, because it seems to make interventions for the purpose of ironing out short-run fluctuations mandatory. (Wilfred Ethier and Arthur I. Bloomfield, *Managing the Managed Float*, Essays in International Finance, no. 112 [Princeton, N.J.: Princeton University, International Finance Section, 1975], p. 22.) The authors recommend that such interventions should be merely permitted. It could indeed be argued that mandatory interventions are incompatible with the amended charter, which gives every country the right to choose the exchange rate regime it prefers. (Ethier and Bloomfield wrote before the text of the amended articles became available.) But it could also be argued that the phrase *as necessary* in the text of Guideline (1) makes the guidelines immune to that criticism.

45. The IMF guidelines define *medium-term* as a period of about four years (IMF *Annual Report for 1974*, Guideline (3)(b), p. 115).

46. Export-weighted foreign currency cost, average of sixty-seven countries. Computed by Office of International Trade, U.S. Department of Commerce. The periods of the dollar-DM rate and the trade-weighted figures are not exactly the same because the latter figures are only available for mid-months.

47. It may be recalled that the Smithsonian realignment of exchange rates was based on what was supposed to be the best expert advice available anywhere in the world, an IMF econometric world model. Actually, the new pattern of exchange rates was proved to be hopelessly wrong within a few months. (It should be mentioned, however, that the American delegation had tried to get a larger devaluation of the dollar which they thought would be necessary to restore equilibrium and confidence.) But the Smithsonian agreement was hailed at the time as a tremendous achievement (and not only by politicians). Even now, hindsight notwithstanding, it is mentioned as an example that it is not utopian to assume that countries will be "able to agree regularly on a consistent structure of spot reference rates." (John Williamson, "The Future Exchange Rate Regime, *Quarterly Review, Banca Nazionale del Lavoro*, June 1975, p. 140.) Consistent perhaps, but totally wrong nonetheless.

48. It should, however, not be overlooked that under the adjustable peg, central bankers and ministers of finance who contemplate a change in the exchange rate--up or down--have to pretend solemnly to the last moment that they would never, never do such a thing--an obnoxious feature of the par value system. Many examples of that painful behavior could be cited, even from the very recent experience in the European snake when the West German mark was appreciated by a few percent.

49. Ethier and Bloomfield, *Managing the Managed Float*; Williamson, "The Future Exchange Rate Regime," pp. 127-44; and IMF *Annual Report for 1974*, Guideline (3)(b) and Commentary, p. 115. See also the interesting pamphlet by Raymond F. Mikesell and Henry N. Goldstein, *Rules for a Floating Rate Regime*, Essays in International Finance, no. 109 (Princeton, N.J.: Princeton University, International Finance Section, April 1975).

50. Ethier and Bloomfield, *Managing the Managed Float*, p. 10.

51. Williamson, "The Future Exchange Rate Regime," pp. 134-36.

52. Ibid., pp. 135-36.

53. If this is the case, it confirms what was said above that floating carries with it a certain self-disciplinary, anti-inflationary incentive.

54. The French franc was not saved by the fact that for many years (1865 to 1914) it was rigidly joined in a one-to-one relationship with the Swiss franc in the so-called Latin Union, which was organized in 1865 by France, Belgium, Italy, and Switzerland, and was joined by Greece in 1868.

55. Balance of payments and exchange rate projections, even for only a year ahead, have been notoriously unreliable. For example see Willett, *Floating Exchange Rates* (forthcoming).

56. Ethier and Bloomfield, *Managing the Managed Float*, p. 11. Italics in original.

57. Ibid., p. 101.

58. For that reason the well-known American proposal of earlier years

to use monetary reserve indicators for changes in exchange rates would require modification.

59. Article IV, Section 3(f). The amended charter substantially repeats this injunction: "These principles [of surveillance over exchange arrangements] shall respect the domestic social and political policies of members." (Article IV, Section 3 [b]).

60. From "The Case Against Capital Controls for Balance of Payment Reasons." American Enterprise Institute Reprint #62. (Washington, D.C.: American Enterprise Institute, 1973), pp. 70-78.

61. Forward Exchange interventions have been tried on a large scale, e.g. by the German Bundesbank but they are essentially very short-run devices. Altogether too much analytic ingenuity has been lavished on operation "mix" and "twist." One prominent practitioner of this game, Harry G. Johnson, has given it up. He "now think(s) that the game of extending Keynesian international economic policy models by introducing further differentiation of the variables is both far too easy for the mathematically competent theorist and not very illuminating for the policy maker." Ineffective or only marginally effective would be a more appropriate description. See Harry G. Johnson, *Further Essays in Monetary Economics*, (London: George Allen & Unwin Ltd., 1972), p. 12.

62. For an excellent analysis of these two types of controls, see Armin Gutowski, "Flexible Exchange Rates vs. Controls" in *International Monetary Problems*, conference sponsored by the American Enterprise Institute, (Washington, D.C.: American Enterprise Institute, 1972).

63. It should not be assumed, however, that the net effect on the capital balance is equal to the reduction in portfolio investment abroad. There are always many opportunities for substitution although it takes time for these repercussions to work themselves out and it is practically impossible to measure them. For example, *foreign* capital in the U.S. is not subject to controls. Investments in Canada are exempted from the controls and investments in LDCs are permitted. It is easy to see that through repercussions on interest levels these three exemptions are likely to become leaks in the dam that is supposed to hold back U.S. capital. Similar considerations hold for the other types of control. The development of the huge Eurodollar market was greatly stimulated by the U.S. capital export controls (along with "Regulation Q") and has become an enormous leak.

64. In January 1974 the French franc was floated and the split market abolished. The system had clearly become too costly and increasingly ineffective. (Added in the proofs.)

65. Gutowski (*loc. cit.*) gives numerous examples of evasions and reactions by the regulatory agencies.

66. The comparative attraction of gold speculation has been greatly increased by capital controls because the yield of competing investments (e.g. in marks or Swiss francs) has been reduced or made negative.

67. This experience strongly influenced Keynes' views on capital controls. In his "Proposals for an International Clearing Union," he said: "There is no country which can, in future, safely allow the flight of funds for political reasons or to evade domestic taxation or in anticipation of the owner turning refugee. Equally, there is no country that can safely receive fugitive funds." (Dictators and revolutionists will heartily agree.) Keynes therefore advocated the general use of capital controls and urged the U.S. and other prospective members of the Clearing Union to "adopt machinery similar to that which the British Exchange Control has gone a long way toward perfecting." But he continued: "Nevertheless, the universal establishment of a control of capital movements cannot be regarded as essential to the operation of the Clearing Union." Unlike some modern controllers Keynes did not want to sacrifice "international loans and credits for legitimate purposes." But he certainly greatly underestimated the difficulties of separating the two, although he realized that capital controls "probably required the maintaining of exchange control for *all* transactions" and "postal censorship." These quotations are from "Proposals for an International Clearing Union," reprinted in Herbert G. Grubel (ed.), *World Monetary Reform Plans and Issues*, Stanford University Press, 1963, pp. 48-73.

We should keep in mind that Keynes wrote during the high tide of post-depression and war-time planning, the time of extreme "elasticity pessimism." One may recall his statement that the trade balance was "a sticky mass" unresponsive to market forces. At that time the potentialities of flexible exchange rates as a method of balance-of-payments adjustment and discouraging disequilibrating capital flows were almost completely overlooked.

68. For a detailed discussion of this argument for fixed rates see my *Money in the International Economy*, 2nd. ed., London, Harrison & Sons Ltd., 1969, pp. 15-17 and my "Comment" on Arthur Laffer's paper "Two Arguments for Fixed Rates," in Harry G. Johnson and Alexander K. Swoboda (eds.) *The Economics of Common Currencies*. (London: George Allen & Unwin Ltd., 1973), p. 35.

69. In principle governments have it in their power by appropriate policies to turn a disequilibrium exchange rate into an equilibrium rate or, to express it differently, to make their forecast with respect to the future equilibrium rate come true. But the appropriate policy often has unacceptable side effects, e.g., too much unemployment, or too much inflation.

70. From "The International Monetary System in the World Recession." *Essays in Contemporary Economic Problems- Disinflation, 1983-1984*. William Fellner, Project Director. (Washington, D.C.: American Enterprise Institute, 1984), pp. 87-129. This selection pp. 89-91; 113-119.

71. One could perhaps argue that the effect of the recession on traded and nontraded goods would have been somewhat different. I do not think that this is an important qualification, however, because there is such a large overlap

between traded and nontraded industries. To be sure, protectionists are using the high dollar and the trade deficits as an argument. But the basic cause of protectionist pressure is unemployment and the recession. And that would not be different.

72. Only those foreign central banks that hold a large reserve of dollars (or gold) or a credit line could do it.

73. For example, the French minister of finance was reported to have "accused Washington of irresponsibility toward the needs of Western Europe. He also warned that the dollar's rise could lead to more belt-tightening in France." He said: "America's partners had rallied round to help when the dollar's weakness in 1978 disturbed the world economy. With the phenomenon now reversed, Washington should do the same in return" (*Washington Post*, April 22, 1983).

74. See "Gains from Disinflation," testimony by Martin Feldstein, chairman, Council of Economic Advisers, before the Joint Economic Committee, U.S. Congress, Washington, D.C., April 22, 1983.

75. See, for example, Michael Mussa, *The Role of Official Intervention*, Occasional Paper 6 (New York: Group of Thirty, 1981), and Martin Feldstein, "Gains from Disinflation." The *Official Report of the International Working Group on Exchange Market Intervention* comes to the same conclusion, though in somewhat veiled and guarded language, which one expects from an international body.

76. It is instructive to consider that in the case of nonsterilizing interventions, the effects of the foreign and domestic parts of the operation--that is, the sale of dollars in the foreign exchange market and the increase in money supply--operate in the *same* direction; both tend to weaken the dollar.

77. See *Deutsche Bundesbank, Auszüge aus Presseartikeln*, no. 75, August 4, 1983, p. 2.

78. See *Deutsche Bundesbank, Auszüge aus Presseartikeln*, no. 77, August 13, 1983, p. 1.

79. See *Deutsche Bundesbank, Auszüge aus Presseartikeln*, no. 75, August 4, 1983, pp. 1-2, 4-5.

6

Trade and Development Policy

Trade Policy[1]

Current Account Deficits Under Floating--
Burden or Benefit?

Under fixed exchange rates a prolonged large current account deficit that does not reflect (is not offset by) autonomous capital flows, in other words, a deficit that mirrors (is financed by) a loss of international reserves, is a "burden" or a deflationary factor, because under the rules of the game it forces the central bank to tighten money. Under floating the balance of payments constraint is removed in the sense that the central bank is no longer obligated to react by tightening money. This does not mean, however, that under floating a country cannot have a prolonged large current account deficit or that a run of such deficits cannot be the subject of legitimate concern.

There is much confusion or even contradictory reasoning on these points. The emergence of a large deficit is regarded by some as a failure of the floating rate system to adjust the balance of payments and as a serious drag on the U.S. economy. As a result, the U.S. government has been urging Germany and Japan to reduce their surpluses or develop deficits by fiscal and monetary expansion in order to lighten the "burden" of weaker neighbors and less developed countries, which have been carrying, it is said, a disporportionately large share of the irrepressible oil deficit. In this connection the United States has been praised as a shining example because it has permitted a deficit in its own balance of payments.

In reality the OPEC surplus is not a burden on the rest of the world, but the opposite. The fact that the OPEC countries have not stepped up their imports *pari passu* with their swollen receipts lightens what is a burden--the oil price increase--at least temporarily. This is implicitly acknowledged when it is urged that the petrodollars should be recycled from the lucky recipients to other less fortunate countries. Recycling is the opposite of relieving the beneficiary countries of the burden of a deficit; it is meant to benefit them by allowing them to run a deficit.

In general, for a less developed country, in fact for any country that wishes to speed up its growth by supplementing domestic capital formation by importing capital from abroad, a trade deficit, however financed, is not a burden but a means of furthering its legitimate or at any rate rational aspiration. It is possible that public or private investment projects financed by borrowing abroad are ill-conceived or over-ambitious and thus turn out to be a burden, or that countries borrow abroad to finance excessive consumption, but that does not change the principle that capital imports if properly used constitute a potentially beneficial option.

Why should the American current account deficit be judged differently from that of other countries? From a cosmopolitan standpoint it can be argued that a rich country should export capital and not import it. But from the national standpoint, from the standpoint of maximizing American GNP or economic welfare, why should the importation of capital be a negative factor? Surely, the statement that the oil importers are better off if the oil exporters do not insist on being paid instantaneously in terms of real goods but accept IOUs instead, applies to rich as well as to the poor oil importer. Furthermore, why should capital imports from other countries such as Japan be judged differently from capital imports from OPEC countries?

There are several possible answers to this question which raise important issues. The straightforward Keynesian answer was given by Edward Bernstein and Paul McCracken. McCracken puts it very lucidly this way:

> From 1975 . . . to 1977, our merchandise trade position has shifted from a $9 billion net export surplus to a $30 billion net export deficit. This is another way of saying that the total demand for output during these two years increased $39 billion more than demand for domestic output, because a part of the . . . increase in [total] demand took the form of enlarged purchases from abroad. . . . If that $39 billion had been spent on [domestic rather than foreign output] employment would have been substantially larger. It is probably safe to assume that this

deterioration in our trade had an employment cost of at least a million jobs.[2]

My trouble with this analysis is the following: True, if our trade balance disappeared, for example because Germany and Japan follow the American advice to inflate or simply because of the depreciation of the dollar, aggregate demand for U.S. output would increase. But can we be sure that this increase in nominal GNP will result in larger output and employment and will not be absorbed by higher prices (inflation)? The orthodox Keynesian answer, adopted by Bernstein and McCracken, is that with much unemployment and underutilized capacity there is no need to worry about inflation. But if that is so, why wait for a change in the balance of payments? Why not simply adopt a more expansionary monetary or fiscal policy?

Here we encounter the problem of stagflation, the coexistence of inflation and unemployment. I have expressed my views on stagflation on other occasions.[3] To repeat briefly: The experience of the last few years has shown conclusively that comparatively high rates of measured unemployment and underutilization of capacity are not incompatible with inflation. Unlike some extreme monetarists, I do not doubt that in the very short run monetary expansion, however brought about, would increase output and employment, in other words would not go entirely into higher prices. But I do believe that because of the long experience with inflation and the resulting high sensitivity of inflationary expectations we are now closer to the extreme monetarist than to the Keynesian position. It follows that we should look at the trade deficit while it lasts as a (small) contribution to the fight against inflation and not as a threat to employment. If and when the trade deficit declines a somewhat tighter monetary-fiscal policy would be required to prevent inflation from accelerating.

Let me put the argument in a somewhat different form. Suppose a current account deficit had not developed in the first place, for example because Germany and Japan had followed the American advice to inflate their economies or to appreciate their currencies sufficiently to keep their emerging surpluses and our deficit at a minimum, or because the United States (horrible thought) had restricted imports.[4] Then demand for U.S. output would have been that much higher. Can we be sure that this increase in nominal demand would have gone wholly or predominantly into quantities (real output and employment) and not into prices? In 1976 and 1977 the United States had a respectable *real* expansion.

Monetary and fiscal policy was, and still is, engaged in a delicate balancing act. It tries to expand nominal demand sufficiently to keep *real* expansion going, but at the same time it seeks to restrain inflation by preventing an excessively fast rise in nominal aggregate demand. Nobody can be quite sure that the actual speed of expansion is the optimal one. But two things should be kept in mind: First, the actually prevailing rate of inflation of 6.5 or 7 percent is generally regarded as too high and unsustainable. Second, moderation in the speed of real expansion is widely viewed as essential for sustained real recovery. Thus, by moderating the speed of expansion the U.S. trade deficit has made a contribution to long-run stability and growth.[5]

It seems wrong to pick out one factor--the foreign balance--and to declare categorically that if it increased then real GNP and employment would be that much larger, without even asking the question how such a change would fit into the present balancing act of overall demand management.

Are there any reasons to believe that an expansion in aggregate demand for "domestic output" brought about by an improvement in the trade balance is in some way more desirable, more effective, and less inflationary than an equal expansion brought about by a domestic monetary-fiscal stimulus? There may be special conditions suggesting an affirmative answer, such as a higher rate of unemployment in the export- or import-competing (traded-goods) industries than elsewhere. This is probably a more important consideration for countries that depend to a much greater extent on international trade than the United States does. Thus, there has been much discussion in Britain on the advantage of "export-led growth" as compared with domestically induced growth. This alleged advantage depends partly on the balance of payments constraint under fixed exchanges (and is therefore no longer relevant) and partly on structural factors such as sectoral unemployment in traded-goods industries due to lack of labor mobility or potential increasing returns to scale in the traded-goods industries. The classical balance of payments constraint does not exist under floating, and I doubt that the structural factors are of much importance for the Untied States.

Structural or Sectoral Aspects and the Protectionist Threat. From a broad global ("Keynesian" or "macro") viewpoint of aggregate output and unemployment (which does not differentiate different sectors of the economy), it makes no difference whether an expansion comes from an improvement in the balance of payments (decline of the external deficit) or from internal monetary-fiscal measures.[6] In the longer run this may be a reasonable position. But how about the short and medium term?

In Europe, especially in Britain, it is widely assumed that there is a significant difference between the foreign trade sector, especially the export industries on the one hand and the domestic, nontraded-goods sector ("sheltered industries") on the other. Industries in the export sector are progressive and competitive, often subject to increasing return to scale (because of external or internal economies), while the sheltered industries are less progressive, often monopolistic, and comparatively backward.[7] There probably is some truth in these statements as far as Europe and Japan are concerned because of the small size of those economies compared with the American economy. But whether true or not in the long or short run, it is, I believe, not possible to argue that in the huge American economy traded-goods industries *as a group* are more competitive, more progressive, and more likely to enjoy increasing returns to scale than the rest of the economy. Nor is there any evidence that there is more cyclical unemployment in the traded-goods industries than in the rest of the economy.

What is true is that there are some comparatively unprogressive, inefficient protected industries and that the impact of the recent surge of non-oil imports on different industries has been uneven, resulting in spotty, above-average unemployment in some areas. Steel, color television, and shoes come immediately to mind. Predictably, this has led to strong protectionist pressures, and the government has given in to many of them by imposing import restrictions in various forms--such as "voluntary" restraints imposed on foreign exporters, also deceptively called "orderly market agreements" (OMAS), and "trigger prices" in the case of steel. If and when the trade balance improves, as a consequence of the depreciation of the dollar in foreign exchange markets or of a more rapid expansion abroad, the import pressure on some of these industries could be expected to abate somewhat.

Nobody can be sure, however, how much relief from import competition the particular industries mentioned will get when the trade deficit declines. The change in the trade balance may come more through an increase in U.S. exports than a decrease in imports. The difficulties of the industries that have been given protection from foreign competition are largely due to long-run structural weaknesses, to a loss of comparative advantage, rather than to temporary cyclical factors. The steel industry probably requires structural changes, a shake-out of high-cost obsolescent facilities which simply cannot compete with the efficient

Japanese steel mills. A special self-imposed handicap of the steel industry is an outsize wage increase which the union of steelworkers obtained early in 1977. This contract put steel workers' wages at the top of the American scale. With this out of the way, unions and management appeared arm in arm in Washington clamoring for protection from foreign competition, as Arthur Okun aptly described the procedure.[8] The protection was duly provided by the notorious price trigger scheme, which went into effect in February 1978 and has already reduced imports and raised domestic steel prices for countless steel users (a fine contribution to the fight against inflation!).[9] The United States is, of course, not the only sinner, nor is it the worst. Neither the European Community (Common Market) nor Japan are models of liberal trade policy--far from it.

At the root of the rising protectionism is (as demonstrated in the above mentioned GATT report, *Trade Liberalization, Protectionism, and Interdependence*) the increasingly stubborn resistance to adjust to changing conditions. This resistance to adjust can be observed in many areas, but it is especially pronounced, for obvious reasons, when the change takes the form of additional imports. Thus when the American steel industry became less competitive internationally after the large wage increase in 1977, it was hardly mentioned that the wage boost had anything to do with the larger imports, and nobody dared to suggest that the wage hike be rescinded. Let me mention one example from another area: When grain prices fell back from the record level that they had reached in 1972-1973 (as a consequence of a crop shortfall and Russian wheat purchases) farmers organized heavy political pressures to force the government to "protect" them. The government complied by raising price supports and acreage restrictions. For good measure import duties and fees for sugar were sharply raised (another contribution to the fight against inflation). But the farmers are not satisfied and even try to organize a "farmer strike."[10] This situation has the elements of a vicious circle. Refusal to adjust reduces the rate of growth, and slower growth makes adjustment more difficult. Trade restrictions are, of course, only one factor among many that slow growth, but they are becoming an important factor. The growing readiness to impose restrictions when imports rise creates uncertainty and inhibits investments that are necessary to exploit fully the opportunities of trade and further division of labor.[11]

To summarize: As far as the United States is concerned, a disaggregated analysis that distinguishes between the traded- and the nontraded-goods sectors does not support the proposition that an expansion resulting from an improved balance of goods and services is less inflationary than an expansion resulting from a domestic monetary-fiscal stimulus. For broadly speaking there is no evidence that the two sectors are different with respect to the volume of unemployment, the chance of developing increasing returns to scale, or other relevant attributes. There exist, of course, some industries that have suffered from large imports-- steel, shoes, color television, and some others. But the troubles of these industries are largely of a long-run structural nature, because of a change in the comparative cost situation, and not merely temporary and cyclical.

However, to say that the steel industry suffers from an adverse shift in the comparative cost situation does not mean, as protectionist propaganda would make one believe, that in the absence of protectionist measures, steel production in the United States would be radically slashed. What it does mean is that there would be marginal adjustments, rationalizations, specialization, a shakeout of some high-cost production facilities, and greater resistance to wage pressure.

In this connection it is well to call attention to a highly significant development in the structure of world trade--the rapid growth of what has become known as intra-industry trade, especially of manufactures: Industrial countries increasingly exchange--that is, export and import simultaneously--variants of the same type of manufactured goods. Among the many examples that could be cited, Irving B. Kravis and Robert E. Lipsey have discovered

> a number of cases in which the size of the U.S. market enables U.S. producers to reach a large volume production for relatively specialized product variants for which markets are thin in any one of the smaller, competing economies. In the antifriction bearing industry, for example, the United States imports commonly used bearings which can be produced in large volume both here and abroad, but the United States has nevertheless enjoyed a net export position in bearings owing to exports of specialized kinds capable of meeting precision needs, resisting heat or rust, or bearing great weight.[12]

Modern trade in manufactures is an enormously complex structure, and the fact that seemingly similar products are simultaneously exported and imported, often through the same ports, is at first blush a baffling phenomenon and gives the impression of wastefulness and inefficiency. But the private actors in the market, manufacturers and dealers, know what they are doing. The research economist may require a major effort to find out what is going on, and the correct solution often eludes him, but the market if left alone solves the most intricate problems with reasonable dispatch and efficiency. The clumsy hands of government regulators and protectionists are bound to play havoc with that delicate mechanism.

Strategic Trade Policy and the New International Economics: A Critical Analysis[13]

In two recent articles[14] I have argued that, using the tools of classical trade theory and making certain unrealistic or even broadly realistic assumptions, it is possible to develop theoretically valid arguments for protection which in actual application are most likely to have negative or even disastrous consequences. Concretely, assuming inelasticities, rigidities, externalities or irrational behavior of certain groups, especially of lowly farmers in less developed countries, the optimum tariff argument for protection can be developed along with the external economies argument for protection which covers the classical infant-industry argument.[15]

In the present article I discuss a new argument for protection which goes under the pretentious name of "strategic trade policy and the new international economics." This theory has been developed in the last five years or so in an extensive and interesting but diffused and excessively repetitious literature.[16]

The proponents of the "new" international economics point out, correctly, that the basic model of classical and neoclassical trade theory on which the case for free trade is based, assumes perfect competition and, therefore, excludes increasing returns to scale. Increasing returns that are internal to the firms in any industry are incompatible with competitive equilibrium; they would lead to monopoly or oligopoly, implying persistently higher profits than in the competitive rest of the economy.

Free traders argue that the existence of local imperfectly competitive firms greatly strengthens the case for free trade. The reason is that the larger the market, the less scope there is for monopolies and oligopolies, and free trade greatly increases the size of the market. In fact, freer or free trade is a potent antimonopoly weapon. Although proponents of the new economics are aware of all that, they evidently believe that many oligopolies would survive under free trade. It would be interesting to have a few plausible examples. But as far as I know, very little has been done on that in the voluminous literature.

I now state briefly the principal conclusions and policy prescriptions of the "new" international economics, their novelty and validity. I take my cue from the latest authoritative summary by Paul Krugman in his paper "Is Free Trade Passé?"[17] which takes into account some of the criticism of the theory. Krugman cites three papers, one by himself, which, written "simultaneously and independently," demonstrate how "economies of scale lead to arbitrary specialization by nations on products" of industries that operate under monopolistic conditions because they enjoy increasing returns. "These models immediately established the idea that countries specialize and trade, not only because of underlying differences, (such things as different endowments of factors of production that are mentioned by traditional trade theory) but also because increasing returns are an independent force," determining the international division of labor.

All this is true, but it is not new. Krugman himself says that it was a major theme in Ohlin's *International and Interregional Trade*, and in an earlier paper he says that the importance of economies of scale has been "widely recognized" and he mentions especially Bela Balassa and Irving Kravis who have argued that scale economies have played a crucial role in the growth of trade of the industrialized countries after the Second World War.[18]

What, then, is new in the "new" economics? The short answer is: the protectionist policy conclusion. The "new" economics has added one more item to the list of theoretically valid arguments for protection. How important is the new argument for protection from the economic point of view and can it be efficiently implemented?--that is the question to which I turn now.

According to Krugman the new economics holds that international "trade is to an important degree driven by economies of scale." This surely is true in the sense that economies of scale give rise to international trade. "That international markets are typically imperfectly competitive" must be strongly doubted, but will not be discussed here. Krugman continues that the new view has suggested two arguments for protection, a wholly new one and an old one. The old one is the external economies argument. It has been reemphasized by the "new" economics, but hardly improves it and need not be further discussed here.

The new idea is that if there are increasing returns and, therefore, monopolistic or oligopolistic firms enjoying excess profits, the government is in a position to shift excess profits from foreign to domestic firms by deviating from free trade, to wit either by imposing import restrictions or by subsidizing domestic firms.[19] Krugman sets up a very simple model that puts the central proposition of the new economics into sharp focus. Suppose there is an industry, say aircraft production, where increasing returns to scale leaves room for only one firm, say Boeing in the United States or Airbus in Europe, to supply the world market profitably. Now suppose Boeing has plans to start production. If it is carried out, it will make large profits and Airbus will be shut out. But, if Europe is alert, it will subsidize Airbus to get ahead of Boeing; the profits will go to Europe and Boeing will be shut out.

The real world is, of course, much more complicated. There exists no industry with only one firm in the world market; there is, after all, McDonnell-Douglas and the Concorde in addition to Airbus and Boeing. Furthermore, there are many industrialized countries, and at this point let us recall that their number has increased since the Second World War. In addition to North America, Western Europe, and Japan, there are now the so-called NICs (Newly Industrialized Countries), Taiwan, South Korea and Hong Kong. Also, some of the "middle income countries," Argentina, Brazil, have developed industrial centers. All this has intensified international competition and reduced the scope for monopolies and oligopolies.

A serious complication of the new economics mentioned by Krugman and other proponents is, in Krugman's words, the fact "that economists do not have reliable models of how oligopolists behave. Yet the effects of trade policy in imperfectly competitive industries can depend crucially on how [oligopolistic] firms behave."

The most serious difficulty of a successful strategic trade policy mentioned by Krugman is what he calls "the general equilibrium" criticism of the policy. "Interventionist policies to promote particular sectors [for strategic reasons], must draw resources away from other sectors. This substantially raises the knowledge that a government must have to formulate interventions that do more good than harm." A policy aimed at capturing external economies runs into the same difficulty. Favored sectors draw resources from other industries. "Again, the government needs to understand not only the targeted sector but the rest of the economy to know if a policy is justified."

Is there a country in the western world that knows all that, one may ask? Krugman is rather vague about that. He ends the discussion by saying "Governments may not know for sure where intervention is justified, but they are not completely without information. However, the general equilibrium critique reinforces the caution suggested by the other critiques." Amen, one is tempted to say.

Be that as it may, Krugman insists that the difficulty--or impossibility, we may add--of formulating the correct policy is not a "defense of free trade." However, he thinks that it is possible to make "a political economy case for free trade," as distinguished from the purely economic case made by traditional trade theorists.[20]

There are two political economy arguments for free trade. The first is the risk of retaliation and trade wars. Every protectionist move risks retaliation, but in the case of strategic policy protection, the risk is very high, because the country in effect tells its trade partners: "We restrict imports from you in order to shift excess profits from your firms to ours." That clearly makes retaliation almost inevitable.

To guard against this danger, Krugman suggests that some simple rule of behavior should be agreed on. Free trade is such a rule. True, the new "theory suggests that [free trade] is unlikely to be the best of all conceivable rules." But since "it is very difficult to come up with any simple rule that would be better, there is a reasonable case for continuing to use free trade as a focal point for international agreement to prevent trade war." Fine, but what is then left of the strategic trade policy?

Krugman's second political economy argument for free trade comes under the heading "Domestic Politics." "Governments do not necessarily act in the national interest . . . Instead, they are influenced by interest group pressures. The kinds of interventions that the new trade theory suggest . . . will typically raise the welfare of small, fortunate groups by large amounts, while imposing costs on larger, more diffuse groups. The result . . . can easily be that excessive or misguided intervention takes place because the beneficiaries have more knowledge and influence than the losers . . . How do we resolve the problem?" The answer, he suggests, "is to establish a blanket policy of free trade, with exceptions granted only under extreme pressure, [that] may not be the best policy . . . that the country is likely to get." Again--what is left of strategic trade policy?

In his last section, "The Status of Free Trade," Krugman comes out strongly for free trade. His last words are: "Free trade is not passé--but it is not what it once was."

What then, is the difference between the old and the new doctrine? I take it for granted that the proponents of the new doctrine agree that the international division of labor along the line of comparative advantage is enormously important and we have seen that traditional economists are fully aware of the importance of increasing returns to scale. On the relative importance of the two factors the opinion of the two groups may differ. I confine myself to saying that the answer depends on how many monopolies or oligopolies remain after free trade has whittled them down.

It will be said that the difference between the old and the new creed is that for the former free trade is the best policy while for the latter free trade is merely a second best. For them the best policy is a policy of active strategic protection. Only if governments are weak and too much under the pressure of special interests to conduct a policy of "sophisticated intervention"--only then can the free trade rule be defended as a second-best.

Actually, there is no difference here between the old and the new creed. The traditional trade theorist, too, knows that there are theoretically valid arguments for protection--the external economies argument and the optimum tariff argument. The latter is akin to the strategic protection argument, because it too is a beggar-thy-neighbor argument that invites retaliation and can lead to trade wars. The classical infant industry argument was dealt a severe blow in Robert Baldwin's reappraisal.[21]

I repeat what I said earlier, the only thing that is new in the "new" economics is that it has added another item to the list of arguments for protection, namely the alleged possibility of shifting "excess" returns or profits from foreign to domestic firms. The appraisal of the new economics must then depend on our judgement about the new importance of this new item.

My conclusion is that it is a very weak argument for protection. We have seen that Krugman himself mentions several serious difficulties of strategic import restrictions which makes one wonder what is left of it. All that applies with equal force, sometimes even with greater force, to strategic subsidies. Retaliation is a good example. It is easier to respond to subsidies of a foreign country by imposing countervailing import duties than to respond to foreign import restrictions.

All this leads Krugman in the end to a strong endorsement of free trade. "Free trade is not passé." Krugman starts his last paragraph by saying "it is possible, then, both to believe that comparative advantage is an incomplete model of trade and to believe that free trade is nevertheless the right policy." Absolutely true. Who would doubt it?

I repeat, all that is new in the "new" economics is to have added one more item to the list of theoretically possible exceptions to the free trade rule, to wit the possibility of shifting, under certain circumstances, excess profits from foreign to domestic firms. But as Krugman himself has shown, this in practice is of very dubious value and should be ignored: "Free trade is still the right policy."

However, all that does not mean that there is nothing the government can and should do to help industry to do better in the world market. On the contrary, in all countries, also in the United States, there is a lot to do in the domestic area to foster innovation and entrepreneurship, for example in the area of education and industrial R&D, removing restrictions and rigidities in the labor market and elsewhere, not to mention taxation and macroeconomic policies. In brief, governments should concentrate on their own functions, which are of vital importance for prosperity and growth of the whole economy. Governments should not squander their limited human and material resources on such dubious policies as strategic and other kinds of protection.

Development Policy

Liberal and Illiberal Development Policy[22]

Free Trade, Like Honesty, Is Still the Best Policy--J.S. Nicholson. I cannot claim to be a pioneer in development economics. But like any economist who is interested in economic policy, I could not avoid thinking and writing about economic growth and development in general. It was then quite natural to apply the general principles of economics to the problems of the developing countries.

Specifically, I came to the problems of development from the theory of international trade. I submit that this is not a bad approach for several reasons. International trade obviously is a matter of utmost importance for the developing countries. Just ask yourself how long it would have taken a developing country--Chile, Egypt, Ghana, Mexico, Nigeria, or any other--to reach its present level of development without international trade? It is no exaggeration to say that international trade has been a major factor in the development that has taken place. This is true not only of the now developing countries, but also of the industrial countries in their early stages of development.

Trade provides imports of commodities at lower cost than they could be produced at home, as explained by the static theory of comparative cost; it also provides imports that could not be produced at home. In addition, trade is the vehicle for the importation of capital, know-how, and entrepreneurship. More on all this later.

It is true, however, that if one samples casually the literature on economic development, one might easily get the impression that trade is a most destructive force that locks developing countries in a vicious circle of poverty. The literature abounds with dire predictions of inexorable deteriorations in the terms of trade and of pernicious "demonstration effects." There is much talk of massive disguised unemployment in developing countries, which is often misinterpreted as being akin to Keynesian unemployment that is curable by monetary expansion and deficit spending and justifies import restrictions. There are strident denunciations of the monopolistic exploitation of the developing countries by monopoly capitalism; this is by no means confined to Marxists and those whom Schumpeter called Marxo-Keynesians.

An extreme example is provided by Gunnar Myrdal. He asserted that "trade operates (as a rule) with a bias in favor of the rich and progressive regions (and countries) and in disfavor in the less developed countries."[23] It is not only that the poor derive less benefit from trade than the rich, but that the poor become poorer if and because the rich get richer. And "by itself free trade would even tend to perpetuate stagnation in the underdeveloped regions" and countries.[24]

Of course, everybody knows that there are situations in which selective trade restrictions can be justified. To put it differently, there exist some widely accepted arguments for tariffs. There is the terms of trade argument that is often called the optimum tariff argument. But the argument most relevant for development economics is the infant industry argument for protection. In fact, the early nineteenth-century proponents of infant industry protection, Alexander Hamilton in the United States and Friedrich List in Germany, can be regarded as early practitioners of development policy.[25] Present-day theorists and practitioners of development economics would do well to familiarize themselves with the literature on infant industry protection, especially with the critical analysis to which the infant industry theory has been subjected by liberal economists such as John Stuart Mill, Frank William Taussig, Alfred Marshall, and others.

Let me make it clear that I use the terms "economic liberalism" and "liberal policy" in the classical nineteenth-century sense of market-oriented, laissez-faire policy and not in the perverted sense that is widespread in the United States and denotes almost the opposite of the classical meaning.

But before going into a more detailed analysis of development economics, I propose to put development economics into historical perspective.

Development Economics and Development Policy in Historical Perspective. The stance of development economics and policies, liberal or illiberal, roughly follows, often with a lag, the stance of general economic theory and policy. This is true even of the development economics of those who claim autonomy for their own brand, "duo-economics," which says that different economic principles apply to developing and developed countries. In my opinion development economics and development policy should be regarded as part and parcel of general economics and economic policy--more precisely, of growth theory and growth policy. I believe in what some development econo-mists call "monoeconomics"; that is to say, the same economic principles apply to developing and developed countries alike. From the adoption of monoeconomics, however, it does not follow that policy prescriptions should be the same for all countries.

In the fifty or sixty years since development economics has emerged as a branch of economics, a big swing in the general stance of economic policy has occurred. A sharp decline of economic liberalism started with the onset of the Great Depression of the 1930s (or possibly earlier--the precise date does not matter) and reached a low point after World War II. It was followed by a revival of liberalism that started in the late 1940s (the precise date again is unimportant).

The Decline of Liberalism. When "the problems of development were thrust upon economists by the breakup of colonial empires in Asia and Africa during the Second World War and shortly thereafter,"[26] faith in liberalism, in free markets, and in free enterprise was probably at its lowest point since the early nineteenth century. No wonder that the stance of much of development economics, too, was far from liberal.

This is strikingly illustrated by an interesting essay by Raúl Prebisch, one of the most influential development practitioners through his work in the United Nations, in the U.N. Economic Commission for Latin

188 *Trade and Development Policy*

American (ECLA) and the U.N. Conference on Trade and Development (UNCTAD). Prebisch relates that in the 1920s he "was a firm believer in neoclassical theories." But "the first great crisis of capitalism," the world Depression of the 1930s, had changed his mind. Thus, Prebisch follows Keynes who during the Depression abandoned his early liberal beliefs (see below). But he goes way beyond Keynes when he continues: "The second great crisis of capitalism, which we are all suffering now, has strengthened my attitude."[27] What Prebisch here refers to is the world recession of the early 1980s that was caused by the fact that the United States and other industrial countries had to step on the monetary brake to curb inflation. To call this a "great crisis of capitalism" is a gross misinterpretation. Actually, there has been no depression in the post-World War II period, if by depression we mean a decline remotely similar to the Great Depression of the 1930s or earlier ones. Moreover, while Keynes later returned to his early liberal beliefs (see below), Prebisch never found his way back.

The story of the decline of liberalism begins with World War I, 1914-18. This war marked the end, or the beginning of the end, of an epoch--the epoch of liberalism, of relatively free trade, of the gold standard, of free migration, free travel without a passport among most countries (excluding Russia but including the United States). True, in the 1920s most countries recovered faster from the ravages of the war than had been expected; trade was resumed and the gold standard restored. But tariffs were higher, and new tariff walls were erected in Central Europe between the successor states of the Austro-Hungarian empire. The United States and some other countries had a severe depression in 1920-21, and the countries on the European continent had high and hyper inflation. The recovery lasted barely eight years, 1921-29.

In the United States the Great Depression lasted from 1929 to 1933. It was followed by a long recovery, 1933-37, but was interrupted by a short (thirteen months) but extremely vicious depression, and full employment was reached only after the outbreak of World War II in Europe when U.S. rearmament went into high gear.

The worldwide depression was greatly intensified when country after country tried to protect employment by raising tariffs and imposing import quotas and exchange control. The volume of world trade shrank by about one-third and its value (in terms of gold dollars) by one-half, the difference reflecting the sharp decline in prices of internationally traded commodities.

Hitler came to power in 1933 at about the same time as Roosevelt. Hitler's economic policy was a great success.[28] Unemployment disappeared in a few years, and for several years prices rose little. Thus he was able to give the German people guns and butter at the same time. This greatly strengthened his position in Germany. The USSR, too, gained economic prestige for two reasons: the immunity of the communist economy to the depression that engulfed the capitalist West and rapid industrialization.[29]

The economic success of the two totalitarian regimes made a deep impression in the West. Along with a fatal misinterpretation of the true nature of the Great Depression (see below), it strengthened the tendency among intellectuals, especially in developing countries, to believe in the superiority of controls and central planning over free markets and private enterprise.

The impact of these traumatic events on the stance of economic policy was powerful. For one thing, the Great Depression spawned the "Keynesian revolution" in economic thinking. Whether it really was a scientific revolution is very questionable, but that Keynes was the most influential economist of the century cannot be doubted. True, the main recommendation firmly associated with his name--that if there is much unemployment, the government should engage in deficit spending--was by no means new. If the policy was applied in situations like the one that existed when Keynes wrote his *General Theory*--a situation characterized by high unemployment, declining prices, and deflationary expectations--the policy would have been widely accepted, even by non-Keynesians. But without Keynes's powerful leadership, which called forth scores of devoted and able followers who enthusiastically preached the Keynesian gospel, the New Economics, the policy would not have been put into practice so fast.

Unfortunately, in the post-World War II period Keynesian economists and policymakers applied the policy in situations very different from the Keynesian situation. The postwar environment was characterized by spotty unemployment, rising prices, and inflationary expectations. Thus Keynesian policies had highly inflationary consequences.

Keynes's followers showed little or no concern about inflation. This was, however, not true of the master himself. In 1937, one year after the publication of his *General Theory*, Keynes became concerned about inflation and urged a shift in policy from fighting unemployment to curbing inflation, although at that time inflation was not very high by post-World War II standards and unemployment was still about 11 percent. We have to distinguish between Keynesian economics and the economics of Keynes.[30]

A Fatal Misinterpretation of the Great Depression. The general picture underlying the Keynesian policy prescriptions was that of a "mature" economy that is subject to more or less continual deflationary pressure, chronic oversaving, and a scarcity of investment opportunities because of a slowdown of technological progress. This theory of secular stagnation has been completely discredited by later developments, but it was very popular in the 1930s and was embraced by Keynes in his *General Theory*.

The theory of secular stagnation is a gross misinterpretation of the nature of the Great Depression. Unfortunately, it was taken up by Raúl Prebisch and thus had a strong impact on development economics. Actually, the Depression of the 1930s would never have been so severe and lasted so long if the Federal Reserve had not by horrendous policy mistakes of omission and commission caused or permitted the basic money supply to contract by about 30 percent. One need not be an extreme monetarist to recognize that such a contraction of the money supply must have catastrophic consequences. According to Joseph A. Schumpeter, who certainly was not a monetarist but recognized monetary forces when he saw them, the collapse of the U.S. banking system in the early 1930s and the implied contraction of money supply "turned retreat into rout"; what would have been a recession, perhaps a relatively severe one, became a catastrophic slump.[31] In other words, the Great Depression was not "a crisis of capitalism," as Prebisch says, but was a crisis of largely anticapitalistic government policy, the consequence of horrendous policy mistakes.[32]

Subsequent Developments. That the Great Depression was not due to an inherent, endogenous instability of capitalism as many Keynesians and Prebisch assume, but was the result of exogenous, avoidable policy mistakes, "adventitious factors" as Schumpeter said, is supported by the fact that during the post-World War II period there were recessions, comparatively mild cyclical declines, but nothing resembling the Great Depression of the 1930s or earlier depressions. This was because there was no deflation, no contraction of the money stock.

This favorable outcome had not been foreseen by Keynesian economists. During the war and for years after the war, Keynesian economists predicted that the dismal interwar experience would repeat itself, that the inherent instability of capitalism would reassert itself, and that therefore expansionary monetary-fiscal policies were necessary. It stands to reason that this stance of the influential Keynesian economists greatly contributed to the inflationary excesses of the World War II period.

This raises the question of whether we have simply exchanged the horror of deflation for the horror of inflation. Far be it from me to minimize the dangers of inflation, but I submit two points. First, even in highly inflationary countries such as Argentina or Israel, the damage done by inflation has not been nearly so great as the consequences of deflation in the 1930s, measured by loss in output and employment.[33] Second, and more important, to call the recent recession caused by disinflation "the second great crisis of capitalism" as Prebisch does is inappropriate, and the policy conclusions derived from this misinterpretation are ill-advised, to put it mildly.

A medical analogy will make clear what I have in mind. Suppose a doctor has a patient who got himself into serious trouble by living for some time on a starvation diet, but later went on an eating binge. The proper treatment would be to put him on a normal diet and let the recuperative forces of the body do their work. It would clearly be inappropriate to put the patient permanently or for a long time under intensive care, using all sorts of devices to monitor and regulate essential body functions such as heartbeat and breathing. But that is precisely what ECLA and UNCTAD prescribed for the developing countries--all sorts of controls. Prebisch himself probably does not go far in   that direction, but his disciples and followers clearly do.

Disintegration of the World Economy. As mentioned above, the Great Depression led to a veritable explosion of protectionism. Under the combined effects of the slump in world output and protectionist measures, world trade fell by about 30 percent in real terms and by 50 percent in nominal terms (gold dollars). The difference reflects the sharp decline in prices of internationally traded commodities. The terms of trade turned sharply against developing countries (exporters of primary products) as they always do in downswings of the business cycle. This was widely misinterpreted as indicating a long-run pattern. It thus led to the famous Prebisch-Singer theory of a secular tendency of the terms of trade of developing countries to worsen--a theory that later research proved to be invalid (see below).

Three interconnected reasons may be roughly distinguished. First, high unemployment made the pressure to protect jobs by shutting out foreign competition almost irresistible. Second, large balance of payments disequilibria were bound to arise, and the prevailing gold standard

mentality made it very difficult for deficit countries to relieve deflationary pressures by devaluation of the currency, let alone by floating;
therefore, they resorted to import restrictions through quotas and
exchange control. Third, free trade conviction among economists,
economic journalists, and intellectuals in general had been weakened and
protectionist views became fashionable.

To indicate the change in general attitude, it will be well to sketch
very briefly Keynes's metamorphosis from a staunch liberal to an all-out
protectionist, because he reflected the view of many others and carried
along many (though fortunately by no means all) of his followers.

In a famous paper, "National Self-Sufficiency," Keynes wrote: "I
was brought up to respect free trade as an economic doctrine which a
rational and instructed person could not doubt . . . As lately as 1923 I
was writing that free trade was based on fundamental truths which, stated
with their due qualifications, no one can dispute who is capable of
understanding the meaning of the words." Ten years later--in 1933--he
summed up his views in the well known passage:

> I sympathize with those who would minimize, rather than maximize,
> economic entanglement among nations. Ideas, knowledge, science,
> hospitality, travel--these are the things which should of their nature be
> international. But let goods be homespun whenever it is reasonably
> and conveniently possible.[34]

When Keynes during the war became involved in planning for postwar economic reconstruction, Bretton Woods, and trade policy, he at
first strongly opposed the liberal trade policy proposed by the U.S. State
Department. In a memo of October 1943 he wrote:

> I am a hopeless skeptic about a return to 19th century laissez faire for
> which the State Department seems to have such a nostalgia. I believe
> that the future lies with (I) state trading for commodities, (II)
> international cartels for necessary manufactures, and (III) quantitative
> import restrictions for non-essential manufacturers.[35]

Harrod writes: "In the preceding 10 years he [Keynes] had gone far in
reconciling himself to a policy of planned trade: these ideas had sunk
deeply in. Even for him with . . . his power of quick adaptation, it was
difficult to unlearn so much."[36] Another great admirer of Keynes, Lionel
Robbins, wrote: "Even Keynes succumbed to the [then] current insanity
. . . A sad aberration of a noble mind."[37]

Keynes later changed his mind, but many of his followers, notably Nicholas Kaldor and the New Cambridge School, have consistently followed the protectionist line.[38] Kaldor recommends protection of manufactures in Britain and other mature countries to stimulate growth. Unlike agriculture and service industries, manufacturing industries are supposed to enjoy increasing returns to scale; hence, protection of manufactures from foreign competition will, it is thought, stimulate growth. Whatever the merits or demerits of a policy of protection for developed countries, it clearly would be highly detrimental for developing countries, especially for the more advanced ones.[39]

Kaldor is wrong when he mentions Germany and France in the late nineteenth century as demonstrating the beneficial effects of protection. In fact, Germany in the crucial years of industrial development had very little protection. The tariff of the *Zollverein*, which preceded the establishment of Bismarck's Germany after the Franco-Prussian War of 1870-71, was very low. for the first ten years or so Bismarck continued the low tariff policy of the *Zollverein*. When he turned protectionist in the late 1870s, the policy was anything but growth promoting. Duties on steel and agriculture, the "Compact of Steel and Rye" as it was dubbed, was inimical to the manufacturing industries.[40]

In his last years Keynes turned sharply against the protectionist-nationalist policies proposed by his erstwhile followers, who in the meantime had become his critics. It was these policies that he had in mind when he wrote in a famous posthumously published paper: "How much modernist stuff, gone wrong and turned sour and silly, is circulating in our system, also incongruously mixed, it seems, with age-old poison." He pleaded that the "classical medicine" should be allowed to work--that is to say, liberal trade policy, convertible currencies, and sound monetary and fiscal policies. "If we reject the medicine from our systems altogether, we may just drift on from expedient to expedient and never get really fit again."[41]

The Changing Tide: The Liberal Revival. The flame of liberalism was sharply dimmed, but never fully extinguished. A tiny flicker was kept alive during the dark days of the Depression by Roosevelt's Secretary of State Cordell Hull, when he initiated the reciprocal trade agreement policy in 1934 and nurtured it into full bloom in the 1940s. After the General Agreement on Tariffs and Trade (GATT) was set up, tariffs were sharply reduced in several rounds of multilateral negotiations.

The reconversion of Keynes to his early liberal beliefs was an important factor in the liberal revival. Keynes's prestige greatly strengthened the liberal cause, and the way in which Keynes's reconversion came about demonstrated the existence of a strong liberal wing among the Keynesians. Keynes's reconversion was largely the result of extensive discussions he had with Roy Harrod, Lionel Robbins, James Meade, Marcus Fleming, and Redvers Opie, when he was working on plans for postwar economic reconstruction.[42]

The liberal resurgence went into high gear in the late 1940s and 1950s when monetary restraint and liberal policies produced economic miracles in several countries. The best known was the German economic miracle which started with the currency reform of 1948 and the simultaneous abolition of all wage, price, and exchange controls by Ludwig Erhard. When the controls, inherited from the Nazi period and continued under the military occupation, were lifted, the German economy quickly rose from the ashes of the Hitler reich.

Revisiting Early Beliefs. Revisiting early beliefs on development economics turned out to be an exciting and, on the whole, enjoyable task. I was pleased that my main thesis seemed to have stood the test of time very well. In fact, statistical material that has become available and new insights have strengthened the case.

As mentioned earlier, I came to the problems of development from the theory of international trade. My approach has been monoeconomic, as it is often called. In my opinion there is only one economics, neoclassical economics in the broad sense, including the theory of international economic policy. This body of theory is broad and flexible enough to handle the problems of the developing as well as of the developed countries. I reject the idea of duoeconomics, a separate theory for the developing countries. From the monoeconomic approach, however, it does not follow that exactly the same policy recommendations apply for all countries.

I have been critical of the view underlying much of development economics that developing countries as a group are set apart from the developed countries and are disadvantaged; that they are characterized by heavy "disguised" unemployment; that their terms of trade have an inexorable tendency to deteriorate (the Prebisch-Singer theory); that they are subject to pernicious "demonstration effects"; that private initiative and market forces can be assigned only a minor role; and that development requires "balanced growth" on a large scale and a "big push" brought about through comprehensive "programming" by the government. One of my main objections, expressed in a 1957 paper, was that this approach suffers from what I called "excessive aggregation."[43] I was then referring specifically to the Prebisch-Singer theory of the secular deterioration of developing countries' terms of trade. But it applies to the whole approach.

It is obvious that the developing countries are a very heterogeneous group, even aside from those that form the core of OPEC and float on a third of the world's crude oil reserves. In fact, even the dividing line between developing and developed countries is arbitrary. Different groupings are possible, although all of them are unavoidably somewhat arbitrary, the borderline between the groups being often a little fuzzy. I suggest the following rough classification. First are the economies in East and Southeast Asia--Korea, Malaysia, Taiwan, and Thailand, as well as Hong Kong and Singapore--that are still referred to as "less developed" but are doing quite well. These economies pursue on the whole liberal, market-oriented policies and obviously are not bothered by the handicaps and afflictions mentioned above from which all developing countries are supposed to suffer. Their success is fully explained by, and confirms, the neoclassical paradigm.

The second group includes potentially rich countries that are in financial trouble and suffer from inflation; some are on the verge of defaulting on their foreign debt. To this group belong Argentina, Brazil, Chile, Mexico, Uruguay, and Venezuela.

The outstanding example is Argentina. It is ironic that Raúl Prebisch's country fits so poorly into his scheme of things. Argentina is a potentially very rich country. Years ago Colin Clark in his pioneering study, *Conditions of Economic Progress*, predicted that Argentina would soon reach the level of the United States and Canada. This was not an unreasonable prediction. Argentina is blessed with excellent human and material resources. Its plight has nothing to do with a "crisis of capitalism." It is simply due to horrendous mismanagement that began with the first Perón regime and was continued by successive military and civilian governments.[44]

To the third group belong Bangladesh, India, and Pakistan, where a large part of the world's poor people live. And in the fourth group, sometimes called the "Fourth World," are some very poor and backward countries, mainly in Africa.

This great heterogeneity of the developing countries makes a shambles of any attempt to apply a separate body of economics, development economics, to all of them. It was, however, a great *poli-*

tical achievement, largely the work of Raúl Prebisch, to bring this disparate group under one umbrella, the caucus of the developing countries. This effective pressure group wields considerable power in the United Nations and other international bodies.

Secular Deterioration of the Terms of Trade. I begin the discussion of the various components of development economics with the Prebisch-Singer hypothesis of the secular deterioration of the developing countries' terms of trade. This was reiterated in Hans Singer's contribution to the first *Pioneers* volume and in a later paper.[45]

I can be very brief because my summary judgment in the 1957 paper that "the alleged historical facts lack proof, their explanation is faulty, the extrapolation [into the future] is reckless and the policy conclusions are irresponsible"[46] has been fully confirmed by later research. I refer especially to Robert E. Lipsey's important book, *Price and Quantity Trends in the Foreign Trade of the United States*, a study carried out with the careful attention to basic data and statistical methods that one expects in a publication of the National Bureau of Economic Research.[47]

Lipsey reaches the following conclusions:

> Two widely held beliefs regarding net barter terms of trade found no confirmation in the data for the United States. One is that there has been a substantial long-term improvement in the terms of trade of developed countries, including the United States; the other, that there has been a significant long-term deterioration in the terms of trade of primary as compared to manufacturing products. Although there have been very large swings in U.S. terms of trade since 1879, no long-run trend has emerged. The average level of U.S. terms of trade since World War II has been almost the same as before World War I.

During the Great Depression the terms of trade of developing countries deteriorated sharply because primary product prices declined much more than prices of manufactures, as they always did in depressions. The cyclical decline was then misinterpreted as a secular change. Since we now know that there has been no secular deterioration in developing countries' terms of trade, it is no longer necessary to dwell on the alleged causes (Engel's law, business monopolies and union power in the developed countries), which would be inadequate anyway, or to comment on the far-reaching policy conclusions (protectionism, leading to "balanced growth," "big push," and inflation), which must be described as ill-advised, to put it mildly.[48]

To further illustrate the futility of forecasting long-run changes in the terms of trade, I mention a school of thought that was the exact opposite of the Prebisch-Singer doctrine. It held that the terms of trade must inexorably turn against the industrial countries because of the law of diminishing returns in agriculture and in extractive industries. This theory goes back to David Ricardo and earlier writers and had a strange fascination for British economists. Alfred Marshall and J. M. Keynes greatly worried about the British terms of trade. The most extreme position was taken by no less than W. S. Jevons in his gloomy book, *The Coal Question: An Enquiry Concerning the Progress of the Nation and the Probable Exhaustion of the Coal Mines.*[49] In our time Austin Robinson has taken up the theme.[50] It hardly needs lengthy arguing that Ricardo's pessimism and Marshall's and Keynes's worries (not to mention Jevons's forebodings of disaster) have proved entirely groundless.[51]

The Demonstration Effect. Another pillar of development economics is the so-called demonstration effect, from which developing countries are supposed to suffer. I quote from my 1957 paper:

> In our era of improved communication and transportation, of high pressure advertising by means of newspapers, radios, film, etc., consumers in poor countries come into quick and intimate contact with the latest products and gadgets developed and consumed in the richer countries. They try to emulate consumption habits which are beyond their means. This reduces the propensity to save and increases the propensity to import. In the sphere of production the consequence of the demonstration effect is supposed to be that capital intensive and highly mechanized methods of production are adopted which are uneconomical for the resource pattern of the poorer countries.[52]

The demonstration effect clearly is not specifically related to the developing countries.

> All of us, even in the most advanced countries, are under pressure by high power advertising to live beyond our means. Everywhere we see and read of things we would like to have and cannot afford. Installment credit makes it easy actually to buy things which we should not buy. Some of us actually are tempted into making foolish purchases, which we later regret; but these slips are quickly corrected and no permanent harm results except if accommodating lax monetary policy leads to inflation.[53]

In the early post-World War II period exactly the same reasoning was used in Europe, especially among Keynesian economists, to explain the "permanent" dollar shortage which then was widely supposed to exist. It was, I believe, in that connection that the term "demonstration effect" was first used by James Duesenberry of Harvard University.

The theory of the demonstration effect shows an unbecoming and unjustified patronizing attitude toward the "natives" on the part of development economists from abroad and their disciples in the developing countries. They grossly underestimate the intelligence and responsiveness to price changes of even businessmen in Korea, Malaysia, and elsewhere, let alone the lowly farmers. All that has been convincingly demonstrated by Peter (Lord) Bauer in numerous writings. While discounting the significance of the demonstration effect in the private sector of the economy, I pointed out that it operates in the area of public policy, the conduct of state enterprises, and the theories that are adopted by the development economists and that underlie their advice to the governments of developing countries.

As I indicated above, when the problems of development were thrust upon the Western world during and immediately after World War II, the faith in free markets and liberal policies was at a low point. The misinterpretation of the nature of the Great Depression and the apparent successes of the totalitarian regimes had made a deep impression on many economists and intellectuals. No wonder that this gave development economics a strong, dirigist, anti-free market, anticapitalist bias.

The most pervasive and damaging example of the demonstration effect is the excessive stress on manufacturing industries and the neglect of agriculture. This has been well described by Harry Johnson in his powerful study, *Economic Policies toward Less Developed Countries*, where he wrote,

> Development plans typically steer a disproportionate share of the available . . . resources toward industry . . . Further, development policy . . . depresses [agricultural] incentives [by raising] the price of industrial inputs for agriculture [and by holding] down the prices received by agricultural producers . . . [Where] an export surplus of agricultural products [exists], it is generally deliberate policy to tax their producers heavily, [reducing] export earnings [and encouraging] the development of alternative supplies from elsewhere.[54]

Needless to add that protection of agriculture in industrial countries damages the developing countries and pushes them further into protectionism.

A striking and depressing example of the lack of confidence in the efficacy of the price mechanism is provided by the theory of the permanent dollar shortage, which was widely held in the early postwar period. It had a strange fascination for British economists. In a more sophisticated form it was embraced by two giants among economists, J. R. Hicks and D. H. Robertson.[55] The theory is based on faulty theorizing and poor judgment and has been disproved and completely discredited by subsequent developments.

The theory had, however, a strong impact on development economics. It became the theory of the "foreign exchange bottleneck." Developing countries cannot increase their export earnings, it is said, because they are faced with inelastic demand for their products; when they try to export more, the price of their exports declines, so that the value of exports remains the same or even declines.

If this were the rule it would show up in a worsening of the terms of trade. There has been no such long-run deterioration. It is perhaps possible to think of individual cases--banana republics--where something like that may have happened. Banana republics seem indeed to be the model the pessimists have in mind. If there are such cases, they should be identified. But to speak of developing-country or primary-product exporters in general is totally unrealistic.

The theory has been extended and elaborated in many ways. The most important extension probably is the so-called two-gap approach to aid and development. The importance of the two-gap approach is enhanced by the fact that its distinguished author Hollis Chenery for many years held a high position in the World Bank. Chenery and his collaborators argue in many publications that developing countries "typically," although with some notable exceptions, run into intractable bottlenecks, or gaps, which make the economy inflexible and unadjustable. These impediments are intractable in the sense that their elimination cannot be left to market forces; they require government action--in particular, foreign aid to afflicted developing countries.[56]

The two gaps are the savings-investment gap and the import-export gap. The trouble arises from the alleged fact that production functions are often rectangular. To state it in the simplest form, the two factors, capital and labor, cooperate in fixed proportions (rectangular isoquants). The capital-output ratio is assumed to be fixed. Hence, if one factor, say, labor, is in excess supply, there will be unemployment, which can be eliminated only by increasing the supply of capital through more saving, foreign aid, or capital imports. The import-export (balance of payments) gap, or bottleneck, occurs if the targeted growth rate and the necessary investment require inputs imported from abroad, which most developing countries cannot obtain by more exports because foreign demand is inelastic.

All this is, of course, in sharp contrast to the neoclassical paradigm, which postulates variable, not fixed, coefficients and elastic demand. In reply to Bruton, Chenery expresses agreement with most of Bruton's analysis, but he disagrees with the neoclassical assumption of variable coefficients and elastic demand.

In my opinion this is not a realistic model of the development process in the countries currently developing or of the early stages of development in the present industrial countries. What I find the most disturbing are the interventionist implications of the approach and the disdain of the efficacy of market forces. The authorities, both national and international, are supposed to know the appropriate or potential growth rate, the volume of investment required, the supposedly fixed capital-output ratio, and so on. This is a tall order, especially for developing countries whose statistics are notoriously deficient. Furthermore, this approach leads to protectionist conclusions. Since the usual methods of balance of payments adjustment--disinflation, devaluation of the currency, or floating--do not work, in the absence of foreign aid the only way out would be direct controls to cut down the imports of "nonessential" goods in order to make room for the imports of "essential" products. Few economists will accept that conclusion.

The apparent success of the Marshall Plan in helping the war-torn economies of Europe to recover made a deep impression on development economists. It suggested to them that foreign aid is a necessary or even a sufficient condition for rapid development. On several occasions I pointed out that this analogy is invalid, irrespective of one's view of the success of the Marshall Plan.[57] It is one thing to assist the economic reconstruction of a war-ravished industrial country; it is a much more difficult and time-consuming task to help a backward country change its way of life and modernize its economy.

Keynesian Economics and Disguised Unemployment. In my 1957 paper I pointed out that development economists eagerly embraced Keynesian economics and "sadly neglected" what I called "the most serviceable types" of neoclassical economics. These include specifically the neoclassical analysis of the infant industry argument for protection, which is, of course, directly applicable to the developing countries.[58]

The theme has been taken up by Albert Hirschman in his brilliant paper "The Rise and Decline of Development Economics" and echoed by Hans Singer.[59] Hirschman speaks (pp. 375-76) of the "inapplicability of orthodox macroeconomics in underdeveloped areas"; Keynes made the "crucial step" from "monoeconomics" to "duoeconomics." He established the "new economics" applicable to situations with unemployment, which "had instant credibility."

All this is, in my opinion, deeply flawed, confusing, and misleading. To begin with, it is not clearly stated what the orthodox macro policy is that failed in the 1930s and is not applicable to developing countries. It probably refers to the views of those who opposed the Keynesian prescription of deficit spending in a deep depression. That view was widespread in British Treasury circles in the City of London and was held by a small but influential group of conservative economists at the London School of Economics, led by F. A. Hayek, Lionel Robbins, and others. (Robbins later changed his mind.)

We have seen already that the Keynesian recommendation of deficit spending in an ongoing deflationary spiral is and was shared by many neoclassical economists such as A. C. Pigou and D. H. Robertson, including some monetarists. It did not require a new economics to make this point. For example, it was the prevailing view of Henry Simons, F. H. Knight, Jacob Viner, Lloyd Mints, and others in Chicago that without gross monetary mismanagement the Depression would not have become so deep, but that after a deflationary spiral had been allowed to develop, government deficit spending was in order, preferably through the operation of the automatic stabilizers, to inject money directly into the income stream.[60] As Milton Friedman, Herbert Stein, and others have pointed out, this climate explains why Keynes did not catch on in Chicago as he did in London.[61]

The development economists who embraced Keynesianism failed to distinguish between Keynesian economics and the economics of Keynes. Keynes himself never lost sight of the dangers of inflation. As mentioned above, one year after the publication of his *General Theory*, he urged a shift from fighting unemployment to restraining inflation. Most Keynesian economists, however, have shown little concern about inflation and have continued to urge expansionary policies throughout the post-World War II period.

In my 1957 article I had a lengthy criticism of the theory that there is widespread disguised unemployment in the developing countries, mainly but by no means exclusively in rural areas. I pointed out that the concept of disguised unemployment originated in Keynesian circles. Joan Robinson seems to have used the term the first time to designate workers who, having lost well-paid positions in industry to which their skill and training entitles them, are doing odd jobs, raking leaves or selling apples to eke out a miserable living.[62]

In a deep depression, Keynesian unemployment, open or disguised, is easily curable by government deficit spending. This is, of course, not applicable in developing countries. The more sophisticated proponents of this theory, W. A. Lewis, Ragnar Nurkse, and P. N. Rosenstein-Rodan, recognize this, but they insist that at least in the more densely populated countries of Asia and Africa disguised unemployment is heavy in rural areas.[63] That means that a fraction of the labor force--25 percent is often mentioned--could be withdrawn without a loss of output. In other words, the marginal productivity of labor is zero or even negative.

Although this situation is not inconceivable in isolated cases, I have strong doubts that it ever existed anywhere on a considerable scale. I have pointed out that the idea of disguised unemployment is associated with the proposition that the capital-labor ratio is fixed; in other words, that the isoquants in the production function are rectangular (or at least angular). I have also demonstrated that the theory of disguised unemployment can be regarded as an extreme and unrealistic version of the theory that in many developing countries, and perhaps in some developed countries too, the quality of labor in agriculture is lower than that in industry; in other words, that agriculture is a backward sector of the economy.

There surely is some truth in this assertion. The process of development will lift backward areas to higher levels though investment in material capital as well as in human capital. There is, of course, much room for public policies to speed up the process of development--for example, by providing better infrastructure and better education.[64] But to speak of disguised unemployment because workers will produce more when better tools, machines, and education become available is totally inappropriate. In that case, everyone is a disguised unemployed, because in the future we will all produce more with better methods of production, better tools, and better education.

Naturally I was very pleased when I discovered that Jacob Viner and Theodore W. Schultz strongly reject the theory. In a well-known article,

"Some Reflections on the Concept of 'Disguised Unemployment,'"[65] Viner has this to say:

> As far as agriculture is concerned, I find it impossible to conceive of a farm of any kind on which, other factors of production being held constant in quantity, and even in form as well, it would not be possible, by known methods to obtain some addition to the crop by using additional labor in more careful selection and planting of the seed, more intensive weeding, cultivation, thinning, and mulching, more painstaking harvesting, gleaning and cleaning of the crop.
>
> I am not aware that anyone has ever given a convincing illustration of a technical coefficient, which is "fixed" in any valid economic sense. [Speaking of the steel industry, he says:] If iron ore, or coal, were as expensive per ton as gold I am sure that the steel industry would find ways of appreciably reducing the amounts of iron ore, or of coal, it uses to produce a ton of steel of given specific character, even though the chemical constituency of the steel were invariant, and, moreover, it would readily find ways of changing the chemical constituency of a ton of "steel" without reducing its suitability for its ordinary uses, and this not only in the long run but in the very short run.

Nobel Laureate Theodore Schultz is just as emphatic as Viner in rejecting the theory of widespread disguised unemployment. He is doubly qualified as a renowned expert on world agriculture and for his seminal work on human capital. He quotes approvingly Viner's statement concerning agriculture cited above, and he sums up his views as follows:

> The conclusion with respect to the doctrine that a part of the labor working in agriculture in poor countries has a marginal productivity of zero is that it is a false doctrine. It has roots that make it suspect. It rests on shaky theoretical presumptions. It fails to win any support when put to a critical test in analyzing effects upon agricultural production of the deaths in the agricultural labor force caused by the influenza epidemic of 1918--1919 in India.[66]

Trade Policies for Developing Countries. I always took it for granted that neoclassical trade theory, as developed by Viner, Heckscher, Ohlin, Meade, Samuelson, or myself is applicable for both developing and developed countries. It never occurred to me that a different theory applies to developing countries. The thesis of duoeconomics came later.

Traditional trade theory includes, of course, the theory of trade policy, which is a branch of welfare economics. Most trade theorists lean toward free trade, but all of them realize that there exist exceptions to the free trade rule. In view of the great diversity of developing countries, the theory of duoeconomics makes no sense. Why should a different theory apply to Argentina and Australia, or to Brazil, Portugal, and Spain?

The classical theory of comparative cost in its modern form presents a greatly simplified model of general equilibrium which lends itself to diagrammatic analysis. It has proved a versatile tool of analysis. Much has been made of the fact that the basic model of comparative cost, like most general equilibrium theories, is static and assumes perfect competition. Development problems, however, are essentially dynamic in nature; therefore, it is argued, a static theory is of no use. But the argument is fallacious. Although the simplest theory of demand and supply is static, nobody would doubt that it is applicable to developing countries.

In my Cairo lectures, I argued at some length that the static nature of trade theory does not deprive it of usefulness in exploring dynamic processes.[67] There is, after all, the method of comparative statics. True, for certain problems, such as the short-run business cycle, comparative statics is of little use. But the trade problem is different. Static gains from trade along the lines of comparative cost enable a country to save and invest more. Furthermore, it attracts capital from abroad and fosters the importation of technical know-how. This means that the static production possibility curve is pushed out. I recalled that classical and neoclassical theorists were fully aware of the dynamic effects of trade. John Stuart Mill, for example, argued at great length that in addition to the direct (static) beneficial effects of an international division of labor according to comparative cost, trade has powerful indirect (dynamic) effects by "placing human beings in contact with persons dissimilar to themselves, and with modes of thought and action unlike those with which they are familiar." This is "principally applicable to [countries in] an early stage of industrial advancement," that is, to what we now call developing countries. According to Mill, "indirect benefits of commerce, economical and moral, [are] still greater than the direct."[68]

I now come to the main question: what is the proper trade policy for developing countries? Most developing countries pursue highly protectionist policies, which are often called--euphemistically-a policy of import substitution, especially with respect to manufacturing industries.

In many cases the results have not been good. The economic landscape in some developing countries is littered and disfigured by white elephants, modern factories unsuited to their productive resources, which either stand idle or operate inefficiently at exorbitant costs, with protection from imports or direct subsidies at the expense of the taxpayer and the traditional export sector--mainly agriculture. The demonstration effect at its worst. Tanzania is a sad example.

As mentioned, most classical and neoclassical trade theorists lean toward free trade but realize that there are exceptions to the strict free trade rule. Some of the arguments for tariffs are discussed below, along with their possible applications to developing countries.

Terms of Trade Argument for Protection. The terms of trade argument comes in two different versions, a static and a dynamic one--the latter applicable specifically to developing countries. The static version, also called the optimum tariff theory, is beloved by trade theorists because it lends itself to elegant mathematical and diagrammatic analysis. It states that any country or group of countries that is confronted with foreign demand for its products with an elasticity of less than infinite can improve its position by imposing restrictions on imports or exports, a duty whose height depends on the elasticity of foreign demand. In other words, any country that, unlike the individual wheat or dairy farmer, is not confronted with infinitely elastic demand for all its products wields some monopoly power which it can exploit in a variety of ways.

The theory has been elaborated in many different ways. But it is not necessary to go into details, for it seems clear that there exists not a single developing country that has any control over its terms of trade. This is more true now than it was earlier because of the tremendous growth of the world economy and a world trade since World War II and the emergence of new industrial centers in many parts of the world, including the Third World and the communist bloc.

This development has made the world economy more competitive than it was and has also made obsolete a theory that was popular among the development economists in the early post-World War II period. This theory holds that the developing countries are confronted by monopolistic markets in their purchases of manufactured goods, and that prices are kept above competitive levels by international private cartels or simply by the absence of price competition among producers operating in imperfect markets.[69] In the early years after World War II, U.S. industry had a quasi monopoly because Europe, Japan, and the communist countries lay prostrate from the ravages of war. But the world economy has completely changed since then. Moreover, even if it were true that developing countries are victims of monopolistic exploitation on the import side, it would not follow that their proper response should be protectionist measures. On the contrary, this response would make things worse.

In the past, many attempts have been made to organize international cartels and collective restriction schemes for rubber, tin, coffee, and the like. All these attempts have failed. The only successful one--for a time--was OPEC. But even mighty OPEC is now in disarray. The mills of markets grind slowly, but powerfully. After some delay, OPEC's monopoly power was undermined by market forces when the high price of crude oil stimulated conservation of energy and induced a successful search for oil outside the OPEC countries.

To sum up, the static terms of trade argument for protection simply does not hold any more, if it ever did. The dynamic version is based on the Prebisch-Singer thesis that the terms of trade of developing countries have a secular tendency to deteriorate. If this were true it could be argued that protection of manufacturing simply speeds up an unavoidable development. But since the Prebisch-Singer thesis is invalid, it cannot supply an argument for protection.

The arguments for protection that appear relevant for developing countries are the infant industry, unemployment, and external economies arguments. These arguments are indeed interrelated.

Infant Industry Argument. In what might be called a synthetic picture of views widely held by supporters of infant industry protection and development economists, I will try to make the case for protection as reasonable as I can.

Unemployment is in the center of the stage. The most reasonable interpretation of the alleged existence of heavy rural unemployment in developing countries is not that the marginal productivity of labor is literally zero, but that the efficiency of labor in agriculture is low, perhaps very low, compared with that of agricultural labor in more highly developed countries and also with that of labor in industry in the developing countries themselves. The lack of an efficient, educated, disciplined labor force is, of course, a great handicap for the development of industries. But inefficient labor can be trained on the job. This is, after all, what happens in the process of development. The crucial question then is, can and should the process be speeded up by providing support to industry through restraints on imports or in some other way-- or should it be left to market forces?

I present two answers to this question: first, the view of the proponents of infant industry protection which is shared by many development economists and, second, that of classical free traders.

Infant industry protection is, to use modern terminology, largely investment in human capital. To make it possible for nascent industries to provide on-the-job training for inefficient and therefore expensive labor, they need "temporary protection" from foreign competitors who are not handicapped by inefficient labor. This applies not only to workers, but also to managers and possibly fledgling entrepreneurs.

Free trade economists, of course, argue that free markets will take care of the problem. Peter Bauer recently restated his view in a powerful article, "Myths of Subsidized Manufacturing."[70] He flatly calls the infant industry argument invalid. "Business people are prepared to finance the early stages of an activity they expect will become viable. Indeed, they routinely do so in manufacturing, trade, transport, and commercial agriculture alike."

For a different view, I first quote a free trader, John Stuart Mill, who says in his *Principles*: "But it cannot be expected that individuals at their own risk, or rather to their certain loss, will introduce a new manufacture, and bear the burdens of carrying it on until the producers have been educated to the [efficient] level."[71]

Mill did not say why he thought that this was not to be expected. An attempt to give a precise reason came much later. What I have in mind is Paul N. Rosenstein-Rodan's theory of the "inappropriability" of labor skills. He explains it this way: "Under a system of slavery it paid the owner to invest in training a slave because the increase in skills would benefit the investor. When slavery was abolished, a worker trained could contract with an outside employer who did not have to bear the cost of his training. Whoever invested in the training of the worker would run the risk of not being able to appropriate the benefit of increased productivity. The training and education of workers under competitive market conditions would therefore be below optimum. This is a widespread phenomenon." In other words, in a free country "there are not mortgages on workers."[72]

There may be some truth in all this, but it surely requires further analysis. The theory must assume that there are institutional rigidities and distortions. For in a fully competitive economy, where factors of production are remunerated according to their marginal productivity, untrained labor would receive a correspondingly low wage. That would mean that the cost of training would be borne by the trainees, not by the trainers. Hence there would be no presumption of underinvestment. Thus the Rosenstein-Rodan effect would not materialize.

True, it can be argued that in many developing countries, just as in industrial countries, wages have become rigid, union power has increased, and government policies have fostered this development through welfare measures, minimum wages, and so forth. Such policies, which in some industrial countries took fifty years or longer to develop, were adopted in some developing countries in a hurry.

But this does not justify import restrictions. In fact, such restrictions are a poor second or third choice. The first choice is clearly to change the policies that cause the rigidities and distortions. The theory can and has been elaborated in many different ways. For example, Robert Lipsey has suggested to me that Gary Becker's distinction between general and specific training can be usefully applied. Becker defines the two types of training as follows:

> General training is useful in many firms besides those providing it: . . . firms would provide general training only if they did not have to pay any of the costs. Persons receiving general training would be willing to pay these costs since training raises their future wages. Hence it is the trainees, not the firms, who would bear the cost of general training and benefit from the return . . . Completely specific training can be defined as training that has no effect on the productivity of trainees that would be useful in other firms . . . If all training were completely specific, the wage that an employee could get elsewhere would be independent of the amount of training he had received . . . The wage paid by firms would also be independent of training. If so, firms would have to pay training costs, for no rational employee would pay for training that did not benefit him. Firms would collect the returns from such training in the form of larger profits resulting from higher productivity.[73]

The general conclusion to be drawn from this analysis would seem to be that a good deal of the cost of on-the-job training can be left to competitive markets, but there surely is a case for public expenditure on education to foster general training.

External Economies and Diseconomies. The problem of external economies plays a great role in development economics.[74] The concept of external economies was first introduced by Alfred Marshall in his *Principles*. It can be defined as influences that flow from the expansion or contraction of one firm or industry to other firms or industries, and that for one reason or another are insufficiently acknowledged by the market or not acknowledged at all--nonmarket interactions for short. Neoclassical writers, for example Jacob Viner, distinguish between technological and pecuniary external economies.

It is easier to think of examples of technological diseconomies than of technological economies. This has become clear in our age of environmental concern. Pollution of air and water are real problems that are dealt with by administrative and legislative actions. Development economists tend to neglect diseconomies when they assert that external economies are more important in industry than in agriculture. This is hardly true of diseconomies.

Tibor Scitovsky defines pecuniary external economies as follows: If industry A invests and expands, it is bound to have pecuniary repercussions on any or all of the following industries: (1) on industries which produce intermediate goods (such as machinery and materials) used by A; (2) through cheapening of A's own products, on industries which use A's products as intermediate goods; (3) on industries on whose products factors used in A spend their additional income; (4) on industries whose product is complementary in use to the product of A.[75] To repeat, according to neoclassical writers these interindustry reactions are not really external; they are reflected in price changes, and market participants take them into account. Development economists such as Rosenstein-Rodan, Scitovsky, and others, however, assert that in the "dynamic context of development these pecuniary external economies become real." Scitovsky puts it this way:

> In the market economy prices are the signalling device that informs each person of other people's economic decision and thus guides production and investment decisions. Market prices, however, reflect the economic situation as it is and not as it will be. For this reason they are more useful for coordinating current production decisions . . . than . . . for coordinating investment decisions, which have delayed effects . . . and should be governed . . . by what the future economic situation is expected to be . . . Hence the belief that there is need either for centralized investment planning or some additional communication systems to supplement the pricing system as a signalling device.[76]

In my opinion this analysis misunderstands the working of a dynamic decentralized market economy. It ignores the role of the entrepreneur and underestimates his capability to foresee the consequences of his action. Of course, any investment carries a certain amount of risk. The larger the investment and the more durable the equipment, the larger the risk. But any adaptation to a change carries uncertainty and risk. The distinction between current production and investment is one of degree. It is therefore misleading to say that the equilibrium theory applies only to the former.

Rosenstein-Rodan and Scitovsky have been quite consistent in their policy conclusion. As Scitovsky put it, to capture the alleged pecuniary external economies, of which the private producers are supposed to be unaware, simultaneous expansion of all industries is necessary. Only complete integration of all industries can do the job.[77] This amounts to a plea for comprehensive central planning.

Using different language, Rosenstein-Rodan reaches the same conclusions. He pleads for a "big push," that is to say, simultaneous expansion of many industries. For good measure he also urges a large investment of social overhead capital by the government to provide an elaborate infrastructure and calls for government programming of the process of economic development; this too amounts to a call for central planning.

Providing a good infrastructure--education, law and order, a good monetary system, and so on--is, of course, vitally important for economic development, and in many developing countries these public services badly need improvement. But when the call for massive expenditures on infrastructure comes on top of a big push to expand many industries through government actions at public expense, the whole program becomes a recipe for economic disaster. It would greatly overburden the weak administrative capabilities of developing countries, overtax their economies, and open the floodgate for corrosive inflation.

The best policy would be to let free markets, in other words, capitalism, do what they do best--develop new industries. Direct investment by foreign corporations should be encouraged, because they provide technological know-how and on-the-job training. Unfortunately, one often finds that foreign companies are denied permission to set up branches in developing countries because this would make life harder for the protected state enterprises. This is development policy at its worst.

As indicated earlier, these theories were developed after the Great Depression and during or immediately after World War II, when faith in free markets was at an all-time low and the prestige of the two totalitarian regimes, Nazism and Bolshevism, and their alleged economic successes were at their zenith. Since then the situation has completely changed. We are now in a position to compare the performance of market economies and centrally planned ones: the German Democratic Republic and the Federal Republic of Germany, the Democratic Republic of Korea and the Republic of Korea, Austria and Czechoslovakia, Greece and Yugoslavia, pairs of countries with similar backgrounds that in the past have enjoyed the same standard of living. Other examples are Taiwan and China, Malaysia and Thailand versus Burma. There can be no doubt that market economies have performed better.

There surely are cases where judicious, temporary restrictions on imports can be justified to help infant industries. For markets are often imperfect, and private investors make mistakes. But market failures and mistakes in the private sector usually correct themselves, possibly in a recession. The business cycle is still with us. In the past fifty years enormous technological advances in transport, communications, and information have made markets much more competitive than they were at the time when new development theories emerged.

Faulty government policies, however, are hard to change. When controls do not yield the intended results, the controls are not abolished but tightened; when the response to a policy of subsidies is not what was expected, the subsidies are raised but the policy continues and infant industry protection is likely to be extended to senility. As Deepak Lal, in his hard-hitting classic, wisely remarked: "Imperfect markets [are] superior to imperfect planning."[78]

Exchange Rate Policies for Developing Countries. Many developing countries suffer from high rates of inflation. If that is the case they should let their currencies float to minimize the adverse effects of inflation on their foreign trade. They should avoid import restrictions for balance of payments reasons, and avoid exchange controls like the plague.

The best policy would be to curb inflation sufficiently to make it possible to peg the currency to a suitable foreign currency, to special drawing rights (SDRs), or some other basket of currencies--but of course they must make sure that the currency is fully convertible into the currency or currencies to which it is pegged without the use of controls.[79] According to statistics of the International Monetary Fund, thirty-four countries peg their currencies to the dollar, thirteen African countries peg to the French franc, eleven to SDRs, and so on.

Proposals have been made, especially in Latin America, to organize regional monetary unions, analogous to the European Monetary System (EMS). In my opinion, this is not a good approach. A monetary union

212 Trade and Development Policy

requires very tight coordination of monetary policy, which is almost impossible to achieve by sovereign states. The example of the EMS is misleading for two reasons: first, the EMS is, after all, backed up by the European Community; second, despite the impressive facade, the EMS has not been an outstanding success from the economic point of view.

Excessive Pessimism. Most of the development literature, both private and official, is imbued with deep pessimism about past performances and prospects for the future of the developing countries. To some extent this pessimism may be regarded as a negotiating stance; for much of the literature, even the unofficial literature, is meant to support demands of the poor countries for foreign aid and other concessions from the rich industrial countries. Whatever the motive, in my opinion, the pessimism is unjustified.

To set the record straight, I can do no better than to quote the world's foremost authority on economic growth, Simon Kuznets. In his magisterial lecture, "Two Centuries of Economic Growth: Reflections on U.S. Experience," Kuznets summed up the results of the enormous amount of research that he and others have done in recent years:

> Even in this recent twenty-five year period of greater strain and danger, the growth in peacetime product per capita in the United States was still at a high rate; and in the rest of the World, developed *and less developed* (but excepting the few countries and periods marked by internal conflicts and political breakdown), material returns have grown, per capita, at a rate higher than ever observed in the past.[80]

In his paper, "Aspects of Post-World War II Growth in Less Developed Countries," Kuznets had this to say:

> For the LDCs as a group, the United Nations has estimated annual growth of total and per capita GDP (gross domestic product at constant factor prices) from 1950 to 1972. The growth rate of per capita product . . . for the twenty-two years was 2.61 percent per year . . . Such growth rates are quite high in the long-term historical perspective of both the LDCs and the current DCS. These high growth rates are largely a recent phenomenon, the result of the post-World War II period of comparative liberalism and liberalization.[81]

Kuznets is, of course, fully aware of the dangers of using broad aggregate measures of growth for the developing countries as a group, given the great diversity among them. He discusses and carefully evaluates possible biases in the procedures. But after everything has been said and done, he stands by the basic soundness of his findings and is puzzled that, despite the "impressively high" growth rates "in the per capita product of LDCs over almost a quarter of a century," the general sentiment in the developing countries is one of dissatisfaction and gloom that "seems to ignore the growth achievements." He conjectures, and gives ample reasons for this conjecture, that "a rise in expectations has produced a negative reaction to economic attainments which otherwise might have elicited litanies of praise for economic miracles."[82]

I suggest three factors that have aroused excessively optimistic expectations. The first one is that the early economic success of the USSR--rapid industrialization and growth, and immunity from the depression that engulfed the West in the 1930s--made a deep impression in the developing as well as in the developed countries. It engendered the belief that through comprehensive central planning governments have it in their power to lift backward countries, in one great leap, to a higher level of development. It took a long time for the persistent conspicuous lag of the centrally planned countries behind the market economies to shake confidence in the superiority of central planning. This issue cannot be further discussed here. I confine myself to asking a simple question: How is one to explain the glaring gap in the per capita GNP and standard of living between such pairs of countries as the German Democratic Republic and the Federal Republic of Germany, Austria and Czechoslovakia, Yugoslavia and Greece--pairs of countries that enjoyed about the same standard of living in the precommunist era?

The second factor to arouse overoptimistic expectations was the apparent success of the Marshall Plan in speeding European recovery after the war. We have seen that the analogy of the Marshall Plan and foreign aid to developing countries is invalid.

The third factor was the great success of the oil cartel in lifting the standard of living in most member countries of OPEC. But mighty OPEC countries have recently fallen on hard times. The high price of crude oil has stimulated conservation of energy and the search for alternative sources. The demand for OPEC oil has sharply declined. The mills of the market often grind slowly, but they always grind powerfully.

Gottfried Haberler
As Development Economist,
by W. Max Corden[83]

Gottfried Haberler is not a development economist as this term is usually understood. He has not written about particular developing countries--that is, currently low-income countries--nor has he focused primarily on their specific problems. But his work is actually highly relevant, both to the analysis of their own policies and to the impact of world macroeconomic developments on these countries. Indirectly, his contributions to trade theory have probably had a greater effect on their policies and the analysis of their policies than the work of some of the development pioneers presented in the first volume in this series.

Above all, Haberler is one of the great figures of international economics in this century.[84] He played a crucial role in the construction of the modern pure theory of international trade by introducing the opportunity cost approach (which replaced the confusing real cost approach espoused particularly by Viner). This new approach clarified the nature of the gains from trade and the law of comparative advantage and went beyond Ricardo's special constant cost case. With further contributions from Lerner, Leontief, and Samuelson (on the gains from trade), and then from Samuelson (incorporating the great Heckscher-Ohlin insights), the foundations of modern pure trade theory were laid. In addition, Haberler's classic textbook, *The Theory of International Trade*, written in his early thirties, has laid the foundation for much later work. It sorted out (and usually demolished) many arguments for protection. It foreshadowed various models and ideas that became prominent later, such as the specific factors model of trade theory.

Most important for the analysis of economic policy of developing countries is his modestly titled but actually quite revolutionary article, "Some Problems in the Pure Theory of International Trade,"[85] which initiated the theory of domestic distortions. In this article he analyzed the implications for the gains from trade of a number of domestic distortions, notably externalities and factor price rigidities. Perhaps his main contribution was to show that immobilities of factors of production (factor specificity being an extreme case) do not affect the case for free trade, but that factor price rigidities do. This pioneering work was subsequently expanded to the analysis of protection and to the consideration of various other cases by Meade, Johnson, Bhagwati, and others. It has been very influential and, in effect, led to a reconstruction of the theory of trade policy.

Gottfried Haberler made his international reputation with *Prosperity and Depression*, first published in 1937 and revised four times after that, the last in 1964.[86] This book critically analyzed numerous pre-Keynesian trade cycle theories, displaying an unsurpassed mastery of the extensive literature in this field and an ability to consolidate and integrate. The later editions took account of Keynes's contributions. Above all, this book showed historical perspective and detachment, something for which Keynes and his followers were not noted. It also foreshadowed numerous ideas that became more prominent later. The book was a tour de force and an immediate success, receiving enthusiastic reviews. Subsequently Haberler has written extensively, but in a less integrative fashion, on domestic and international macroeconomic issues, particularly on the international monetary system and (skeptically) on various reform proposals.

His paper here speaks for itself. It is utterly clear, written in Haberler's usual simple, unpretentious style. It certainly does not require summarizing. What comes through is his historical sense, his constant awareness of the contributions of earlier scholars, and his breadth of approach. A good part of it might be regarded as rather negative, because he reviews his criticisms over the years of a whole range of questionable arguments that were temporarily fashionable. For this reason I have drawn attention to his important positive contributions. In my view he has been consistently correct, one reason being that his arguments are always carefully qualified, a characteristic to which I shall return. Many of the criticisms he made seem obvious today, but it is worth noting that Haberler was right *at the time*, not afterwards. As a discussant of his paper I suffer from the serious disability that I agree with him almost entirely and know of no way of saying better what he has already said so straightforwardly. No doubt criticisms can be made from points of view with which I have little sympathy. To me it seems hard for a reasonable person to disagree.

Something must be said about Haberler's style or approach. It does not appeal to those who like drama or flamboyance. Some might argue that if ideas are to make an impact they must be stated in extreme form. Haberler, however, is too scholarly, has too much knowledge of and respect for the contributions of scholars of earlier times, and is too aware of the qualifications to most simple propositions to engage in the sort of bold generalizations or statements, and spurious claims to originality, which are often found effective for maximum impact.

Is he a constructionist or a skeptic? Obviously, he is a constructionist about the uses of the neoclassical model. He uses it continuously, and he shows, for example, that static models are useful even in a dynamic world and that, in any case, the theory does not ignore dynamics. (Quite early, in his well-known *Survey of International Trade Theory*,[87] however, he called for improvements in a dynamic direction, a call that has, in fact, been heeded by subsequent contributors to trade theory.) He is a constructionist when he refutes silly arguments against trade theory, which take simple heuristic models (such as Samuelson's factor price equalization model) literally and criticize trade theory because one cannot observe results that appear to follow from very simple models. With his continual and sensible use of neoclassical theory he is indeed an archconstructionist. But Haberler is, of course, also a skeptic, not only about the numerous unsound generalizations and confused arguments to which he refers in his paper, but also about more recent extreme arguments on the neoclassical side, namely (as I have mentioned) the theory of rational expectations.

Is Haberler a utopian or a pedant? He is definitely not a pedant. Indeed, pedantry irritates him, and he has never been fond of excessive formal theorizing (note his skeptical references to the elaborations of the terms of trade argument for protection). At the same time, his style is certainly nonutopian. He is too much of a skeptic and too judicious. But, in a sense, he *is* a utopian, while recognizing the short-term costs that may be involved in getting to Utopia. He does believe that a system of free markets and free trade (subject, I need hardly add, to some qualifications) is the most efficient way of organizing an economy, and he has consistently advocated moving in that direction. Although he does not suggest that Utopia would result, he has no doubt that great improvements could, in many cases, be brought about by moving in that direction. And, in a manner of speaking, the Utopias--or at least the role models--do exist, though never, of course, perfect.

In referring to Argentina, Haberler used the phrase "horrendous mismanagement." No doubt this could be used about the economic policies of many other countries, although Argentina may have given the world some of the most dramatic examples. Indeed, in many countries at many times there is "horrendous mismanagement," and economists like Haberler spend their time preaching against it and hoping to improve things with their preaching. In a sense, we are all management consultants, often not too successful on our advocacy, but always optimistic that we can do some good, this being a particular form of utopianism. But this raises the thought that there is more in heaven and earth than horrendous or wise management. There are larger issues on which Haberler has not touched but which are relevant to the issues he discusses.

To some extent, politicians and political behavior are endogenous, reacting to pressure groups and reflecting deep-seated historical attitudes. Thus, a belief in planning and regulating when there are economic problems, and in restricting imports when a local industry is in trouble, comes naturally to people all over the world. The extent of these beliefs depends, among other things, on collective memories of earlier events, especially crises, as well as on ideologies that may have originated far back in history. Politicians who engage in horrendous mismanagement rarely see themselves as free agents, and the question is to what extent economists can actually affect events by clarifying issues and explaining consequences. Clearly, the varying impact of economic advice and preaching and the explanation of why horrendous policies were actually followed are important matters for study but somewhat outside the tradition in which Haberler has been writing.

Gottfried Haberler has been a "liberal" economist--defined in the continental European sense--all his life. He has believed in free markets and free trade and has been unsympathetic to interventionist policies. For many years, notably in the late 1930s, these views were not in fashion. After World War II they came back into fashion in Germany and to some extent in the United States, but they were quite out of tune with the conventional wisdom of the new field of development economics. In the 1970s the advantages of the market system, the need for liberalization, and an awareness of the excessive costs of import substitution in developing countries came to be widely, though not universally, accepted by students of developing countries and practitioners of development economics. I need not go into details here, since this is so well known. Various writings, such as those by Ian Little, Tibor Scitovsky, and Maurice Scott,[88] played a role, but possibly even more important were the success stories of the outward-looking newly industrializing economies, notably Korea and Taiwan. In effect, Haberler was a precursor, who kept the free market or liberalization flame alight. Now, when one rereads him, one finds much that is obvious, quite moderate, and close to the mainstream. In assessing him, one should assess the whole of this school of thought and its battles with the protectionists.

Notes

1. In "Reflections on the U.S. Trade Deficit and the Floating Dollar." *Contemporary Economic Problems*, William Fellner, Project Director. (Washington, D.C.: American Enterprise Institute, 1978), pp. 215-222.

2. Paul W. McCracken, "The Dollar and Economic Growth," *Wall Street Journal*, January 26, 1978. On the basis of an essentially similar type of reasoning Edward Bernstein, focusing on the balance of goods and services and GNP rather than on trade and employment, reached the conclusion that the real GNP growth (and therefore employment) has been significantly reduced by the deterioration of the balance of payments.

3. See, for example, William Fellner, ed., *Contemporary Economic Problems 1976* (Washington, D.C.: American Enterprise Institute, 1976), pp. 255-272, and William Fellner, ed., *Contemporary Economic Problems 1977* (Washington, D.C.: American Enterprise Institute, 1977), p. 277.

4. I abstract here from possible foreign reaction to such a policy.

5. For an excellent general discussion of the problem of the relation between national stability and growth on the one hand and the degree of openness (degree of "international interdependence") on the other hand, see Richard Blackhurst, Nicolas Marian, and Jan Tumlir, Trade Liberalization, Protectionism, and Interdependence" *GATT Studies in International Trade*, no. 5 (Geneva, 1977), pp. 34-38.

6. It is true, however, that with rigid wages any expansion of real GNP whether resulting from domestic factors or from the foreign sector, requires an accommodating monetary expansion.

7. See, for example, Nicholas Kaldor, "Conflicts in National Economic Objectives," *Economic Journal*, vol. 81 (March 1971), pp. 1-16. Kaldor advocated export-led growth through devaluation or floating which he contrasts with consumption-led growth stimulated by domestic fiscal-monetary measures. Similarly, the so-called Scandinavian model of inflation, which enjoys much popularity on the European continent, is based on the alleged backwardness of the nontraded-goods sector. (See, for example, Helmut Frisch, "Inflation Theory 1963-1975: A 'Second Generation' Survey," *Journal of Economic Literature*, vol. 15, no. 4 [December 1977], p. 1305ff.)

8. Okun has spoken of a new variant of the wage-price spiral as follows: "A big wage hike is followed by a major price increase and then by a joint pilgrimage of business and labor executives to Washington to demand that the government stop foreign sellers from increasing their share of the American market" (see Arthur M. Okun, "The Great Stagflation Swamp," *Challenge*, vol.

20 [November-December 1977], p. 9).

9. See the article "Anti-Dumping Measure Cuts into Foreign-Steel Flows: Domestic Prices Firming," in the *Wall Street Journal*, February 23, 1978. According to news reports the American move was not unwelcome in Brussels because it made it easier for the Commission of the European Community to institute similar protectionist measures.

10. The farmer strike need not be taken very seriously. While the government subsidizes and finances strikes of industrial workers by generous welfare payments, food stamps, and unemployment benefits for workers idled by strikes (including, in some states, the striking workers themselves), we have not yet reached the stage where striking (that is, nonproducing) farmers can apply for welfare and unemployment benefits.

11. See the above mentioned GATT report in regard to all this.

12. Irving B. Kravis in *The Technology Factor in International Trade*, Raymond Vernon, ed. (New York: National Bureau of Economic Research, 1970), p. 289. Other examples can be found in Irving B. Kravis and Robert E. Lipsey's massive monograph *Price Competitiveness in World Trade* (New York: National Bureau of Economic Research, 1971). See also H. G. Grubel and P. J. Lloyd, *Intra-Industry Trade* (New York: Halsted, 1975), and the GATT Report, *Trade Liberalization, Protectionism, and Interdependence* for an evaluation of the phenomenon of intra-industry trade.

13. From *The Political Economy of International Trade*, Ronald W. Jones and Anne O. Krueger, editors, (Oxford, Basil Blackwell, 1990), pp. 25-30.

14. "Liberal and Illiberal Trade Policy: The Messy World of the Second Best," in Wietze Eizensa, E. Frans Limburg and Jacques J. Polak (eds.), *The Quest for National and Global Economic Stability*, The Netherlands: Kluwer Academic Publishers and Cambridge, Mass.: MIT Press, 1988, and the "Introduction" in Gottfried Haberler (ed.), *International Trade and Economic Development*, San Francisco, Calif.: International Center for Economic Growth, 1988.

15. Robert E. Baldwin, "The Case Against Infant Industry Tariff Protection," *Journal of Political Economy*, May-June 1969, 77, pp. 295-305, gives a masterly criticism of different versions from Alexander Hamilton and Friedrich List to Gunnary Myrdal and Paul Rosenstein-Rodan.

16. I list some publications which I have found especially useful. Gene M. Grossman and J. David Richardson, "Strategic Trade Policy: A Survey of Issues and Early Analysis," *Special Papers in International Economics*, No. 15, (Princeton, NJ: Princeton University Press, 1985). Paul R. Krugman, "Strategic Sectors and International Competition" in Robert M. Stern (ed.), *US Trade Policies in a Changing World Economy*, (Cambridge, Mass.: MIT Press, 1987). Elhanan Helpman and Paul R. Krugman, Market Structure and Foreign Trade: Increasing Returns, Imperfect Competition, and the International

Economy, (Cambridge, Mass.: MIT Press, 1985). Paul R. Krugman (ed.), *Strategic Trade Policy and the New International Economics*, (Cambridge, Mass.: MIT Press, 1986). This last is a collection of the most important papers of the new trade theory with a critical analysis by Gene M. Grossman, "Strategic Export Promotion: A Critique," pp.47-68.

17. Paul R. Krugman, "Is Free Trade Passé?," *Journal of Economic Perspectives*, 1987, 1(2), pp. 131-44.

18. See Paul Krugman, "Increasing Returns, Monopolistic Competition, and International Trade," in *Journal of International Economics*, 1979, 9(4), pp. 469-79.

19. See James A. Brander and Barbara J. Spencer, "Export Subsidies and International Market Share Rivalry," *Journal of International Economics*, 1985, 18(1), pp. 83-100.

20. Traditional trade theorists, too, have put forward political economy arguments for free trade. See, for example, Robert E. Baldwin, "The Political Economy of Protectionism," in *Import Competition and Response*, J. N. Bhagwati (ed.), (Chicago, Ill.: University of Chicago Press, 1982).

21. Robert E. Baldwin, "The Case against Infant Industry Protection," *Journal of Political Economy*, May-June 1969, 77, pp. 295-305.

22. Reprinted from "Liberal and Illiberal Development Policy," *Pioneers in Development: Second Series*. Gerald M. Meier, ed. (Oxford: Oxford University Press, 1987) pp. 51-83.

23. Gunnar Myrdal, *Development and Underdevelopment*, 50th Anniversary Commemoration Lectures (Cairo: National Bank of Egypt, 1959), p. 29.

24. Gunnar Myrdal, *An International Economy* (New York: Harper, 1956), p. 2.

25. Alexander Hamilton is also claimed as an early practitioner of industrial policy.

26. See Gerald M. Meier's masterly introduction, "The Formative Period," in *Pioneers in Development*, Gerald M. Meier and Dudley Seers, eds. (New York: Oxford University Press, 1984), p. 5.

27. "Five Stages in My Thinking on Development," in Meier and Seers, *Pioneers in Development*.

28. Hourly wage rates, nominal and real, did not change much, but real annual earnings increased sharply because unemployment disappeared and the work week returned to its normal length. The situation changed two or three years later when rearmament hit its full stride and price controls clouded the picture. For details, see Gerhard Bry (assisted by Charlotte Boschan), *Wages in Germany, 1871-1945* (Princeton, N.J.: Princeton University Press, 1960).

The Nazis' economic successes did not go unnoticed in the Third World. Hitler's economic wizard, Hjamar Schacht, who was acquitted by the Nuremberg tribunal of war crimes, was after the war retained as a consultant by some developing countries. Interestingly, his advice proved to be too conservative for the governments that consulted him.

29. This prestige was by no means accorded only by outright fellow travelers and Soviet sympathizers.

30. The title of a famous book by Axel Leijonhufvud, *On Keynesian Economics and the Economics of Keynes: A Study of Monetary Theory* (New York: Oxford University Press, 1968). See also T. W. Hutchinson, *Keynes Versus the Keynesians...?* Hobart Paperback no. 11 (London: Institute of Economic Affairs, 1977).

31. See "The Decade of the Twenties," *American Economic Review Supplement* (May 1946), reprinted in *Essays of J. A. Schumpeter*, Richard V. Clemence, ed. (Cambridge, Mass.: Addison-Wesley, 1951), p. 214.

32. I discuss the misinterpretation of the Great Depression further in *The Problem of Stagflation: Reflections on the Microfoundation of Macroeconomic Theory and Policy* (Washington, D.C.: American Enterprise Institute, 1985); also to appear in *Political Business Cycles and the Political Economy of Stagflation*, Thomas D. Willett, ed. (San Francisco, Calif.: Pacific Institute for Public Policy, forthcoming).

33. We have become familiar with stagflation, the vicious form of an inflationary recession. And the possibility of an inflationary depression cannot be entirely excluded. I have given reasons why I think that this is unlikely in "The Great Depression: Can it Happen Again?" in *The Business Cycle and Public Policy, 1920-80*, a compendium of papers submitted to the Joint Economic Committee of the U.S. Congress, November 28, 1980; reprinted as AEI Reprint no. 118 (Washington, D.C.: American Enterprise Institute, January 1981).

34. *Yale Review* (Summer 1933), pp. 755, 758.

35. Quoted in R. F. Harrod, *The Life of John Maynard Keynes* (New York: Harcourt Brace, 1951), pp. 567-68.

36. Ibid.

37. Lionel (Lord) Robbins, *Autobiography of an Economist* (London and New York: Macmillan, 1971), p. 156.

38. See Nicholas (Lord) Kaldor, "The Nemesis of Free Trade" (1977), reprinted in his *Further Essays in Applied Economics* (New York: Holmes and Meier, 1978), and *The Economic Consequences of Mrs. Thatcher: Speeches in the House of Lords 1979-1982* (London: Duckworth, 1983).

39. But there can be no doubt that it is very bad advice for the developed countries, too. Kaldor does not make it clear whether he assumes internal or external economies to be the reason for increasing returns. He does not even mention this vital distinction. With regard to internal economies, the enormous advance of transportation, communications, and information technology has progressively undermined the strength of local monopolies, enhanced the importance of large free trade areas, and made protectionist policies increasingly more costly and obsolete. External economies are attached

not merely to manufacturing industries; service industries are equally important.

40. Agricultural protection was politically motivated to help the Junkers (large estate-owners in Germany); see Alexander Gerschenkron, *Bread and Democracy in Germany* (Berkeley: University of California Press, 1943). The protection of the steel industry enabled the German steel cartel to dump steel at low prices abroad. This was helpful for steel-using manufacturing industries, especially in the free trade countries, Great Britain and the Netherlands, but was resented by the German manufacturing industries.

41. See John Maynard Keynes, "The Balance of Payments in the United States," *Economic Journal*, vol. 56, no. 222 (1946), p. 186.

42. See *The Collected Writings of John Maynard Keynes*, Donald Moggridge, ed. (London: MacMillan and Cambridge University Press, 1980), vol. 26, for the extensive exchange of letters and views. Unfortunately, Prebisch never returned to his early liberal beliefs as far as I know.

43. See my paper, "Critical Observations on Some Current Notions in the Theory of Economic Development," *Industria*, no. 2 (Bologna: Societa Editrice Il Mulino, 1957).

44. The irony is heightened by the fact that Prebisch had been fully aware of the mismanagement.

45. "The Terms of Trade Controversy and the Evolution of Soft Financing: Early Years in the U.N.," in Meier and Seers, *Pioneers in Development*; and "Ideas and Policy: The Sources of UNCTAD," *IDS Bulletin*, vol. 15, no. 3 (July 1984), pp. 14-17.

46. "Critical Observations." See also my "Terms of Trade and Economic Development," in *Economic Development for Latin America: Proceedings of a Conference Held by the International Economic Association*, Howard S. Ellis, ed., assisted by Henry C. Wallich (London: Macmillan, 1961); and "The Liberal International Economic Order in Historical Perspective," in *Challenges to a Liberal International Economic Order*, Ryan C. Amacher and others, eds. (Washington, D.C.: American Enterprise Institute, 1979). My views on the terms of trade were foreshadowed in or based on what I said more than fifty years ago in *The Theory of International Trade*, 1st German ed., 1933, rev. English ed. 1936.

47. Princeton, N.J.: Princeton University Press for the NBER, 1963; the quotation that follows in the text is from p. 76. The coverage of Lipsey's volume is more comprehensive than the title suggests. The book also contains price, quantity, and terms of trade indexes for the United Kingdom and continental industrial Europe, which come mainly from C. P. Kindleberger, *The Terms of Trade: A European Case Study* (New York: Technology Press of M.I.T. and John Wiley, 1956). See also the extension of Lipsey's work in Irving B. Kravis and Robert E. Lipsey, "Prices and Terms of Trade for Developed Country Exports of Manufactured Goods," in *The Economics of Relative Prices*, Bela Csikos-Nagy, Douglas Hague, and Graham Hall, eds.

(New York: St. Martin's, 1984), pp. 415-45, which confirms and strengthens Lipsey's conclusions.

48. On the policy conclusions, see also Bela Balasa, "Comment," in Meier and Seers, *Pioneers in Development*, pp. 304-11.

49. 1st ed., London 1865; see especially chap. 13 of the 3d ed., A. W. Flux, ed. (London, 1906). Keynes related that Jevons had the courage of his convictions. He

> laid in such large stores not only of writing-paper, but also of thick brown packing paper, that even today [1936], more than fifty years after his death, his children have not used up the stock he left behind him of the latter; though his purchases seem to have been more in the nature of a speculation than for his personal use, since his own notes were mostly written on the backs of old envelopes and odd scraps, of which the proper place was the waste-paper basket.

Keynes's *Essays in Biography*, new edition, with three additional essays edited by Geoffrey Keynes (New York: Horizon Press, 1951), p. 266.

50. "The Changing Structure of the British Economy," *Economic Journal* (September 1954).

51. There exists an extensive literature on the terms of trade. A large part was reviewed by T. Morgan, "Trends in Terms of Trade and Their Repercussions on Primary Producers," in *International Trade Theory in a Developing World*, Roy Harrod, ed. (London: International Economic Association, 1963), pp. 52-95. See also his "The Long-Run Terms of Trade Between Agriculture and Manufacturing," *Econometrica* (1967); Kindleberger, *The Terms of Trade*; and P. T. Ellsworth, "The Terms of Trade between Primary Producing and Industrial Countries," *Inter-American Affairs* (Summer 1956). There is no support for the Prebisch-Singer hypothesis in any of these works.

52. "Critical Observations."

53. Ibid.

54. Washington, D.C.: Brookings Institution, 1967, pp. 70-71. See also Arnold C. Harberger and David Wall, "Harry G. Johnson as a Development Economist," *Journal of Political Economy*, vol. 92, no. 4 (August 1984), p. 623.

55. J. R. Hicks, "The Long-Run Dollar Problems: Inaugural Lecture," *Oxford Economic Papers* (June 1953); and D. H. Robertson, *Britain in the World Economy* (London: Allen and Unwin, 1954). For further references, see P. T. Bauer and A. A. Walters, "The State of Economics," *Journal of Law and Economics*, vol. 18, no. 1 (April 1975), p. 5; and Gottfried Haberler, "Dollar Shortage?" in *Foreign Economic Policy for the United States*, Seymour Harris,

ed. (New York: Greenwood Press, 1948), p. 426.

In the 1920s J. M. Keynes argued in his famous dispute with Bertil Ohlin that Germany would not be able to pay reparations because demand for German exports abroad was inelastic. It is now generally agreed that Ohlin was right and Keynes's elasticity pessimism was wrong. Alfred Marshall had also emphatically rejected the idea of inelastic demand for a country's exports.

56. The list of publications and country studies in which the theory has been developed is impressive. I mention a few: Hollis Chenery with Irma Adelman, "Foreign Aid and Economic Development: The Case of Greece," *Review of Economics and Statistics*, no. 48 (February 1966); Hollis Chenery with A. Strout, "Foreign Assistance and Economic Development," *American Economic Review*, no. 56 (September 1966); and Hollis Chenery and Moises Syrquin, *Patterns and Development, 1950-1970* (London: Oxford University Press, 1975). Especially useful is Henry Bruton, "The Two-Gap Approach to Aid and Development," *American Economic Review*, no. 56 (September 1966), and the reply by Chenery, "The Two-Gap Approach to Aid and Development: A Reply to Bruton," in the same issue of *American Economic Review*. The theory has been sharply criticized by Deepak Lal in *The Poverty of "Development Economics*," Hobart Paperback no. 16 (London: Institute of Economic Affairs, 1983).

57. I myself share the general view that on the whole the Marshall Plan was a very constructive and beneficial policy, even though the advice of the U.S. administrators of the plan to the recipients of aid was not always the best.

58. I discussed the infant industry protection in *The Theory of International Trade*.

59. See Albert Hirschman's essay in *The Theory and Experience of Economic Development: Essays in Honor of Sir W. Arthur Lewis*, Mark Gersovitz, Carlos F. Diaz-Alejandro, Gustav Ranis, and Mark R. Rosenweig, eds. (London: Allen and Unwin, 1982); and Hans Singer, "Ideas and Policy: The sources of UNCTAD."

60. Similar views were expressed in Germany by conservative economists such as Albert Hahn and Wilhelm Röpke. They spoke of "secondary deflation," which enormously aggravated the cyclical decline caused by "structural maladjustments."   The secondary depression required strong expansionary measures, including government deficit spending.

61. Milton Friedman, in "The Monetary Theory of Henry Simons," *Journal of Law and Economics*, vol. 10 (October 1967), p. 7, writes:

> There is clearly great similarity between the views expressed
> by Simons and by Keynes--as to the causes of the Great
> Depression, the impotence of monetary policy, and the need
> to rely extensively on fiscal policy. Both men placed great
> emphasis on the state of business expectations and assigned a

critical role to the desire for liquidity [on the] 'absolute' liquidity preference under conditions of deep depression . . . It was this that meant that changes in the quantity of money produced by the monetary authorities would simply be reflected in opposite movements in velocity and have no effect on income or employment.

See also Herbert Stein, *The Fiscal Revolution in the United States* (Chicago: University of Chicago Press, 1969), and "Early Memories of a Keynes I Never Met," *AEI Economist* (Washington, D.C.: American Enterprise Institute, June 1983); and J. Ronnie Davis, *The New Economics and the Old Economists* (Ames, Iowa: Iowa State University Press, 1971).

62. See Haberler, "Critical Observations," p. 3.

63. Rosenstein-Rodan in a famous article refers to East European countries. His figures have been critically analyzed and found wanting by Berdj Kenadjian, "Disguised Unemployment in Underdeveloped Countries," *Zeitschrift für Nationalökonomie*, vol. 21 (1961), pp. 216-23, part of a Ph.D. dissertation, Harvard University, 1962.

64. In my 1957 article, "Critical Observations," I pointed out that the argument has been used to advocate protection for industry so that inefficient labor can be drawn from agriculture and educated on the job in industry. This is, of course, the infant industry argument for protection. The scope and limits of the argument have been thoroughly discussed in the classical and neoclassical literature by John Stuart Mill, Alfred Marshall, Frank W. Taussig, and others.

65. In *Contribuicóes a Analise do Desenvolvimento Económico* (Rio de Janeiro: Livraria Agir Editora, 1957), pp. 346-49.

66. *Transforming Traditional Agriculture* (New York: Arno Press, 1976), p. 70.

67. *International Trade and Economic Development*, 50th Anniversary Commemoration Lectures (Cairo: National Bank of Egypt, 1959). See also my paper "An Assessment of the Current Relevance of the Theory of Comparative Advantage in Agricultural Production and Trade," *International Journal of Agrarian Affairs*, vol. 4, no. 3 (May 1964). Both papers are reprinted in *Economics of Trade and Development*, James D. Theberge, ed. (New York: Wiley, 1968).

68. See John Stuart Mill, *Principles of Political Economy*, Ashley edition (London: Longmans, Green, 1909), Bk. 3, chap. 17, sec. 5, pp. 581-82. On Mill's theory see Hla Myint, "The 'Classical Theory' of International Trade and the Under Developed Countries," *Economic Journal* (June 1958), pp. 317-37; reprinted in Theberge's *Economics of Trade and Development*.

69. See, for example, *The Economic Development of Latin America and Its Principal Problems* (New York: ECLA, 1950). The theory was endorsed by Nicholas Kaldor; see his "Stabilizing the Terms of Trade of

226 Trade and Development Policy

Underdeveloped Countries," paper submitted to the Rio de Janeiro Conference organized by Yale University, January 1963.

70. *Wall Street Journal*, December 26, 1984.

71. Ashley edition, p. 922. Mill was fully aware of the great danger, not to say certainty, that in practice infant industry protection will be carried from "infancy to senility," to quote Bauer again.

72. See Rosenstein-Rodan's contribution to Meier and Seers, *Pioneers in Development*, pp. 209-14, summarizing and updating the conclusion of his well-known article, "Problems of Industrialization of Eastern and South-Eastern Europe," *Economic Journal*, vol. 53 (June-September 1943), pp. 202-11.

73. Gary Becker, *Human Capital*, 2nd ed. (Cambridge, Mass.: National Bureau of Economic Research, 1975), pp. 19-20, 26-28.

74. This section is based on my paper, "An Assessment of the Current Relevance of the Theory of Comparative Advantage to Agricultural Production and Trade," *International Journal of Agrarian Affairs*, vol. 4, no. 3 (May 1964).

75. Tibor Scitovsky, "Two Concepts of External Economies," *Journal of Political Economy* (April 1954); reprinted in *The Economics of Underdevelopment: A Series of Articles and Papers*, A. N. Agarwala and P. Singh, eds. (London: Oxford University Press, 1963), p. 305.

76. Ibid., pp. 305-06.

77. Ibid., p. 304.

78. *The Poverty of "Development Economics,"* p. 106.

79. Since this was written, the *Economist* (May 18, 1985, p. 73) has taken up the subject. It points out that "many developing countries are still letting their exchange rates become overvalued. The results are always bad, sometimes disastrous." In other words, many developing countries use controls to prop up the exchange rate.

80. Richard T. Ely Lecture, *American Economic Review*, vol. 67 (February 1977), p. 14 (emphasis added). Kuznets's findings about growth in the developing countries are reported at some length in his *Economic Growth of Nations: Total Output and Production Structure* (Cambridge, Mass.: Harvard University Press, 1971), chap. 1, and in "Aspects on Post-World War II Growth in Less Developed Countries," in *Evolution, Welfare, and Time in Economics: Essays in Honor of Nicholas Georgescu-Roegen*, A. M. Tang, E. M. Westfield, and James E. Worley, eds. (Lexington, Mass.: Lexington Books, 1976), chap. 3. Kuznets's findings have been confirmed in an important paper by Irving Kravis and Robert Lipsey," The Diffusion of Economic Growth in the World Economy, 1950-1980," in *International Comparisons of Productivity and Causes of the Slowdown*, John Kendrick, ed. (Washington, D.C.: American Enterprise Institute, 1984), pp. 109-52; they use later data for 1950-80, which have become available since Kuznets wrote.

81. Kuznets, "Aspects of Post-World War II Growth," p. 40.

82. Ibid., pp. 40-41.

83. This is an abridged version of the comment on Haberler's "Liberal and Illiberal Development Policy," which appeared immediately following the essay in *Pioneers in Development: Second Series*, pp. 84-103.

84. For a fuller survey, see Robert E. Baldwin, "Gottfried Haberler's Contributions to International Trade Theory and Policy," *Quarterly Journal of Economics*, vol. 97, no. 1 (February 1982), pp. 141-48.

85. *Economic Journal* (June 1950).

86. 1st ed., Geneva: League of Nations, 1937; 5th ed., Cambridge, Mass.: Harvard University Press, 1964.

87. Princeton, N.J.: International Finance Section, Princeton University, 1955.

88. *Industry and Trade in Some Developing Countries: A Comparative Study* (London: Oxford University Press, 1970).

About the Book and Editors

Paul Samuelson judges that Gottfried Haberler's work "should qualify him for about two-and-a-half Nobel Prizes in economics—one for his quantum improvement in trade theory beyond Ricardo's paradigm of labor's comparative advantage, one for his definitive synthesis of business cycle theory, and beyond these his policy wisdom over a period of six decades." It is Haberler's "policy wisdom" that serves as the basis for this comprehensive collection of the eminent economist's work.

Throughout the book, Haberler's contributions demonstrate the clarity of his analyses for exploring the complex economics of policy issues and for identifying key governmental responses to problems of unemployment, trade, and development. Presenting Haberler as the eclectic economist he is, the editors show that far from being an ideologue, Haberler is an economist who uses whatever approaches and theories are appropriate for the problems he considers. The portrait that emerges is one of a multifaceted thinker, able to choose freely among competing theories and to effectively apply them to complex and demanding policy issues.

Richard J. Sweeney is Sullivan/Dean Professor of International Finance at Georgetown University, **Edward Tower** is professor of economics at Duke University, and **Thomas D. Willett** is Horton Professor of Economics at Claremont McKenna College and the Claremont Graduate School.

Index

For Product Safety Concerns and Information please contact our EU representative GPSR@taylorandfrancis.com Taylor & Francis Verlag GmbH, Kaufingerstraße 24, 80331 München, Germany